THE FALKLANDS WAR

CHANNEL FOUR

THE FALKLANDS WAR

Denys Blakeway

Sidgwick & Jackson
LONDON

In Association with
Channel Four Television Company
Limited

For Denise

Author's Acknowledgements

I am grateful to Hugh Scully, who first had the idea for a television series on the Falklands War and who was commissioned to make it by Channel Four, for having given me the opportunity to write this book. His deep knowledge of the Falklands conflict and his understanding of the complex issues which lay behind it have been an invaluable help to me. I am grateful to many others who have been of considerable assistance: Barbara Dean, for her transcription of the interviews; Mary FitzPatrick, for her research; Heather Briley, for her research in Buenos Aires; Cdr C. L. Johnstone-Burt OBE RN (Ret.) and Jasmine Blakeway for their careful reading of the text; and Paul Watkins for his design of the book. Above all, of course, I must thank my wife, who produced our baby while I produced this book, who never once complained, and gave me the best advice and encouragement.

Page 1: Tracer fire during an evening air raid on 30 May 1982, seen from on board *Canberra* in San Carlos Water
Frontispiece: A Sea Harrier takes off from the deck of HMS *Invincible*

First published in Great Britain in 1992 by Sidgwick & Jackson Limited

Copyright © 1991 Denys Blakeway/Fine Art Productions

The Channel Four series on the Falklands War is made by Fine Art Productions and produced by Denys Blakeway

Designed by Paul Watkins

Maps by Jess Jethwa/Mission Incorporated

ISBN 0 283 06101 4

Typeset by Parker Typesetting Service, Leicester
Printed by BPCC Hazell Books, Aylesbury, Bucks
Member of BPCC Ltd.

for Sidgwick & Jackson Limited
18–21 Cavaye Place
London SW10 9PG

Contents

PROLOGUE

SHORTLY before Christmas, in December 1977, HMS *Dreadnought* slipped her moorings in Faslane and headed out to sea. Having tested her buoyancy tanks, and ensured all systems were working, she dived and headed south at speed. Until the departure only the Captain had been aware of the nature of the mission, and the submarine's destination. Once at sea he was able to share his knowledge with *Dreadnought*'s crew. He told them that the nuclear powered hunter-killer was heading at top speed for the Falkland Islands, and that they had permission to apprehend and, if necessary, to sink any Argentine naval ships taking part in an invasion of the Islands.

Late in the same year, 1977, Admiral Juan Jose Lombardo received a call from the Fleet Commander of the Argentine Navy, Admiral Jorge Anaya. Anaya ordered Lombardo to report to him immediately at the naval base of Puerto Belgrano, close to Buenos Aires. He was to keep his visit absolutely secret. Lombardo was commander of the Navy's submarine force in Mar Del Plata, a naval base 200 miles to the south. As he made the journey northwards he had time to ponder the reason for his summons.

Neither he nor Anaya much cared for one another although they had much in common. They were both hard and ambitious men; they were both tainted with the bloody excesses of the 'dirty war' being fought at that time by the armed forces against the people of Argentina; and both men shared a consuming passion: the desire to end nearly a century and a half of Argentina's humiliation at the hands of an old colonial power. Since 1833 Britain had, in their view, illegally occupied the Malvinas Islands, or the Falklands as the English called them. Argentina had been cruelly denied a piece of her patrimony.

To the men of the Argentine Navy the occupation of the Malvinas was a particular slight. They considered that the position of the Islands, 300 miles away from the south coast of Argentina, was of immense strategic importance to the control of the seas. If the Navy was to contribute to Argentina's development as a regional superpower and a bulwark against communist expansion, these important islands, the equivalent to a permanent aircraft carrier in the South Atlantic, would have to be retaken.

But the dishonour was more profound than the mere humiliation of being denied a strategic asset. The Argentine Navy was modelled on the Royal

Navy. The uniforms of the two navies were almost identical, the only difference being that the Argentine uniform bore a wide black stripe down the right trouser leg as a tribute to the memory of Lord Nelson.

For years the Royal Navy had supplied many of Argentina's ships, both new and second hand. The aircraft carrier *25 de Mayo*, the pride of the fleet, had seen service in the Royal Navy as HMS *Venerable* in the 1950s. By 1977, as part of the armed forces' massive expansion and re-equipment programme, the decision had been taken to buy two brand new Type 42 Exocet-armed destroyers from the British. HMS *Endurance*, the Royal Navy's Ice Patrol Ship in the South Atlantic, was a regular visitor to Argentina's naval ports, and her crew were welcomed as brothers-in-arms.

And yet, the Malvinas: always there, always a nagging sore, always a block to the true friendship which should have existed between the two services, the one so closely modelled on the other.

Now, however, Britain appeared to be in permanent decline. Throughout their naval careers Lombardo and Anaya had watched as the British withdrew from colonies and reduced their fleet. By some perverse twist, however, the Malvinas was one of the very few remnants of Empire which had bucked the trend and actually refused to decolonise and break away from the old country. The Islands' inhabitants, brought in over the years by the British to settle in the barren and desolate terrain, had resolutely refused all attempts to make them change their minds and accept that their destiny lay with Argentina.

More perversely still, in their view, the British Foreign Office had agreed that the Islands should return to Argentina. In 1968 a junior minister, Lord Chalfont, negotiated a Memorandum of Understanding which accepted the transfer of sovereignty. But the House of Commons in London, egged on by the Falkland Islanders and their powerful lobby, had blocked the transfer when details of the deal were leaked to the press and Parliament.

To the Argentine Navy there was always a solution which would settle the problem once and for all: the occupation of the Islands by force. As Lombardo approached the huge and monolithic edifice of the Navy's headquarters he considered whether this was the reason behind his summons to see Admiral Anaya. Anaya and his men were nicknamed 'the Gorillas' by colleagues because of the hard-line attitude they took to the question of the Malvinas. In the year since the Admiral had left his post as Naval Attaché in London to take up the position of Fleet Commander he had deliberately increased the tension in the South Atlantic. In October 1977 he ordered his ships to fire on and arrest seven Soviet and two Bulgarian trawlers fishing in Falklands waters without Argentine permission. A crewman had been badly injured. Before that an Argentine destroyer had fired at the British research ship, the RSS *Shackleton*, in February 1976, after it refused an order to stop when sailing close to the Falkland Islands.

During the same period relations with Britain had entered one of their periodic troughs. Argentina had not replaced her Ambassador in London and had suggested that Britain follow suit. The press in Buenos Aires was more hostile than usual, hinting at the necessity of an invasion to solve the problem once and for all.

Lombardo himself had been active in the campaign to recover the Malvinas, and had carried off one of Argentina's most daring coups against the British. In November 1976, he had taken part in a secret mission to establish a permanent base on one of the uninhabited dependencies of the Falkland Islands. He chose Southern Thule, in the South Sandwich Islands, 1,000 miles south of Port Stanley. The military command had been entirely satisfied with the operation which gave Argentina a footing on British claimed territory. When a helicopter from HMS *Endurance* discovered the base in December 1976 the British Government decided to accept the occupation as a *fait accompli* and did nothing more than protest in secret. It was a success of which Lombardo was justly proud.

The two men, Anaya and Lombardo, faced each other inside the naval headquarters: both proud, both extremely reserved, and both passionate nationalists. Their mutual ambition to repossess the Malvinas had made them rivals. The Fleet Commander had a simple question for his Submarine Chief: could Argentina's new German built diesel-electric submarines find and attack a British nuclear-powered submarine in the waters around the Malvinas? Lombardo gave his Commander a one word reply. 'No.'

To hunt and kill a submarine in a wide area of water such as the South Atlantic is almost impossible. What is needed to trap the quarry is an area

Admiral Jorge Anaya, Argentina's most passionate advocate of the re-conquest of the Malvinas of confluence: a narrow isthmus, or straits, through which the submarine is forced to pass. In the Second World War German U-boats were at greatest danger of detection and sinking in the straits of Gibraltar through which they had to pass to gain access to the Mediterranean. No such passageway existed near the Malvinas. Lombardo could never, therefore, guarantee to find and kill the British submarine.

With Lombardo's emphatic 'no' collapsed Anaya's dream of repossession of the Malvinas in 1977. The Fleet Commander had drawn up a plan for invasion that year if sensitive diplomatic talks at the time did not result in British concessions on the sovereignty question. But Argentine intelligence had been tipped off by the British Security Services that an SSN – a nuclear-powered hunter-killer submarine, HMS *Dreadnought* – was in the area. To attack would be to court destruction of an invasion force and national humiliation. Although Anaya submitted his plan for an invasion, it was rejected out-of-hand by the ruling Military Council.

By a deft piece of diplomatic and military footwork Britain had thwarted an invasion. Only now, fifteen years later, are enough pieces of the complex jigsaw in place for the full story to be told. James Callaghan, the British Prime Minister at the time, has justly claimed credit for the success of the operation to prevent the invasion. As a young man he had served in the Royal Navy during the Second World War, and shortly after the war he had been a member of the Board of Admiralty. Ever since he retained a visceral sense of the importance of sea power.

When Callaghan became Prime Minister in April 1976, he remembered from his Admiralty days the existence of a naval chart, prepared once a week, which showed the disposition of all the ships of the Royal Navy. The Ministry of Defence, no doubt to its chagrin, was duly ordered to send a copy of this chart once a fortnight to the Prime Minister. Callaghan would study it, and if he considered that there might be trouble in some far away spot, suggest a naval deployment to the region.

This almost obsessional interest in the affairs of the Royal Navy was motivated not only by a desire to show the flag, but also out of a deeply held belief that the small issues, 'the pimples on the map, like Hong Kong, Belize, Gibraltar, the Falklands', could cause the greatest trouble and might even unseat a Government. Large issues in the world, according to Callaghan, were 'like a huge liner'; they took a long time to change course and moved very, very slowly. If a small pimple were about to become a troublesome boil, the rapid deployment of a small naval task force might help settle things down.

In 1977 the British Government was not unaware of the increasingly aggressive noises coming from Argentina. The policy was to conciliate Argentina by asking for talks, and allowing the illegal occupation of South Thule to continue under protest. In November the Joint Intelligence Committee, Whitehall's clearing house for intelligence information, told Ministers of increasing Argentine frustration and warned that military action could not be ruled out if there was no progress in forthcoming talks.

Callaghan took action. He ordered a reluctant Ministry of Defence to assemble a small task force of two frigates and one nuclear submarine. The two frigates remained miles away from the Falklands; HMS *Dreadnought* travelled directly to the area. The operation had to be entirely covert. If it were made public it would either provoke an Argentine armed response before the submarine arrived on station, or – once the force was in place – damage any prospects of progress in the negotiations. But if the force was secret how could the Argentine Government possibly react to its presence and cancel any invasion plans? The answer was simple. The Prime Minister directed his Security Chief, Sir Maurice Oldfield, to instruct MI6 to let the right people in Argentina know that a British submarine was operating in the area.

Admiral Anaya's question to Lombardo about his ability to find and destroy a British submarine was thus based on the knowledge that a British boat could be operating somewhere in the South Atlantic. And Lombardo's negative response killed any hopes of an invasion of the Malvinas that year.

It was a lesson which Britain forgot, but which Argentina remembered. Less than five years later, in 1982, when, once again, relations were at their most strained over the Falklands issue; when, once again, a Falkland Island dependency was occupied by an Argentine force; when, once again, a series of diplomatic talks were taking place between the two countries, Admiral Anaya and Admiral Lombardo were all too aware of the absence of a British nuclear submarine in the area. This time they could invade with impunity.

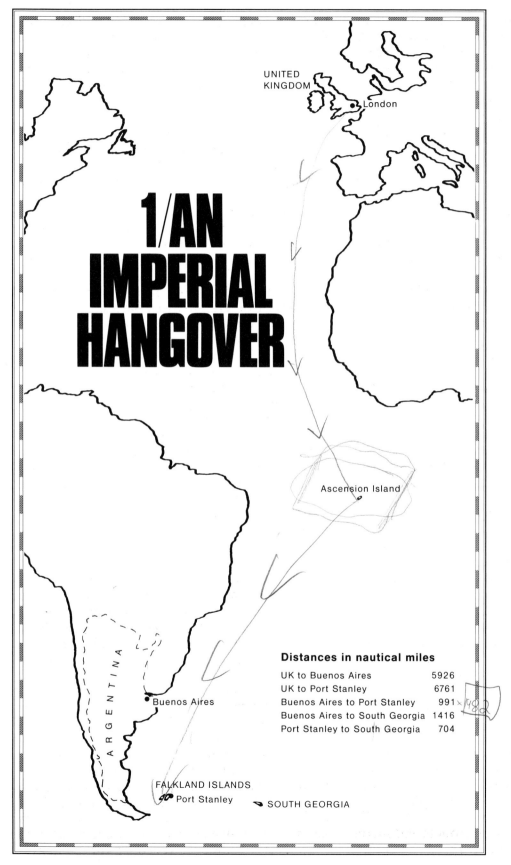

1/AN IMPERIAL HANGOVER

UNITED KINGDOM

London

Ascension Island

ARGENTINA

Buenos Aires

FALKLAND ISLANDS
Port Stanley   SOUTH GEORGIA

Distances in nautical miles

UK to Buenos Aires	5926
UK to Port Stanley	6761
Buenos Aires to Port Stanley	991
Buenos Aires to South Georgia	1416
Port Stanley to South Georgia	704

THE appointment of Peter Carrington, sixth Baron Carrington, as Secretary of State for Foreign Affairs in May 1979, was greeted with the muted joy typical of the Foreign Office when it gets the man it wants. The arrival of a radical and reforming Prime Minister in the shape of Margaret Thatcher had aroused deep fears that the ship of state could be heading unnecessarily for stormy waters. The urbane and patrician Lord Carrington, however, was the ideal man to pour oil where it was needed, and calm the excessive zeal of the Prime Minister, whether she was dealing with matters of the EEC budget, or Britain's settlement of the Rhodesian question.

The Foreign Office had long been regarded with deep mistrust by politicians of all persuasions. Left and right alike suspected it of an eagerness to appease opponents and sell Britain's interests down the river. Margaret Thatcher was no different. She had come to view the Foreign Office as a hot-bed of treachery and sought throughout her premiership, with little success, to impose her own agenda on this wayward Office of State.

Students of British foreign policy have long regarded the issue of the Falklands as a perfect example of the mutual mistrust which exists between the Foreign Office and the House of Commons. The diplomats hoped that Lord Carrington would rise above this political squabbling and impose a settlement which would be the product of Foreign Office thinking; which would be acceptable to the Islanders; and which would appease even the most virulent Labour and Conservative backbencher. After all, had he not achieved this with the creation of Zimbabwe, overcoming the doubts of Mrs Thatcher and the right wing of the Conservative Party? The Falkland Islands were, however, a different problem, and one to which there was no solution. Lord Carrington was destined to find that this pimple in the affairs of state would destroy his career.

It had not helped the career of another Peer in a previous administration. In 1965, fourteen years before Lord Carrington became Foreign Secretary, Argentina achieved a success at the UN which became the driving force behind Foreign Office policy towards the Falklands. On 16 December 1965 the General Assembly voted by a large margin to approve Resolution 2065. The resolution recognised the existence of the dispute and called on the two countries to 'proceed without delay' to a solution. The Argentine diplomats managed to link the resolution to the United Nations' commitment to worldwide decolonisation. In the preamble to the Resolution there was a reference to 'the cherished aim of bringing to an end everywhere colonialism in all its forms, one of which covers the case of the Falklands Islands (Malvinas)'. The rights of the Islanders to self-determination, another UN governing principle, were ignored.

In December 1965 the Labour Government of Harold Wilson had been in power for more than a year. George Brown, then Foreign Secretary, determined that a solution should be found within the context of the United Nations' resolution. The Foreign Office was in complete agreement. Alun Gwynne Jones, whom Harold Wilson created Lord Chalfont and brought into Government originally for his expertise on disarmament, found himself in 1965 in the unexpected position of being a Minister of State at the Foreign and Commonwealth Office with responsibility for Latin American affairs. This, of course, included the Falkland Islands. When Chalfont arrived at the Foreign Office he found that the policy was already in place, regardless of his own views as a Minister. 'The view was,' he remembers, 'that the Falkland Islands were a kind of hang-over from imperial days, that there was no really intelligent reason why they should remain in the position they were in at that moment.'

The Foreign Office advised their new Minister of State that talks should begin as soon as possible with the Argentinians about a change of status. Officials pointed out that the Islands were many thousands of miles from Britain, but only 300 miles from Argentina, that they were run down and lacking in investment, and that their population of less than 2,000 was in decline. Above all, these tiny islands, with their small but obdurate population, were perversely obstructing the development of relations with an entire continent.

Lord Chalfont assented. A team of diplomats from both sides started negotiations in earnest almost immediately with the object of the eventual hand-over of sovereignty to Argentina. The talks were held in secret in London and Buenos Aires and proceeded well, if slowly. Britain and Argentina, aside from the issue of the Falklands, had a great deal in common. Many thousands of British people had settled in Argentina over the years: the country was home to the largest British community outside the Commonwealth. The British had established the country's railway system, and for years they had controlled the beef market.

The negotiations were held in a spirit of mutual understanding and a desire to settle a problem which, it was agreed, should no longer be allowed to cloud an otherwise natural and strong friendship. The eventual product of the talks, three years later in 1968, was a 'Memorandum of Understanding' in which the British accepted, for the first time, the principle that sovereignty should be transferred to Argentina. The memorandum stated unequivocally that 'The Government of the United Kingdom as part of such a final settlement will recognise Argentina's sovereignty over the Islands from a date to be agreed'. The agreement also said that the sovereignty changes had to be made on the firm understanding that the Islanders' interests would be taken into account.

The word 'interests' was of crucial importance. From then on the question of the 'interests' and the 'wishes' of the Islanders dominated the dispute, stood in the way of any settlement and finally led to war. If the wishes of the Islanders were paramount a settlement would, clearly, be impossible. The people of the Falklands had no wish whatsoever to become Argentine. If, on the other hand, their interests alone were considered by London and Buenos Aires, and their wishes were ignored, then no such problems arose and a settlement could be reached quickly.

In 1968 Lord Chalfont was happy to bow to Argentine demands that 'wishes' be deleted and replaced by 'interests' in the Memorandum of Agreement. The professional diplomats in the Foreign Office believed that, in Chalfont's words, the Islanders' 'emotional attachment to the United Kingdom and British citizenship distorted their view of what was really in their best interest'. In other words, London knew better than the Islanders what was good for them, and that was to become citizens of Argentina.

In order to encourage the Islanders to develop a liking for their neighbours in Argentina the two sides agreed that the transfer of sovereignty would take place after closer links had been established between the Falklands and the mainland. There would be educational exchanges, tourism, and, most importantly, the Islands would be made increasingly reliant on Argentina for their communications with the outside world, and their everyday needs. British transport links with the Islands would be cut.

Lord Chalfont's disinterested view that the agreement was the best thing for the Islanders had little relevance to the political realities of the day. He was a recently appointed Peer with no experience of the House of Commons. Details of the Memorandum of Agreement, which was not legally binding, soon leaked to the Falkland Islanders and caused the predictable storm of outraged horror. On 27 February 1968 four unofficial members of the Falklands Executive Council sent an open letter to every Member of Parliament. The emotional contents of the letter drew the politicians' attention to the secret talks:

Are you aware that negotiations are now proceeding between the British and Argentine Governments which may result in the handing over of the Falkland Islands to the Argentine? Take note, that the inhabitants of the Islands have never yet been consulted regarding their future, they do not want to become Argentines, they are as British as you are . . .

The letter ended with an appeal to Members of all sides to help the Islanders in their fight against the transfer of sovereignty. That help was readily given. On the right MPs such as Sir Bernard Braine rallied to the nationalist cause:

The Falkland Islanders spoke English, they had sent their sons to fight in two world wars on our side. They were a small, loyal, decent community, and they were entitled to the protection which only a British Parliament could give them.

On the left, Peter Shore joined in the battle against what he saw as a perfidious attempt by Argentina at 'reverse colonialism'. Liberals and Scottish Nationalists from the Highlands and Islands also answered the call, fearful that a precedent might be set for trampling on the wishes of minorities and isolated communities in the British Isles. A head of steam was building which the Government could not ignore.

In 1968 a Falkland Islands lobby was established in London. It was made up of an unlikely coalition of Socialist and Conservative MPs, Falkland Islanders resident in Britain, the Falkland Islands Company, Antarctic explorers, members of the forces who had served in the South Atlantic and assorted British eccentrics. It was called The Falklands Islands Emergency Committee and its purpose was to give the Islanders a voice in any negotiations over the transfer of sovereignty.

Lord Chalfont visits the Falkland Islands in 1968. His reception was, in his words, 'less than enthusiastic'

In November 1968, Lord Chalfont, with some courage, given the strength of feeling building against him, made the arduous journey to the Falklands, to explain the Government's policy. Unsurprisingly, he ended up listening while the Islanders explained their views to him. Today he recalls that his reception was 'less than enthusiastic':

There were, first of all, Union Jacks galore, the quay side was alive with fluttering Union Jacks, punctuated only by a few rather dispiriting messages saying, 'Chalfont go home'. Things of that kind! Some of them rather less polite than others.

The message was clear and unequivocal. The Falkland Islanders wished to remain British. They were not interested in closer ties with Argentina. That was the end of the matter.

During Chalfont's absence in the Falklands the lobby in London was working at full steam. Hostile articles appeared in the press and questions were asked in both Houses. To the Cabinet the deal with Argentina was beginning to look distinctly shaky.

Lord Chalfont's political reception on his return was little better than that which he had experienced in the Falklands. The House of Lords gave him a very rough ride on 3 December 1968. While in the House of Commons it was made plain to the new Foreign Secretary, Michael Stewart, that any deal involving the transfer of sovereignty would not be acceptable. On 11 December 1968 the Cabinet decided that, on the basis of the very hostile attitude of Parliament to the Memorandum of Agreement, no settlement of the Falklands issue could be made which did not take the *wishes* of the Islanders into account. Lord Chalfont and the Foreign Office were utterly defeated. But Chalfont had the last word. In a report for the Cabinet he wrote: 'Unless sovereignty is seriously negotiated, and ceded, in the long term we are likely to end up in a state of armed conflict with Argentina.'

The feeling in Argentina after the rejection of the Memorandum was one of frustration, incomprehension and hurt pride. Senior diplomats, like Enrique Ros, the Counsellor at the London Embassy who negotiated the agreement, felt that London had reneged on a deal which had been negotiated in good faith. Ros believed – and still believes – that the Falkland Island Company, the major landowner in the Islands at the time, 'took notice of the existence of this memorandum and moved the lobby in Parliament in order to stop it'. His views were shared by many Argentinians who could not understand how such a small and insignificant group of people could hold such sway in Britain.

Although Britain could no longer offer Argentina a transfer in which only the interests of the Islanders would be considered, talks continued over the years and under different administrations. In 1977, when tension increased and an invasion seemed likely, James Callaghan took action to prevent Argentine aggression. Otherwise both Labour and Conservative policy remained consistent throughout: that a handover of sovereignty would be in the best interests of Britain, if not the Islanders, and that everything should be done to persuade the recalcitrant Falklanders of this.

As planned, a series of communications agreements were signed in which Argentina agreed to supply fuel oil and air links to the Islands. Tourism between the Falklands and the mainland increased. Many Islanders sent their children to school in Buenos Aires and conducted business with Argentina. But their love for Argentina did not grow. It diminished.

KEEP THE FALKLAND BRITISH

2/THE ROAD TO WAR

IN MAY 1979 Margaret Thatcher took office, quoting St Francis of Assisi, 'where there is discord, may we bring harmony'. Her Foreign Secretary Lord Carrington took her at her word and set to work on the Falklands. Carrington realised that something had to be done:

It was quite clear that it was impossible to go on doing absolutely nothing. The impatience of the Argentines was running out, and it was necessary to make some kind of movement, and there were some difficult decisions to take.

At the time the Falklands were regarded as a relatively trivial issue in the affairs of state. They were rarely discussed in Cabinet. The usual forum for discussion of the problem in the South Atlantic was a Cabinet sub-committee, called the Overseas Defence Committee, which was chaired by the Prime Minister, and included the Foreign and Defence Secretaries among its members. Even this committee rarely actually discussed the matter. Instead the issue of the Falklands would be noted in minutes sent by the Foreign Secretary to his colleagues.

Carrington personally favoured the Foreign Office line: that some sort of settlement had to be reached, and preferably one which involved handing sovereignty to Argentina. The best option was thought to be 'leaseback', in which sovereignty was given to Argentina, and the Islands then leased back to Britain for a time long enough for the Islanders to accept the change.

Barely a month after the General Election in May 1979, which brought the Conservatives to power, Carrington had instructed his junior, Nicholas Ridley, to hold exploratory talks with his Argentine opposite number. It became clear at the talks that the position had not changed: Britain could make no concessions without the Islanders' agreement; Argentina, on the other hand, wanted the Islanders to play no part in a settlement.

Carrington bombarded his colleagues with minutes and memos, urging them to reach a decision about what to do next, and recommending leaseback as the best option. But the Prime Minister was not to be rushed. Responding to a memo of 20 September 1979, she postponed a decision until a meeting of the Overseas Defence Committee. The Foreign Secretary was forced to tell an Argentine diplomat at the UN that the Falklands were extremely low on his list of priorities. It was an unintended insult to a nation which regarded the Malvinas as a focus of national identity, and which gave the matter top priority on the country's agenda. It also confirmed the Foreign Ministry's view in Buenos Aires that the British were not seriously interested in a settlement. Enrique Ros was Deputy Foreign Minister at the time:

Most of the time they (the British) were not interested in the subject, although they recognised the existence of the problem because the issue was registered in the United Nations. But they never thought it was an important issue. There are so many other problems in the world, I mean why should they care about these windswept islands down in the South Atlantic?

Three weeks later, on 12 October 1979, Lord Carrington sent a more strongly worded memo to the Defence Committee in which he warned that continuing talks without making concessions on sovereignty carried a serious threat of invasion. The Prime Minister was not to be moved. She decided that discussions of the matter by the Committee would have to be postponed until after the Rhodesian problem had been settled. Finally, after yet another minute from Lord Carrington urging talks on sovereignty, the Defence Committee discussed the issue on 29 January 1980. It was one of the very few occasions until the conflict itself that the Falklands were discussed by Ministers. At the meeting they agreed that talks should take place, but only after written consent had been obtained from the Islanders' Council. Six months later, after talks about talks had been held in New York, the Prime Minister agreed that a solution on the basis of leaseback should be attempted.

It was a tremendous victory for Carrington and the Foreign Office. The Prime Minister had accepted the principle that British sovereign territory should be handed to Argentina, with the proviso that the views of the Islanders be taken into account. This was much further than many of her colleagues in the Conservative Party would wish her to go. To the right, the idea of accepting the principle that territory could be handed over to another power was anathema. To Lord Carrington, the idea was the best option:

I mean you can't negotiate about nothing, and therefore something had to be found, some way had to be found ... which might be acceptable to the Argentinian Government and might be acceptable to the Falkland Islanders, and the more I looked at it the more I thought that the leaseback situation was the one which was, I wouldn't say the most likely to succeed,

Oppression in Argentina: from 1976 to 1982 the military dictatorship imposed a reign of terror. Thousands of young men and women were abducted by the armed forces, never to be seen again

but had the least objections to it. Because if you've got a long enough leaseback, say a hundred years or something of that kind, the world is going to look a very different place in a hundred years from what it does now. And you will certainly have bought quite a lot of time.

Just as Lord Chalfont had been despatched to the Islands before him in 1968, so Nicholas Ridley was sent down south to test the waters of the South Atlantic in 1980. And, like Lord Chalfont, he found them to be icy cold. The Islanders were in no mood to accept leaseback. They had, as the Foreign Office desired, developed links with Argentina. The problem was that they did not like what they saw.

Rex Hunt, the Colonial Governor, had recently arrived in the Islands. Hunt, a kindly but shrewd Colonial Officer of the old school, quickly recognised the strength of Islander feeling:

They felt that the Argentines were arrogant and inefficient, and I'm afraid they were both of that. They were trying to win the hearts and minds of the Islanders and that's why I think they'd had the communications agreements and they laid on the airline and some of the fuel and they were trying to woo the Islanders to make them see that they would be better off as part of Argentina; but they'd completely failed to do that by the time I arrived here in 1980 and relations were very poor.

The Islanders were in no mood to accept leaseback. They made this plain to Ridley, but grudgingly accepted that talks should continue about further economic ties. In their view, the issue of sovereignty should be taken off the agenda.

Nicholas Ridley returned to London, and like Lord Chalfont before him, faced the full wrath of the Falklands lobby in the House of Commons. Only rarely do Conservative backbenchers turn on one of their own and tear them apart, but on this occasion they vented their full wrath on Ridley for daring to mention the possibility of a transfer of sovereignty.

Richard Luce, who inherited the poisoned chalice from Ridley, was in the House that day, and remembered that his colleagues on the back benches 'reacted with the utmost ferocity'. Ridley was left pale and shaken. Julian Amery summed up the feeling of the Conservative Party as he spoke in the debate:

Is my Hon Friend aware that his statement is profoundly disturbing? Is he also aware, certainly the Falkland Islanders are, that for years – and here I speak from some experience – his Department has always wanted to get rid of this commitment?

Ridley rejected the inference that the Foreign Office, and not he, had been making policy, and

replied that 'the Government as a whole have taken the decision to take this initiative'. Yet he was isolated. Lord Carrington, as a member of the House of Lords, had been unable to prepare the ground for him in the Commons, and the Prime Minister, who had sanctioned the initiative, remained silent.

The anger of the Commons was compounded by their knowledge of the nature and behaviour of the regime in power in Buenos Aires. On 23 March 1976 a coup in Argentina led by General Jorge Videla overthrew the Peronist Government and put a military regime in place. The following year the Junta began what it grandiosely called 'the Process of National Reorganization'. The avowed purpose of this Process was to put an end to left-wing terrorism which had plagued the country for six years before the coup. But this aim soon became lost in a general battle against liberal or left-wing thought. Thousands of young men and women, generally university graduates of leftish persuasion, 'disappeared'. Abducted by men from the military, they were tortured and killed. The exact number to have disappeared is unknown: estimates range from 10,000 to 20,000.

Amnesty International alerted Sir Bernard Braine to events in Argentina. Braine was hor-rified by what he discovered, not just because of the terrible nature of the oppression, but also because of the British Government's apparent determination to ignore the matter. Braine built up a dossier of the Junta's killing and torture as the evidence came to him of bodies which had been dropped from the air by naval aircraft into the sea; of children forcibly taken from their parents for adoption by 'respectable' citizens; of still more bodies, weighed down by concrete, dis-covered in the River Plate by British seamen:

I started compiling a list: priests were abducted for protesting against this violation of human rights, their bodies found on the roadside a day or two later, with their eyes gouged out, and when the local bishop objec-ted to it, he too was run off the road in his car, and left to die by the roadside. Former Argentinian diplomats who raised their voices were killed. University profes-sors, teachers were killed. Students who protested were killed. Argentina became a graveyard.

Braine was incensed by the lack of British protest at what was going on. In Parliament he named three British citizens who had disappeared in Argentina, and asked for action by the Foreign Office to discover their whereabouts. No effective action was taken: 'One can only assume that they were regarded as expendable,' he remarked later.

15

What infuriated Braine and many other back-benchers was the fact that negotiations on the transfer of sovereignty over the Falklands were continuing with such an unspeakable regime; that Ministers like Nicholas Ridley were travelling to Buenos Aires, making no protest about human rights abuses, but readily talking about the possibility of a transfer of sovereignty under a leaseback deal.

One simply couldn't grasp why it was that a British Minister was negotiating with gangsters of this kind. The very least that one would have expected of them was to say, before we get down to any business, our information is that there are a number of British subjects, not many but there are some, included in these thousands of disappeared people. Where are they? That should have been the first condition for any negotiation.

Sir Bernard Braine's outrage had a deep resonance on the opposite side of the House. The left wing of the Labour Party regarded the Junta as a fascist regime, which it naturally detested. Once more Labour members joined with those who were usually their most bitter opponents, and made a political solution of the Falklands problem an impossibility. The reception given to Ridley on his return from the Falklands was an expression of collective disgust and anger. Opposition to lease-back was now an unstoppable force.

The Cabinet Defence Committee met on 29 January 1981 and agreed that leaseback should not just be put on the back burner, it should be taken right off the stove. The only policy which remained was to continue talking in the hope that something might turn up. The Ambassador in Buenos Aires, Anthony Williams, scornfully called this a decision 'to have no strategy at all beyond a general Micawberism'.

Politically, a settlement was now out of the question. Militarily, the Chiefs of Staff had advised on numerous occasions that the Islands were indefensible without a substantial commitment which no Government could possibly afford, and which the Treasury would never allow.

The only thing left was to talk, in the hope that conflict might be averted. In the words of Lord Carrington, 'It was pretty awful, we all agreed on that; and there didn't seem to be another solution.' But the policy of talking would only work if the British Government made it plain that it was absolutely committed to deterring Argentine military action. This Mrs Thatcher's Government failed to do.

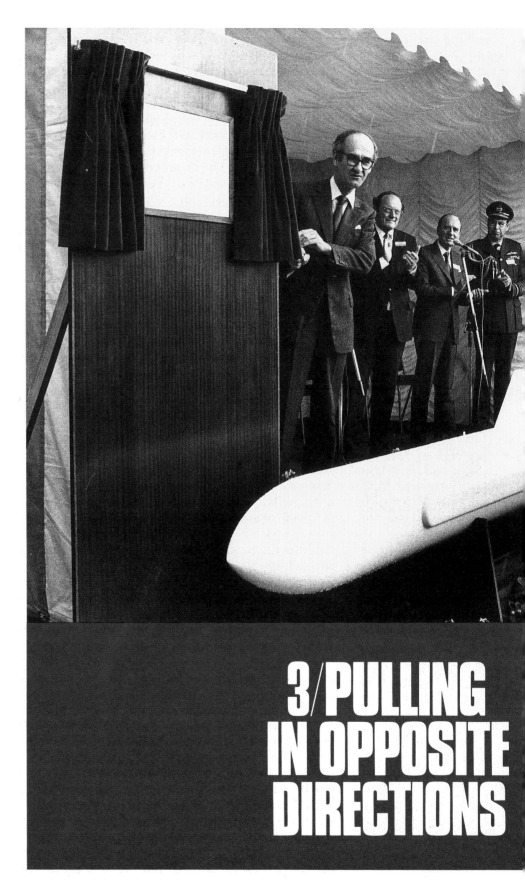

3/PULLING IN OPPOSITE DIRECTIONS

John Nott unveils a new missile. His proposed cuts in Britain's surface fleet outraged the Royal Navy. The First Sea Lord, Admiral Sir Henry Leach (right), led the campaign against the Government's defence review

Eed ARLY in June 1981, the Defence Secretary, John Nott, published a radical Defence Review. Its contents infuriated the Royal Navy, alarmed the Foreign Office and led the Argentinians to believe they would soon be able to invade the Falklands with impunity.

John Nott's Review, published as a Government White Paper, proposed that the Navy's surface fleet be slashed. The consequences were that one of its carriers, HMS *Invincible*, was to be sold to the Australians, another, the elderly *Hermes*, was to be phased out. The specialist amphibious ships, *Intrepid* and *Fearless*, would be taken out of service earlier than scheduled. Most importantly for the Falklands, the Ice Patrol Ship, HMS *Endurance*, would be withdrawn. Britain, it appeared, was declaring that the United Kingdom should have no defence role outside NATO, and certainly, no commitment to the Falkland Islands at a time when diplomacy had reached an impasse. Foreign and defence policy were completely out of kilter.

Rarely has a single man been regarded with more suspicion by the Royal Navy than John Nott, the architect of the proposed cuts. The Senior Services' deep distrust of the Defence Secretary was personified by the Chief of Naval Staff and First Sea Lord, Admiral Sir Henry Leach. The two men could not have had more different temperaments. Nott was considered by some to be nervous and hyperactive; his behaviour often struck colleagues as erratic and lacking in self-confidence. Leach, by contrast, seemed solid and calm. The son of a naval captain who died at sea during the Second World War, he was obviously and resolutely confident of the role of the Royal Navy and absolutely determined to defend it from interfering politicians. Today the Admiral no longer attempts to hide the problematic working relationship he had with Nott and blames him for turning a deaf ear to advice based on many years of naval experience.

The principle which lay behind the Defence Review was, in John Nott's words, 'the need to end the task force mentality of the Royal Navy'. In 1981, when he became Defence Secretary, the Ministry was some £600m overspent and had reached a position where it could no longer pay its bills. Cuts had to be made. Nott decided they should be made on the basis of a review of the role of the armed forces, rather than on some arbitrary budgetary principle. He took the view that the Royal Navy should not be equipped for independent British operations, led by carrier task forces, wherever they might be required in the world. In future, the Navy would operate only as part of a larger NATO force defending the West against the Soviet Union. Above all, there could be no defence policy for the remote fag-ends of empire like the Falkland Islands.

The idea that Britain should withdraw from its outstanding imperial commitments because they were too expensive appeared ill-judged and immoral to the First Sea Lord, Sir Henry Leach:

We still did have places of sovereign territory with British citizens, and the Falklands was a classic example, and as such, being British citizens, so they were entitled to British law and British defence, and

how were you going to provide that defence if you didn't have the capability to form a task force to provide that defence? It was as simple as that.

John Nott was unmoved by such arguments. He had the support of the Treasury, and, more importantly, the Prime Minister. The cuts would go ahead.

The Ice Patrol Ship, HMS *Endurance*, was of little consequence in the fight over naval cuts when compared to the carrier *Invincible*; but it was of immense importance to the Falkland Islands. The thinly armed 3,600 ton ice-breaker, with its complement of thirteen officers and 106 men, was ill-equipped to fight a battle at sea. She was, nevertheless, a symbol of Britain's presence in the area and commitment to the defence of the Falkland Islands. She cost little more than £4m *per annum* to keep on station in the South Atlantic for six months every year. Yet she was a favourite for scrapping whenever the question of defence cuts arose. Even the Navy was prepared to see *Endurance* go if it meant saving a more modern frigate, or preserving a new weapons programme. John Nott had little difficulty in adding *Endurance*'s name to the long list of casualties of his Defence Review.

But the Foreign Office was much less happy to see the departure of the Falklands' guard ship. With negotiations leading nowhere, the diplomats did not believe it made sense to withdraw the one obvious symbol of Britain's commitment to defend its sovereign territory. Immediately the Defence Review was made public Lord Carrington wrote to John Nott, on 5 June 1981, urging him to retain HMS *Endurance*. It was the beginning of a long and fruitless correspondence with his opposite number in Defence on the future of the ice-breaker. John Nott was not to be moved. He firmly believed that defence policy could not afford to cater for the Foreign Office's every need.

Lord Carrington considered that the Islands did at least merit the presence of HMS *Endurance*. It was not so much the importance of the ship itself, but, as he said later, 'it was the signal of our intention to withdraw the *Endurance* that was important'.

It was a signal which was received loudly and clearly in Buenos Aires. Admiral Jorge Anaya took note of it, and linked it to the diplomatic situation at the time: 'With negotiations near to being frozen, Great Britain announced the imminent retirement from service and scrapping of HMS *Endurance*, as part of a decision of major importance linked to the withdrawal, without replacement, of two aircraft carriers', he wrote later in his account of the causes of the conflict. His fellow Admiral, Juan Jose Lombardo, was similarly impressed:

The fact that they withdrew the *Endurance* was yet another indication that the English wanted to get rid of the Malvinas, stop spending money on them, and stop worrying about the Malvinas question ... it was yet another sign that the English weren't terribly bothered about these South Atlantic islands.

Argentine diplomats, men like Nicanor Costa Mendez, who had years of experience of watching developments in the South Atlantic, drew the same conclusion. Britain was losing interest. Their suspicions were confirmed by two other concurrent developments. In 1981 the Conservative Government introduced a Nationalities Bill which denied full citizenship to many of the Falkland Islanders. At the same time it was announced that the British Antarctic Survey's grant would be reduced, forcing a partial withdrawal from South Georgia, the Falkland Islands dependency.

Many in Britain warned that these decisions would send the wrong signals to Argentina. James Callaghan, who had acted so promptly to prevent an invasion in 1977, was particularly concerned:

I said they would give the wrong signals to the Falklands, to the Argentine Government, and they did ... We were withdrawing from other things. We were withdrawing from Hong Kong at the same time. We seemed to be lessening our commitments. Now, all right, that's a sensible thing to do in many ways. But you've got to do it in an orderly way, in a way that you do not expose the Falkland Islands, as they were exposed, by our failure to protect them properly.

Admiral Sir Henry Leach did everything he could to save the Royal Navy from the cuts. Out of desperation he broke all the rules. He briefed the media; he spoke to senior members of the Opposition; he pleaded with the Prime Minister.

I was desperate for the sake of the country to try to prevent, at all costs, this utter decimation of the Royal Navy, and I risked, therefore, being sacked, and I think quite honestly the only reason I wasn't sacked was that if I had been, the whole truth would have come out, instead of only bits of it.

It was to no avail. The Prime Minister and her Secretary of State for Defence were determined that the cuts should go ahead.

Three men with a mission. The Argentine Junta: (left right) Brigadier Lami Dozo, President Galtieri and Admiral Anaya

4/THE MILITARY OPTION

O N 8 December 1981 General Leopoldo Galtieri toppled Argentina's President, General Roberto Viola, and came to power as leader of a new military Junta. Although Sir Henry Leach was unaware of it at the time, Galtieri's arrival was the answer to his prayers.

General Galtieri owed his position to Admiral Jorge Anaya. Galtieri had initially been reluctant to become part of the Military Government. A convivial and heavy drinking soldier, who modelled himself on the colourful American war hero, General Patton, he had little time for politics. His sole wish had been to become Commander-in-Chief of the Army. But Admiral Anaya, who as head of Argentina's small Navy could never command enough influence to become President, exercised enormous influence over Galtieri. He persuaded the simple-minded General that he was a man of destiny who could reverse Argentina's historic humiliation at the hands of the British. According to Oscar Cardoso, the leading Argentine authority on the Malvinas conflict, 'It didn't take much to convince Galtieri. He's not very bright, you know, and doesn't have a very articulated view of himself and the world.' Anaya, the passionate 'Malvinista', quickly persuaded Galtieri that the recapture of the Islands would gain immense public support and prestige for an unpopular and oppressive military dictatorship.

On 12 December 1981 Jorge Anaya travelled to the Argentine Navy's largest base, Puerto Belgrano, to hand over command to Vice-Admiral Juan Jose Lombardo. Lombardo had been appointed Commander of Naval Operations to replace his old rival Anaya. The two men completed the hand-over formalities with little of the warmth and mutual congratulation which might be expected between old colleagues:

My relationship with Anaya was not one of friendship. I was never a good friend of Admiral Anaya's; I wasn't on close terms with him. What's more, he's a reserved man and basically I am too, so we're not very communicative; we're not the sort who have a lot of friends.

No mention was made of the Malvinas during the ceremonies. Lombardo's mind had been occupied with more pressing matters: in particular, Argentina's dispute with Chile over the Beagle Channel. Until a Papal mediation in the long-standing quarrel over territorial rights had been accepted, it had seemed that Argentina's next battle would be with Chile. The three services had been

The Argentine Navy's
Officers Club in Buenos
Aires, where secret
planning for the invasion of
the Malvinas took place

gearing up for war with their neighbour, and had
filed away the question of the Malvinas.

The two men travelled together on the aeroplane back to Buenos Aires. While seated next to
each other Anaya leant over and issued Lombardo with a simple order:

He said to me, and it was a complete surprise, that I
had to prepare a plan to capture the Malvinas. He told
me to do it in the utmost secrecy, and to do it alone. It
was really a shock to me because, well, it was something
new and important and I could see it was dangerous as,
regrettably, it turned out.

Four years before, in 1977, Anaya had made his
own plan for the capture of the Malvinas. That
plan had been thwarted by a single British nuclear
submarine in the South Atlantic. This time, however, it appeared that the British had little interest
in the region. The sudden appearance of a submarine was highly unlikely, given the fact that the
solitary British naval ship in the waters of the
Malvinas, HMS *Endurance*, was being withdrawn.
But, above all, Anaya explained to Lombardo,
secrecy was of the essence. If the British learned
of the plans, they could reinforce the Islands
rapidly, and make a landing impossible.

Lombardo says he was 'completely surprised' by
the order, but as the two men were hardly on
speaking terms, he felt unable to explore the
matter further with his Commander-in-Chief in
the constrained setting of an aircraft cabin.
Instead he arranged for a more formal discussion
three days later. It took place on 18 December
1981, in the ornate Officers' Club in the centre of
Buenos Aires' most fashionable shopping district.
Anaya, whose thin face and tight-lipped manner
gave him a harsh and forbidding appearance, was
monosyllabic in his response to Lombardo's questions. But his short answers gave the Admiral the
information he needed. The operation was to be a
tri-service matter; it was to be planned as a contingency, not a firm intention. As the despised Falklanders, the 'kelpers' as he called them, were
supposedly being 'liberated' from colonial rule
there were to be no injuries among them. The
same applied to the small garrison of Royal
Marines on the Islands, for diplomatic reasons.
Most significantly, Lombardo was to make no
plans for the subsequent defence of the Islands
from a British counter-attack. One was not
expected.

On 8 January 1982 the Junta met to endorse
Anaya's plans and give formal backing to Lombardo's planning. Four days later, on January 13,

the Junta met once more, and appointed a small
staff to aid the Admiral in his work. There was no
dissension among the members of the ruling
troika. Galtieri was happy to lead his nation to the
glorious fulfilment of its national dream; Anaya's
burning desire was well known; the third, and
perhaps most moderate of the Junta, Brigadier
Basilio Lami Dozo, the head of the Air Force, did
not raise his voice in protest.

Lombardo set to work with his small team of
senior naval officers. Planning took place in an
annex of the Officers' Club in the centre of
Buenos Aires in order to prevent the prying eyes
and gossip which would have been inevitable in
the huge bureaucracy of the Navy headquarters.
So secret was the work that typewriters were for-
bidden; only handwritten notes could be made.

The capture of the Islands had been planned so many times before: countless exercises and war games had played out the invasion of the Malvinas and secret reconnoitring parties had landed on the beaches almost annually (including one led by Lombardo himself in 1966) – that the actual scheme of the operation did not take long to put together. Its timing was determined by three factors: the weather, the training of conscripts, and the ability of the British to respond.

Lombardo decided that Operation *Rosario*, as the invasion was code-named, should take place in the southern winter when conditions in the South Atlantic would be so appalling as to deter any British counter-attack. This ruled out an early operation in March or April 1982, and made June to September the most favourable period.

As the operation was to involve the army, allowances had to be made for the training of conscripts. Not being a fully professional service, the Argentine Army relied on conscripts for its manpower. They usually began their National Service in March. Some time was required, therefore, for them to pass through their basic infantry training.

Finally, the British defence cuts would not begin to take effect until the summer, when the sale of the carrier HMS *Invincible* to the Australians would be completed, and the Ice Patrol Ship HMS *Endurance* withdrawn. For Lombardo, all the factors pointed to a date in July:

For the sake of choosing a day, we decided on 9 July, which is a national day, the day of Argentinian Independence. So we thought, well, let's set the date as 9 July, but it was just a rough indication, there was no definite order to say that was the date.

With military planning under way, the Junta could concentrate on the political rationale for their plan. Since the war Anaya has written his own confidential account of the reasoning behind the operation, *The Secret Story of the Malvinas War*. It is a somewhat contradictory and splenetic account of a military action of which he had long dreamed, but which was to bring about his own downfall, and the collapse of the military dictatorship.

In his *Secret Story* Anaya outlines his world view at the time that planning for Operation *Rosario* had started. In his idiosyncratic and rather curious outlook, Argentina's position at the end of 1981 and beginning of 1982 was satisfactory. The military regime had succeeded in stamping out 'guerilla activity'. Outside Argentina 'the virulence of anti-Argentine propaganda on human rights had diminished', with the arrival of the friendly Reagan administration. The dispute with Chile was on the way to resolution by Papal mediation. Relations with another troublesome neighbour, Brazil, were also on the mend. Only Britain stood in the way as an impediment to Argentina's development as a regional superpower and bulwark against the expansionism of Marxism in the South Atlantic.

The rejection of leaseback in the House of Commons, motivated by the Falkland Islanders' lobby, together with the perfidious British ability to negotiate endlessly without any progress, meant that an alternative solution to the Malvinas problem had to be found. In Anaya's words:

The hardening of the British position was obvious, and the large number of events suffered by us personally: the British ability to throw up obstacles, take advantage of incidents, create diversions, advance and retreat without losing ground, made it absolutely clear that it was essential to have a fall-back plan. This had never been considered as a national objective, but now it came into its own.

The fall-back plan was, of course, the recovery of the Islands by military force.

The diplomatic aspects of the 'fall-back plan' were discussed with the Foreign Ministry, and in particular, the new Foreign Minister, Dr Nicanor Costa Mendez. Costa Mendez was a veteran Malvinista, having negotiated the problem of the Islands with George Brown, the British Foreign Secretary, at the UN in 1965. He was also typical of many Argentine diplomats in being something of an Anglophile – he was an Oxford graduate – yet at the same time he seethed with resentment at what he considered the patronising manner of British diplomacy, and the fruitlessness of seventeen years of negotiations.

Costa Mendez shared the world outlook of the Junta: he believed that Argentina had a manifest destiny in the Southern Hemisphere to fight Marxism, preserve the Catholic faith and to dominate the region. Obviously, the Malvinas stood in the way of this so long as they remained British.

He did not react negatively when he was informed of the existence of a secret group studying the possibility of retaking the Islands. Instead, the Foreign Minister emphasised the need to continue negotiations while planning for war. The

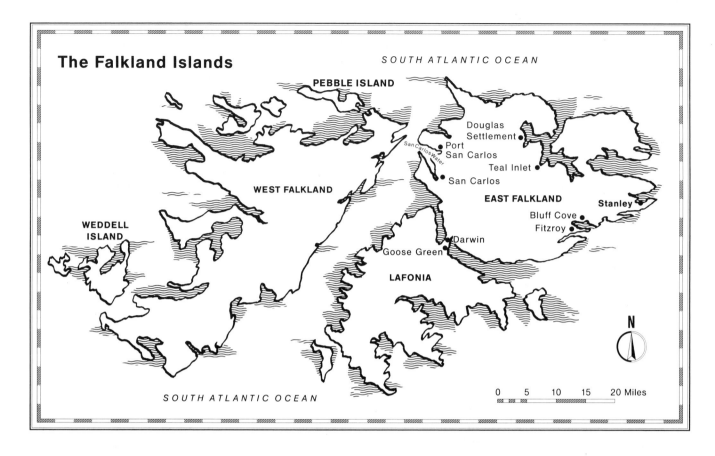

The Falkland Islands

next session was due to take place at the end of February at the United Nations. If these talks were fruitless, and if Britain reacted negatively to Argentina's proposal for a permanent negotiating commission with regular meetings to discuss the transfer of sovereignty under a fixed timetable, then the 'fall-back' military plan could be considered in tandem with diplomatic pressure at the United Nations.

Argentine diplomats were aware that Britain's position at the United Nations was not strong. Non-aligned nations tended to support Argentina in a matter regarded as a colonial issue. If the issue was taken to the General Assembly, after the likely failure of talks, Argentina would most probably gain world support for its cause. That achieved, the military option could take place as a legitimate action to recover illegally held colonial territory.

The Junta was also under the impression that the United States would support Argentina in its cause. The arrival of the Reagan administration in 1980 had brought with it renewed friendship and co-operation between the two countries. Prominent in President Reagan's entourage were

right-wing ideologues who had considerable sympathy for the Latin-American dictatorships in their battle against communist subversion. Jeane Kirkpatrick, the US Ambassador to the United Nations, was a particular friend of Argentina, and author of an influential essay, *Dictatorships and Double Standards*, in which she argued that there was a qualitative difference between 'authoritarian regimes', like Argentina, which opposed Marxism, and 'totalitarian regimes' which espoused communism.

Argentina responded to this new found legitimacy with undisguised eagerness. The traditional non-aligned stance of the country's diplomacy was thrown over in favour of a partnership with the United States in the battle against the expansionism of the Soviet Union and its Marxist ideology in Central America. In November 1981, shortly before he became President, General Galtieri visited the United States and was feted by the Reagan administration as a conquering hero. In response Galtieri announced the new partnership: 'Argentina and the United States will march together in the ideological war that is beginning in the world,' he declared.

The first stage of the 'ideological war' was the battle against the Sandinista regime in Nicaragua. In Argentina, the United States found an ideal partner in its clandestine war against the socialist government of this small Central American state. The Junta readily agreed to be the conduit through which the United States could provide military aid to the Contra rebels fighting to overthrow the Sandinistas. The arrangement benefited both sides. The United States was able to gain a valuable ally in the fight against communism in the Southern Hemisphere; Argentina was able to regain legitimacy in the West, and benefit from a partnership with the world's most powerful nation.

The Junta embarked on a programme of diplomatic pressure. Prominent visitors from the United States were reminded of Argentina's longstanding claim to the Malvinas. It was hoped that the new-found friendship would bear fruit in any conflict with Great Britain if not in direct support from the United States, at least in forceful neutrality. Admiral Anaya was particularly conscious of Britain's humiliation at the hands of the Americans in 1956: 'The last disproportionate British reaction with emphasis on confrontation before negotiation', he wrote in his *Secret Story*, 'was that carried out by the minister Anthony Eden in 1956 – the Suez crisis – and that had failed precisely due to pressure from their allies, the United States . . .'

The men of the Junta believed that history would repeat itself once Argentina had recaptured the Malvinas: a British military force on the way to recover the Islands would be forced to withdraw, just as Anthony Eden had been made to pull out of the Suez Canal zone.

There were other recent precedents which gave the military dictatorship confidence that the British would accept humiliation rather than face military conflict. In particular, the Junta was conscious of the withdrawal from Rhodesia in April 1980, and the creation of independent Zimbabwe, which, in Anaya's words, 'had impelled Great Britain to behave in a pacifist way, having to swallow a strong dose of insults to British feelings'. The Junta was convinced that the United Kingdom had to accept this 'well-publicised defeat for British prestige' because of pressure from the United States.

In the first place, however, force was to be subordinate to negotiations. Pressure on Britain was to be increased on all diplomatic fronts: in the UN, in London and Buenos Aires, and in Washington. The problem with this twin-track policy of diplomacy and negotiation, however, was that diplomatic pressure involved the use of veiled threats of military action. While plans for the invasion of the Malvinas were being prepared in complete secrecy, a series of hints that action was being contemplated if talks failed began to appear in the press, and rumours spread in the diplomatic community in Buenos Aires. Fortunately perhaps for Argentina, these warning signs of impending military action were ignored in London.

On 24 January 1982, the right-wing nationalist Iglesias Rouco revealed Argentine policy in its entirety in his column in the Buenos Aires newspaper, *La Prensa*. He wrote that Argentina was increasing diplomatic pressure on Britain, that diplomats would press Britain for a negotiating timetable which would finally settle the issue in favour of Argentina, and that if these failed, discussions would be broken off. He concluded that the United States would support Argentina in any action, not excluding military action. The article was planted by the Junta, with whom Rouco had excellent relations. Three days after it appeared the Foreign Minister, Nicanor Costa Mendez, delivered a note to the British Embassy which outlined Argentina's position at forthcoming talks in the UN. It made clear that recognition of sovereignty was the '*sine qua non* for the solution of the dispute' and proposed a permanent negotiating commission with a time frame for the transfer of sovereignty. Barely a week later, on 7 February 1982, Iglesias Rouco wrote again in *La Prensa* that if Britain was not prepared to accede to Argentine demands for a fixed timetable, military action to recover the Islands could not be excluded.

In case the message had not got through, the *Buenos Aires Herald*, Argentina's English language newspaper, published an editorial on 9 February 1982 which drew attention to the strong rumours circulating in the city of military action:

From a military point of a view such an operation would no doubt succeed, as there are very few British troops on the Islands and there has been no indication of large-scale reinforcements being dispatched from the homeland despite the occasionally warlike talk going on here. This suggests that the British either refuse to believe the rumours or even if they think they are true it would be a mistake to act on them. If the latter is the case the Foreign Office is playing a very peculiar game indeed, because it would plainly be better for a Britain resigned to losing the Islands, to see them handed over gracefully after friendly discussions than to see them snatched away . . .

The British Embassy in Buenos Aires began to take notice of the rumours. The Ambassador, Anthony Williams, reported to London that Admiral Anaya appeared to be 'in the driving seat' and that negotiations would now go through a 'test period' to see if anything could be achieved. At the same time Colonel Stephen Love, the British Military Attaché, became alarmed.

Colonel Love appeared to his colleagues and the British community in Buenos Aires as a typical military officer; indeed, his rather formal manner and measured delivery made him seem almost a caricature of the type of upright and honourable man which Sandhurst and Camberley tend to produce. Such men do not have a reputation for brains, nor was an intellectual approach expected of them when they came as Military Attachés to the Embassy in Buenos Aires. Life consisted of the usual round of cocktail parties and dinners with colleagues from other embassies and military men in the Argentine armed services. It was a pleasant if undemanding existence.

But Colonel Love's conventional exterior hid a keen and sharply perceptive mind. He, at least, was aware of the changing atmosphere and increasing tension in relations with Britain over the problem of the Islands:

The press was the big factor, this chap Iglesias Rouco, who I think most certainly was having all his stuff planted just to get a reaction, was writing the most virulent stuff and increasingly hawkish in its output, in La Prensa and all the other newspapers; and it was on the television and people were talking about it. And this was, I think, a little unusual, even among the English in Buenos Aires, the old established English, who had been there a long time. These were people who had always just accepted that the problem was there, but suddenly they were worried.

Given the British community's concerns, Love decided that his military mind 'should start to switch on'. He saw that negotiations did not look as though they would lead much further:

We either changed, they changed, we agreed to do nothing or there was going to be a crunch. I felt that my problem was to identify what that crunch could be and to make quite certain that my masters knew what the bottom line was.

The Colonel approached his Ambassador and suggested a trip to the Falklands to assess the ease with which the Islands could be taken by an Argentine force. Anthony Williams readily assented. But Love needed to get permission from London, as the Falkland Islands were not part of his remit. At first permission was refused, but the Ministry of Defence eventually relented, on the understanding that Love would pay for his own trip, and take his family with him in order to give the appearance of a holiday, rather than an intelligence gathering excursion.

While in the Falklands Colonel Love made a brief assessment of the Islands' defences: he visited the small Royal Marine detachment at their barracks in Moody Brook; he inspected the terrain, and he looked at the beaches surrounding Port Stanley. The outlook from Buenos Aires was clear:

The Falklands, in my view, was a ripe plum waiting to fall into the hands of any professional military machine which like the Argentine armed forces would have wished to have occupied them. I think probably we knew that before going there, but it was nonetheless reinforced when one looked at the size of the Royal Marine detachment in Moody Brook and looked at the vulnerability and the number of places which anybody could land.

Love's perspective came from his knowledge of the methods and abilities of the Argentine armed forces. He was well aware that they were very practised at the *coup de main* operation, in which an army seizes the key locations of the enemy in a surprise attack:

They had studied it, they had used it in their own capital city on numerous occasions. And to unseat an administration, and an administration not very well armed at that, would have been easy. And there were a hundred ways in which it could have been done.
The timing would have depended very much on the weather. It would depend very much, in my view, on the state of training of the conscript army which they would be probably using, and these conscripts would not have been trained to the sort of standard that I would have thought they would have liked them to have been until later on in their winter, June/July time. All of which led me to the view that if anything was going to be done it could be done comparatively easily and it would have been done the second half of the year if they had been planning such a move.

Love briefed the Ambassador on his fears when he returned to Buenos Aires. He was particularly concerned that he would be unable to give a clear and timely warning that an attack was about to take place. The Embassy's manpower simply

HMS *Endurance* seen at anchor in Port Stanley. The proposed scrapping of the Ice Patrol Ship sent the wrong signals to Buenos Aires

could not stretch to watching Argentina's navy and army bases for signs of suspicious military activity.

On 2 March 1982 Colonel Love wrote a paper which he sent to the Governor of the Falkland Islands, Rex Hunt, and copied to the Ministry of Defence and the Foreign Office.

It said that the *coup de main* operation was clearly a very easy option for the Argentine military to take and that the Governor could quite easily be put in the bag, that the small Royal Marine detachment could easily be overpowered, that there was nothing really which we could do about it. It said also that, in my view, the Argentine military were capable of doing it, and that finally unless very special arrangements were made and made pretty quickly there was no further warning that I could give from my post in Argentina.

Love's views were received with the tired indifference which seems to have characterised so much of Whitehall's dealings with the Falklands before the conflict. A Foreign Office official merely wrote in the margin of the report, 'It says nothing that we don't already know.' The Military Attaché in Buenos Aires heard nothing:

There was no reaction. This had been, if you like, one of the characteristics of the reportage from my desk back to London throughout, one doesn't expect an answer to every little thing you send back . . . But I had hoped that such a letter would have sparked a few questions. Do you really mean this? Aren't you over-emphasising it? Haven't we been here before? Isn't this all hype? But no, silence, complete silence, and so one gets the feeling, you know, they know it all backwards.

Meanwhile, in London, the Foreign Office was preparing for the next round of talks with Argentina at the United Nations, due to take place at the end of February 1982. Although he did not know of Colonel Love's paper, Lord Carrington was not unaware of the increasing tension in the region. His efforts to protect British interests in the South Atlantic centred on the Ice Patrol Ship, HMS *Endurance*. On 22 January 1982 he wrote to John Nott for the second time, stating that the decision to withdraw HMS *Endurance* would be seen as a political gesture of a lack of commitment to the Falkland Islands. He suggested a discussion of the matter. John Nott refused to talk further about the ship and declined to reverse his decision. Mrs Thatcher herself confirmed Nott's decision less than three weeks later in a written reply to a question in the House of Commons.

By this stage Carrington was becoming increasingly concerned. A week after Mrs Thatcher's intervention he wrote for the third time to John Nott expressing his continued anxiety about the withdrawal of HMS *Endurance*. But John Nott was not to be moved:

I recognised that the Foreign Office felt it was a mistake to withdraw *Endurance* and I respect that view, but I was in the middle, if you remember, of a very public and difficult Defence Review. And to have removed yet another frigate from the Navy's precious surface fleet and said we are keeping *Endurance* instead of a serious naval asset rather than one which was foundering and was falling to pieces and needed replacing, would have just been impracticable at the time.

And indeed, it was part of the Defence Review's proposals that we should deploy serious defence assets, a couple of frigates, to the Falklands, every year, and perhaps that wasn't noticed by the Argentinians.

A policy of financial stringency, imposed by the Prime Minister and backed up by the Treasury, lay behind the defence cuts. John Nott simply did not have access to the funds to pay for all Britain's worldwide defence commitments. Lord Carrington had found this out for himself when he had turned in desperation to the Treasury for extra funds to protect the Falklands in an emergency:

I mean if you look at the money involved in keeping *Endurance* it was absolutely nothing at all, but the Secretary of Defence had the Treasury to contend with. I mean when I suggested that some preliminary measures ought to be taken, I mean long before all this happened, about supplying the Falkland Islands if they were cut off from the mainland, the Treasury said that if that's what I felt it ought to be done on the Foreign Office vote. Well, I mean, how could it be done on the Foreign Office vote?

But events were taking place in the South Atlantic which would soon make the Treasury's niggardliness irrelevant. On 16 December 1981 Constantino Davidoff set off from Buenos Aires on board the Argentine naval ice-breaker, the *Amirante Irizar*. His destination was the Falkland Islands' dependency, South Georgia. Davidoff, a buccaneering Argentine businessman, intended to inspect a disused whaling station at Leith with a view to dismantling it for scrap, and return a few months later to start work. In 1979 he had signed a contract with the Edinburgh-based firm, Christian Salvesen, which managed the station for the British Government. The contract gave him the option to purchase and dispose of old equipment.

More than two years after he had signed the contract Davidoff appeared to be taking up his option. He informed the British Embassy in Buenos Aires of his visit to South Georgia in a letter which arrived after his departure. He did not, however, comply with the formal entry requirements on his arrival at Leith. These obliged foreign nationals to report to the British Government representative at the port of Grytviken for formal entry clearance. As Argentina regarded South Georgia as its own sovereign territory, asking for formal entry clearance presented obvious difficulties.

The British Antarctic Survey base commander at Grytviken informed Rex Hunt in Port Stanley of Davidoff's landing at Leith. The Governor was incensed by what he heard. A naval ship had gone into British waters without permission, and landed a party who had agreed in a contract to comply with the laws of the Falkland Islands' dependencies, yet had flagrantly breached them:

I wanted that contract to be wound up, and I wanted a case to be taken against Davidoff for landing illegally in South Georgia, and a protest to be made to the Argentines. The Foreign and Commonwealth Office decided against taking any action against Davidoff, under the Falkland Islands Dependencies laws, but they did instruct our Ambassador in Argentina to make a formal protest about the illegal landing in South Georgia.

Anthony Williams was most reluctant to make any protest at all. His belief was that the matter was of little importance, and that Hunt was over-reacting as usual to the smallest Argentine action.

Relations between Port Stanley and the British Embassy in Buenos Aires were not as good as they might have been. Although contact between the two British outposts was almost always cordial, they were worlds apart in outlook and background. Hunt and Williams personified the difference. Rex Hunt was the archetypal Colonial Officer. He had served all over the world administering Britain's remaining imperial possessions with the loyalty and efficiency for which his service was renowned. A straight speaking Yorkshireman, he could get on well with anyone, from a Falklands shepherd to a visiting Peer. Above all, he was convinced of the right of the Islanders to remain British if they so wished. The late Anthony Williams, on the other hand, was the epitome of a professional British diplomat. His approach was intellectual and urbane. He specialised in Spanish and Latin American affairs and had little time for the views of the Falkland Islanders which, he believed, obstructed the development of relations with South America.

The two men represented different services. Although the Diplomatic Service had merged with the Commonwealth Relations Office – the renamed Colonial Service – in 1965, the differences remained. The diplomats regarded the colonial officers with a certain amount of contempt. They had not, after all, had to pass the stringent entry examinations required of Foreign Service officers; they were not, in the main, 'Oxbridge'; they tended to 'go native' and support the interests of their colonies rather than those of British foreign policy.

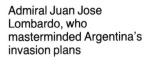

The outlook, therefore, from Port Stanley and Buenos Aires was very different. This clash of personalities and views led to a clash of advice from the two centres to London, and – quite naturally – a confused response. On almost every issue the British Embassy advised London to accommodate Argentina, while Port Stanley counselled a tough and uncompromising response. Colonel Love remembers the differences:

As far as Argentina was concerned, we in the embassy had a lot to do with the Argentines. We liked them, we saw their faults but we got on with them. We had to, and we understood very clearly where we had a mutual interest.

In Port Stanley, divided by that fateful strip of water, what could they make of Argentina? Argentina was a gun-toting collection of people who were quite unable to run their own country, had obvious designs on the Falklands' own sovereignty and future life-style. What could they think but that they were very much a bunch of thugs? And they did not fit into their view as to how their life was going to go on at all. As far as London was concerned, well, I suppose London was the referee that had to make what it could from both our views.

It was no easy matter for London to referee. The Foreign Office had little time to spare for working out the best policy to follow when offered two sets of conflicting advice. The result was that both Stanley and Buenos Aires had considerable autonomy in their actions and that important events were often ignored, and insignificant developments frequently exaggerated.

When the British Ambassador was instructed, on 4 January 1982, to lodge a formal protest about the landing of Davidoff on South Georgia, he demurred. A formal protest was much less than the Governor in Port Stanley wanted, but to the Ambassador it was a dangerous escalation of a minor incident. Five days later the Foreign Office in London, having learned of the presence of a naval ship in South Georgia, the *Amirante Irizar*, ordered Williams to lodge the protest. This time he complied reluctantly. The protest was rejected out-of-hand by the Argentine Foreign Office.

Rex Hunt was correct to have been suspicious. On 20 December 1976, exactly five years before Davidoff made his first landing on South Georgia, a Wasp helicopter from HMS *Endurance* had discovered the Argentine military base which Admiral Lombardo had set up on Southern Thule, in the South Sandwich Islands. As Britain had done no more than issue formal protests the base had remained on the island. This occupation of a Falkland Islands Dependency was judged a signal success by the Argentine authorities. Southern Thule had become, in effect, Argentine territory.

In 1981 Admiral Lombardo proposed a more ambitious but similar scheme: the occupation of South Georgia.

We were going to affirm our rights, and it was going to cost very little – in every sense of the word because from the point of view of monetary cost it wasn't going to cost us anything because it was just another operation within what the Navy normally does. And from the point of view of political cost, it was judged that the same applied, because in the event of the English reacting, we could always back out, withdraw and say that it had been a landing to carry out a meteorological or hydrographical investigation or whatever.

Lombardo's plan was accepted both by the Navy and the Foreign Ministry. It was code-named 'Operation *Alpha*', and the detailed planning was handed to more junior officers in the Navy. The plan which they produced was simple. A group of about fifteen servicemen would embark on an Argentine naval ice-breaker for the duration of the Antarctic summer. At the end of the season the ship would divert to South Georgia and deposit the small force who would spend the winter on the island. Lombardo explains:

That Operation *Alpha* was going to be carried out around April 1982, when the English had already gone back to England, so that it was physically going to be more difficult for them to come back, and moreover, it would possibly go unnoticed for some time. So, in June or July, right in the winter, we were to appear, carrying out meteorological reports and radio ham jobs etc. so that the world would know that there were Argentinians living on those islands. That was the idea of Operation *Alpha*.

When it was learned that Davidoff was planning to visit South Georgia in December, and return later in March 1982, Operation *Alpha* was modified to use the scrap-metal merchant's visit as a cover. The Argentine Navy offered Davidoff the use of their ships, and supplied some manpower of their own.

None of this was known to the British at the time. But Rex Hunt drew his own conclusions, which were not far from the truth:

All the indications were that we were losing interest in the Falkland Islands. It started I think way back when the Argentines took Southern Thule in the '70s and we didn't do a thing about it: we just made a customary protest every year, but we didn't act firmly then, and I think that gave the Argentines the idea that they should carry on pushing, that's why I reacted so strongly when they landed in South Georgia illegally, because I was convinced that had we not reacted firmly, that would have become another Southern Thule and we wouldn't have got the Argentines out of South Georgia again, they would have stayed.

Davidoff returned with his party to Buenos Aires and, on 23 February 1982, visited Anthony Williams at the British Embassy. He apologised for the problems caused by his visit and stated his intention to return with a salvage party. He asked for details how best to proceed so as not to cause an incident. The Ambassador passed this request on to Port Stanley, but no reply was received before Davidoff's party had left for South Georgia for their second visit.

On the diplomatic front, meanwhile, Argentina was increasing pressure as planned, but in a haphazard and shambolic manner. On 27 February 1982, Richard Luce, the Minister of State for Foreign Affairs, met his opposite number, Enrique Ros, for scheduled talks at the United Nations in New York. The two men got on with each other. They were both accomplished negotiators, and both displayed the tact and charm which they thought civilised nations should use when conducting complex talks. They met frequently in two New York East Side restaurants, each side taking it in turns to host the talks. The agenda mainly concerned the establishment of a permanent negotiating commission. At the end of the talks the two sides issued a joint communiqué which declared that the meeting 'had taken place in a cordial and positive spirit', and that Argentine proposals had been considered in detail. Both sides agreed to inform their Governments accordingly.

The joint communiqué infuriated the Junta. They could not understand why Ros, contrary to all instructions, had behaved in such a friendly and diplomatic manner to the British. Admiral Anaya considered it yet another example of the ability of British diplomats to manipulate gullible Argentines. This was unfair to Ros, who was neither gullible nor easily manipulated, but firmly believed that the negotiations should be conducted in a positive spirit of co-operation.

When the mild-mannered Ambassador Ros returned to Buenos Aires he was kept in no doubt about his disgrace. Officials from the Foreign Ministry boarded his aeroplane before he could disembark at Buenos Aires, and told him that he was to avoid the press and speak to no one about the joint communiqué. It had been torn up. In its place the Argentine Foreign Minister, Nicanor Costa Mendez, had issued his own unilateral statement which had little to do with the talks, but a great deal of relevance to Junta policy. In a broad hint that military action would be contemplated, should Britain fail to accede to requests for a fixed timetable for the transfer of sovereignty, the unilateral communiqué stated that 'Argentina reserves the right to put an end to the proceedings and to choose freely the procedure which best suits its interests'.

When Richard Luce returned to London, having visited Washington to ask for US help 'to keep things cool', he had an urgent meeting with Lord Carrington:

And I remember that Lord Carrington and I were pretty surprised, and worried by the reaction that appeared to be developing in Argentina. *La Prensa*, one of the leading newspapers, was saying some pretty aggressive things and clearly sparked by the military regime. Clearly they were feeling restless. That wasn't in keeping with the atmosphere of my negotiations, and therefore we were worried by that and wanted to clarify things and try and overcome some of the misunderstanding.

Luce and Carrington reviewed the situation on 5 March 1982. Their intelligence briefings indicated that Argentine military action would probably only take place after a series of hostile diplomatic and economic measures against the Islands: most probably a vote in the General Assembly of the UN, and the abrupt cutting off of the Islands' communications with the outside world.

Two days before, on March 3, shortly after returning from Washington, Luce had reassured the House of Commons that all necessary steps were in hand 'to ensure the Islands against unexpected attack'. It may have been the right way to quieten a suspicious Commons, but it sent the wrong signals to Buenos Aires. It gave Argentina the impression that Britain was preparing to fortify the Falklands against any Argentine attack. This was not the case. When Luce and Carrington discussed military measures at their meeting on March 5 they decided not to take any steps to reinforce the Islands.

A Foreign Office official revealed the events of 1977 to Luce and Carrington when they met on March 5. He told them how Jim Callaghan had ordered the despatch of a small task force of two frigates and a nuclear-powered submarine to the South Atlantic. Carrington was informed that Argentina had not been made aware of the deployment. On hearing this he decided not to request the immediate despatch of a task force.

If there was a point of no return, this was it. Lord Carrington was misinformed when he was told that Argentina had not been made aware of the previous task force. Maurice Oldfield, the head of MI6, *had* told the Argentinians covertly of the probable presence of a submarine in the South Atlantic.

Even if the Argentinians had been unaware of the presence of the Royal Navy in 1977, the availability of naval support in a period of tension must have been extremely helpful to hard-pressed diplomats seeking to avoid conflict. Admiral Sir Henry Leach was the commander of the 1977 task force:

It did mean that at any point that the politicians desired, they could say to Argentina, 'We have got in position', wherever it was, 'Now stop it, or else', and that meant you would save time, whereas if you'd said that from back in UK, the Argentines could have done their arithmetic just as well, and they would have said, 'Well, they can't do anything about it for three weeks, we'll give it a run'.

Although Luce had reassured the House of Commons that measures were in hand to defend the Islands from a surprise attack, he and the Foreign Secretary firmly rejected taking precisely the measures required. As the crisis unfolded over the next four weeks, the two men must have wished many times that they had requested a nuclear submarine to proceed to the area when the opportunity had presented itself. With hindsight, Carrington ruefully admits, '... it would have been much better to do it earlier, but if we all knew how events unfolded before we actually had to take decisions, it would be much easier.'

Mrs Thatcher now became aware of the problem. Although she had endorsed John Nott's decision to withdraw HMS *Endurance*, she realised that military measures might be necessary to defend the Falklands and deter an attack. After reading of hostile comments in the Argentine press after the New York talks, she wrote 'we must make contingency plans' in the margin of a briefing paper. On March 8, three days after Carrington and Luce had rejected the submarine option, the Prime Minister's Private Secretary passed on this message to the Foreign and Commonwealth Office. It drew no response. Officials merely pushed it on to the agenda of the next Cabinet Defence Committee.

On the same day Mrs Thatcher raised the matter with the Defence Secretary. She asked John Nott how quickly a task force could be deployed to the Falkland Islands. Four days later his department replied that it would take about twenty days. No mention appears to have been made of a submarine, whose passage would have been some eight days faster.

The Ministry of Defence was anxious not to become involved. A deployment of even a small task force to the South Atlantic would have made a mockery of the proposed defence cuts which were based on the philosophy that the Royal Navy no longer had a role outside NATO's area. A return to gun-boat diplomacy was precisely what John Nott was hoping to prevent once and for all.

ON 19 March Constantino Davidoff's team returned to South Georgia as planned. Davidoff had told the British Embassy of his team's intention to start work on dismantling the whaling station at Leith ten days before their arrival. No objections were raised. Davidoff also informed Salvesens, the Edinburgh company with whom he had a contract. Salvesens informed Rex Hunt in Port Stanley, and the Foreign Office. But when the party of sixty men landed they once again ignored British entry procedures. This time they went further and raised an Argentine flag.

The United Kingdom representative on South Georgia, the chief of the British Antarctic Survey team, reported this infringement to Port Stanley, who passed the news on to London. There followed the usual dispute between the Embassy in Buenos Aires and the Governor in Port Stanley on how to respond, with London acting as referee. Rex Hunt believed, rightly as it turned out, that the Davidoff party was a front for a permanent Argentine occupation of the Islands. Anthony Williams thought the matter was a minor infringement of immigration procedures, which he called 'trivial and low-level misbehaviour'. Lord Carrington had to arbitrate:

It was difficult I think to make a judgement as to whether that was the preliminary for an Argentinian assault on the Falklands, or whether it was just a try on. Certainly the Embassy in Buenos Aires took the view that it was not very important, because when I decided that there was no way we could let Davidoff stay, and we had to clear him out ... the Embassy said don't make such a fuss about this, it disturbs the good relations that we've built up with the Argentinians and you're making a mountain out of a mole hill. And so there were differences of opinion about it, but it was quite clear I think that things were on the move, but the intelligence assessments at the time were still that it was not going to happen ... that there was going to be gradual build up.

Rex Hunt advised that HMS *Endurance* be used to remove the Argentine men. London agreed. *Endurance* was ordered to set sail for South Georgia with a party of marines on board. There followed a period of confusion in which *Endurance*'s orders were countermanded and reinstated as Ministers in London responded to conflicting advice from Port Stanley and Buenos Aires. The British Ambassador was instructed, meanwhile, to inform the Argentine Ministry of Foreign Affairs that Britain took the matter very seriously. Meanwhile HMS *Endurance* continued her voyage.

The Junta in Buenos Aires was shocked and alarmed by the strong British diplomatic reaction and the despatch of HMS *Endurance*. They had planned for increasing diplomatic pressure, followed only if necessary by invasion of the Malvinas later in the year. The landings on South Georgia were part of the navy's semi-official plan, Operation *Alpha*. The naval staff who planned it had predicted a repetition of the low-key British response to the occupation of Southern Thule.

The Argentine Military Government was chaotic and poorly managed. As is so common in armed forces, the three services jealously guarded their own projects, and fought tooth-and-nail for the advancement and prestige of their own interests. Operation *Alpha*, a naval project, was typical of this rivalry.

Now that the British seemed to be waking up to events in the South Atlantic, the Junta would have to act fast. What Anaya feared most was the deployment of a British nuclear submarine. If that were to happen, all his carefully laid plans would be ruined once again. It was essential, therefore, that an invasion plan be set in motion if the slightest indication arose that Britain might be ready to send a task force. The strong response to the landing party on South Georgia seemed to indicate that Britain was preparing just such a contingency, as Anaya wrote in his *Secret Story*:

The landing was converted into an 'incident' and then magnified by Great Britain to justify, through using it, to the international community its decision to NOT NEGOTIATE and to lay a foundation for a later military backing up of the Malvinas, in aid of an eventual exploitation of the area's resources.

It was a wildly inaccurate reading of the British response, but it was one which was to lead to war.

As Britain demanded the removal of the Argentine party on South Georgia, and implied that – if necessary – force would be used, the Junta went into action. It was agreed that Britain's demands could not be complied with. HMS *Endurance*'s small detachment of marines would be no match for the Argentine forces in the area.

The Junta was becoming increasingly concerned about the situation in the Malvinas. Admiral Juan Jose Lombardo, who was celebrating his birthday in Uruguay, was ordered to end his holiday and return to Buenos Aires. Before returning to the capital, he paid a visit to Puerto Belgrano to see what ships were available for an operation.

Grytviken in South Georgia, a disused whaling station and the headquarters of the British Antarctic Survey. HMS *Endurance* lies alongside the jetty

Lombardo then returned to Buenos Aires and was summoned to meet the Junta. At the meeting he was asked to find out the earliest date by which an invasion force could be ready to set sail for the Malvinas. Two days later, on March 23, he informed the Junta that a task force could set sail on March 28:

We, the Argentinian Navy, normally have our ships quite well prepared, and also what we were going to use for the operation was less than half of the ships available. So, from the point of view of the National Navy, it wasn't too difficult to do it and the co-operation which we required from the Army was at that point very limited, that is, the number of people from the Army that had to embark was very small – I think we took about sixty men, that's all.

As the Junta was learning that an invasion force could be made ready extremely quickly, the first reports of the landing of the scrap workers at Leith in South Georgia were appearing in the press in London. These magnified the crisis, and when seen in Buenos Aires, were interpreted as yet more evidence of a new British belligerence. The *Evening Standard* of March 23 headlined its report 'ARGENTINE INVASION OF SOUTH GEORGIA ISLANDS'. On the same afternoon, Richard Luce again reassured the House of Commons that it was the duty of any British Government to defend the Islands to the best of its ability. This was immediately reported to Buenos Aires where the Junta interpreted his comments as a sign of British intentions to reinforce the Malvinas.

That afternoon, London decided on a strong line. The Foreign Office ordered Anthony Williams to tell the Argentine Ministry of Foreign Affairs that HMS *Endurance* was proceeding to Leith to remove the remaining Argentines. London's strong response to the landing of the scrap metal workers alarmed the British Ambassador. Having delivered the message with extreme reluctance, he hurried back to the Embassy and telegraphed the Foreign Office, warning that an over-reaction could do lasting damage to relations between the two countries. At the same time he instructed Stephen Love to reiterate his warning that Argentina could capture the Falklands quickly and easily. Love complied:

I pointed this out, I think, in a signal that I sent at about this time, saying that with reference to my original assessment of the bottom line, as I call it, in the Falkland Islands, the worst scenario would be the following: that if *Endurance* were used to take off those men there was a definite risk that the Argentine Navy might have intercepted her and would have tried to retake those chaps, and that it could very definitely in my view have raised the temperature and escalated the possibility of a military coup against the Falklands.

London now listened to this advice, quite contrary to that coming from Port Stanley, and ordered HMS *Endurance* not to proceed to Leith, where the Argentines were based, but to sail instead to Grytviken, the British base, and monitor developments from there.

But the diversion of *Endurance* was too late to calm the situation. Admiral Anaya ordered the naval supply ship, *Bahia Paraiso*, with a party of fourteen marines to reinforce the scrap workers. To argue, as the leaders of the Junta have done since the crisis, that the *Bahia Paraiso* was diverted from the Antarctic to reinforce South Georgia in the face of British over-reaction to a trivial incident is disingenuous. The Argentine Navy had always intended that the marines be sent to Leith to join the scrap workers. They were the group which comprised the official side of Operation *Alpha*.

These men had been hand-picked by Admiral Lombardo as part of the plan to establish a permanent base on the Island. They were not an innocent group returning from the Antarctic to Argentina, as was later claimed, but an élite force of ultra-nationalists, led by the notorious Lieutenant Alfredo Astiz, who were going to reclaim a piece of territory they believed to be Argentine.

The arrival of the *Bahia Paraiso* on March 24 was observed by the Royal Marine detachment who had sailed with HMS *Endurance*, and who had been diverted to Grytviken. The 22-year-old Lieutenant Keith Mills was in command:

We set a small observation post on Jason Peak, on the other side of the bay from Leith, and the guys with their powerful binoculars were able to see what was actually going on. Although not in that much detail because even with powerful binoculars, at three kilometres or more it is still very difficult to get detail. And one day that week, a ship came in, an Argentine ship. And we thought this is it, they're on their way and this ship's come to pick them up. Anyway, it transpired that this ship hadn't come to pick them up at all, but was actually unloading stores and, far from wanting to leave, it looked as if they were planning to make their stay a little bit more permanent than they had intended.

London was informed by *Endurance* of the arrival of the *Bahia Paraiso* and the establishment of what looked like a permanent base. Lord Carrington began to review his options. They were extremely limited. Intelligence assessments were still advising that the crisis would probably develop in stages, starting with the termination of supplies and communications to the Islands. If this were to be the case, money – which the Foreign Office did not have – would be needed to pay for the replacement sea and air services to the Islands. As part of the attempts to lead the Islands to the Argentine point of view, the Foreign Office had previously agreed to the complete severing of British services. Now the Falklands were totally dependent on Argentina. Carrington appealed to the Treasury once more for the extra emergency funds from the Contingency Reserve. Less than a week before the invasion, the Chief Secretary to the Treasury peremptorily told the Foreign Secretary that the money would not be made available.

The Ministry of Defence was no more helpful. Without a nuclear submarine on station – an option which Carrington and Luce had rejected at the beginning of March – there was nothing which could be done. *Endurance* was dangerously exposed. Her almost complete lack of armament made her no match at all for Argentina's Exocet-equipped navy. The Foreign Secretary was advised by officials that there was a real risk of military confrontation, 'which Britain was in no position to win'.

Britain was in a hopeless position. Any attempted military reinforcement, as the Embassy in Buenos Aires was constantly warning, could precipitate an invasion of the Falklands.

The Junta in Buenos Aires were, by now, extremely alert to any signs that Britain might be preparing to reinforce the Islands and send a nuclear-powered submarine into the South Atlantic. They noted that a party of marines, led by Major Michael Norman, had embarked on the *John Biscoe* in Montevideo, to join the marine detachment in Port Stanley. These men were the scheduled replacement, but the Foreign Office had gained Ministry of Defence agreement that the outgoing detachment's departure be delayed, so as to 'doublebank' the garrison during this difficult time.

Intelligence sources also informed the Junta on March 25 that a Royal Navy logistical ship, the *Bransfield*, had left Punta Areñas in Chile. This information was incorrect. The *Bransfield* was a civilian survey ship, and had nothing to do with the Royal Navy. But the Junta appears to have been keen to read any signs of British activity as an indication of the full-scale reinforcement of the Falklands, and the start of the dreaded 'Fortress Falklands' policy.

In London, on March 25, Lord Carrington briefed the Cabinet on the situation. It was the first time for more than a year that members of the Cabinet had discussed the matter. The Foreign Secretary explained to his colleagues the difficulty of the situation: that HMS *Endurance* could remove the Argentine party, but if this led to military confrontation Britain would be in no position to defend the ship, nor the Falkland Islands. The Cabinet agreed that the question of the future of *Endurance* might have to be reconsidered, but no decision was made on how to solve the problem of the illegal landing on South Georgia.

John Nott was absent in the United States, and was unable to defend his decision to withdraw *Endurance*. However, on the following day, March 26, he spoke on the telephone to his junior, Gerry Wiggin, and ordered him to write to Lord Carrington confirming that the Ministry of Defence could not justify paying for the Ice Patrol Ship's retention.

The letter was typical of the disarray in British policy. While the Foreign Office was facing a crisis which it could barely handle with HMS *Endurance*, the Ministry of Defence was ensuring that even this insignificant ship be removed. On the same day, March 26, the Ministry of Defence glumly informed the Prime Minister that if the Islands were invaded by Argentine forces the chances of retaking them were very slim indeed.

In Buenos Aires on March 26, as the decision to withdraw *Endurance* was confirmed in London, the Junta issued orders for the invasion fleet to set sail. There was unanimous agreement amongst the Commanders-in-Chief that the invasion of the Malvinas had to be brought forward. It appeared to them that Britain was preparing to reinforce the area with a naval force which would, in their view, be disastrous. Argentina would be humiliated in South Georgia if the scrap workers were removed forcibly. Any progress towards the transfer of sovereignty would become impossible as Britain renewed its commitment to the Falkland Islands. There was no alternative. Action had to be taken fast.

Nicanor Costa Mendez concurred. While it would have been much better, in his view, to invade later in the year, something had to be done immediately for Argentina to have any chance of success in negotiations. He emphasised the overriding need to carry out the military operation without causing British casualties. If Argentina occupied the Islands without causing physical harm, he advised, serious negotiations could begin from a position of moral and physical strength. At the meeting of the Commanders-in-Chief no consideration was given to a British military response to the planned invasion. The possibility does not seem to have crossed the Junta's collective mind.

In London the British Government was reluctantly becoming aware that events were taking place which were beyond its control. A telegram was received from the British Ambassador on March 27, the day after the Junta had ordered the invasion of the Malvinas. By this time even Anthony Williams had realised that things were not as innocent as they seemed. In the telegram he admitted that the Argentines had been 'playing us along' and that the Foreign Minister was being duplicitous in his handling of the South Georgia incident. On the next day Williams reported that Costa Mendez had issued an uncompromising statement in which he refused to back down on the South Georgia question, and closed the door to any immediate diplomatic settlement.

Having worked almost continuously for three days the Argentine amphibious forces were ready to put to sea on March 28. Rear-Admiral Carlos Busser was in command of the operation:

The equipment was in very good condition because we had kept it serviced, and therefore it wasn't difficult to gather together. But it was very hard work. Some of my people had to remain in the General Staff building from the 24th to the 28th without going home, almost without sleep. Of course they slept, but they did in the building, on a chair or sofa when they could. They would rest a bit and then carry on working. On the 28th we were ready to set sail; everything was on board, all the equipment was in working order, our personnel were equipped and there were no problems.

On Sunday, March 28, the Argentine invasion fleet set sail on the 1,000 mile journey south to the Falklands. It was led by the British-designed *Santissima Trinidad*, the latest Exocet-equipped Type 42 destroyer, and included in support the elderly aircraft carrier, *25 de Mayo*. In all, the force consisted of fourteen ships, about half the Argentine surface navy. The landing force was concentrated on board the amphibious landing ship, *Cabo San Antonio*, and was made up of 904 men, mostly marines. So great was the need for secrecy that few of the men of the task force were aware of their destination when the ships left Puerto Belgrano.

The following morning, Monday March 29, Mrs Thatcher and Lord Carrington travelled to Brussels to debate the European Community budget. Before the Community meeting they agreed that a nuclear-powered submarine be sent covertly to the South Atlantic as soon as possible.

The decision led to an unprecedented confusion in Government. The Ministry of Defence considered that it would be a good thing if the despatch of a submarine appear in the press as a warning to the Argentine Government. At the same time, ITN's Defence Correspondent, in Gibraltar observing the Royal Navy's exercise *Spring Train*, reported that a nuclear-powered submarine, HMS *Superb*, had been seen leaving harbour. That Monday evening ITN ran the story that *Superb* was heading for the Falklands.

The next day, Tuesday March 30, the *Daily Telegraph* confirmed the report, with a briefing from the Ministry of Defence that it was the first of two boats sailing south. The news was flashed from the Argentine Embassy in London to Buenos Aires by the Commercial Attaché, Minister Molteni.

The story was bogus. *Superb* was not sailing south, but heading north to return to base. British submarines did not set sail for another two days. Frank Cooper, then Permanent-Under-Secretary at the Ministry of Defence, believed that the Argentines should be warned:

I think it became known by the press that a submarine had sailed ... And they printed it, and assumed that the submarine was going to the South Atlantic. It was not in fact going to the South Atlantic, so the Ministry of Defence, I think decided quite rightly, and very sensibly, they were not going to correct the press on this particular occasion ... But it happened to suit everybody's book, to give the impression that there was a submarine on its way.

It did not suit the Foreign Office's book. Officials there were well aware that the news that a submarine was on its way could only spur the Argentine Junta into action. Richard Luce was horrified when he heard the bogus news story:

To me, that was one of the most serious things that happened throughout the whole of that crisis. And I was deeply shocked, indeed, my principal private secretary said to me when he heard that news, that the headline was coming out the next morning, late at night, he went out in the garden and was physically sick because we realised the damage that was going to do.

The text of Molteni's telegram which was received in Buenos Aires at 11.30 am on March 30 read: '... papers widely report the sending of one or two nuclear-capacity nuclear submarines (*sic*). Certain newspapers maintain having received confirmation from the British Government that the submarine *Superb* sailed from Gibraltar on Thursday, March 25.'

The Junta immediately calculated their window of opportunity. They knew that the passage of a nuclear submarine travelling at speed was about twelve days. They could expect, therefore, that an invasion would be impossible after April 6 at the earliest. They had no time to lose. The operation would proceed as planned.

From the perspective of Buenos Aires the news that a submarine was on its way confirmed the view that Britain was acting in an arrogant and aggressive manner over the question of South Georgia. Argentina simply could not back down. If, as Britain suggested, the scrap workers were removed by an Argentine ship, or if, as the Governor in Port Stanley wished, their passports were stamped by a British representative, the Junta believed a fatal legal precedent would be established. Argentina would be forced into accepting British sovereignty over a dependency of the Falkland Islands and, by extension, over the Falklands themselves. Military action was the only way out, swiftly taken while the possibility existed. There could be no going back.

Between March 30 and 31 a violent storm broke out in the South Atlantic which slowed the invasion force and led to a change of route. In London intelligence was received on March 30 of the position of the task force some 800–900 miles north of the Falklands. The Ministry of Defence concluded that the ships were probably only exercising, though this was unusual for the time of year, and recommended against the sending of

President Reagan. The problem of the quarrel between two allies over an 'ice-cold bunch of rocks' perplexed him

surface ships to the South Atlantic. A second submarine, however, was prepared for departure south.

As usual, the Ministry of Defence was reluctant to take action. When Lord Carrington urged, on the same day, that a third submarine be sent, his request was refused. The Ministry also counselled against sending the group of eight warships exercising off Gibraltar, arguing that 'there was no sign' of Argentine plans to invade the Falklands. This was an obvious misreading of intelligence, given the fact that it was known that an Argentine task force was heading south at that moment.

On Wednesday March 31 Rear-Admiral Busser, in command of the landing force aboard the *Cabo San Antonio*, signalled Buenos Aires that the storm had forced the postponement of the invasion by one day to Friday, April 2. The signal was intercepted, passed to GCHQ, the Government's signals intelligence centre in Cheltenham, decoded and transmitted immediately to the Ministry of Defence, the Foreign Office and the Joint Intelligence Committee.

The truth which the Government and officials had been hiding from for so long was now staring them in the face. John Nott, back from the USA, sought an immediate meeting with the Prime Minister. He found her in her rooms in the House of Commons, where he was joined by Richard Luce (Lord Carrington was away in Israel), Humphrey Atkins, the Lord Privy Seal, and officials from the Ministry of Defence and the Foreign Office. The outlook seemed grim indeed. A landing was about to take place on British sovereign territory about which nothing could be done. Britain would be humiliated in the eyes of the world. The future of Mrs Thatcher's Government seemed extremely shaky.

When Mrs Thatcher sought advice from the Ministry of Defence about the possibility of retaking the Islands both Mr Nott and his officials were deeply pessimistic. They referred to previous studies commissioned by the Joint Chiefs of Staff which had argued that a repossession would require a massive force and would have no guarantee of success. Without air cover, which had been removed from the Royal Navy in previous cuts, the mission would be hazardous in the extreme. It would also be a logistical nightmare, with no possibility of reinforcement and resupply from the air.

Mrs Thatcher's salvation came in the form of Admiral Sir Henry Leach, the First Sea Lord and Chief of Naval Staff. Leach had been away on a day's visit to a naval establishment in Portsmouth, and did not return to London until about six o'clock in the evening. When he reached his office he discovered two briefs awaiting him: one advising that no military action be taken in the circumstances, and the other that an invasion was imminent:

These two briefs did not add up and I had an immediate and acute feeling, 'What the hell's the point in having a navy if you're not going to use it?'

John Nott, the Defence Secretary, was even then being briefed, I wasn't sure to which brief, so I rushed along to get in on the act, quickly, and in fact he wasn't in his office, he was being briefed in the House of

Commons and so I went down there as quickly as I could, got held up by that splendid policeman in the Central Lobby, rescued by a Whip and treated hospitably by them.

In due course the Defence Secretary was located with the Prime Minister and I was asked to go in, and I joined them and we took it from there, and the Prime Minister asked me a number of questions, of course, which I was able to answer, fortunately.

In that single meeting Sir Henry was able to demolish, for the time being at least, the whole basis of the proposed Defence Review. The Prime Minister had been warned that sending a task force to repossess the Falklands was a risky business which ought not to be contemplated. Now she received welcome and contradictory advice:

She was undoubtedly seeking positive, actual data, on which to make her own mind up as to whether this thing was on or not, and one of the more pertinent ones (they were all pertinent, but this was particularly pertinent and almost the final crunch) was, 'Could we do it?', against all the risks as we'd previously discussed.

And I said, 'Yes, we could, and in my judgement, we should', which was not my business because that was a political matter, and she was on to that in a flash, 'Why do you say that?', and I said, 'Well, because I think if we don't, or if we do it half-heartedly, and are not completely successful, we shall be living in a different country, which counts for very much less'.

Mrs Thatcher's response was immediate. Leach was ordered to prepare a task force. The decision as to whether it should sail or not would be taken later.

After the meeting John Nott remained alone with the Prime Minister:

... I did say to her that I thought that it was an exceptionally difficult task and that the landing, an opposed landing on the Falkland Islands without proper air cover, was going to prove a very difficult task indeed. I certainly was cautious about it at that stage.

It was a caution which many others, including senior serving officers in the Army and the Royal Air Force, shared, but which the Royal Navy rejected totally.

During the same meeting an urgent message was sent to President Reagan. Mrs Thatcher asked the US President to talk to General Galtieri as quickly as possible and to urge him not to use force. The Prime Minister's request was received at 4.00 pm* in Washington, on the same day, Wednesday March 31. At that stage the United States did not share the British sense of alarm at events in the South Atlantic. The Falklands hardly figured on the State Department's agenda,

and were unheard of in the White House. The British Ambassador, Sir Nicholas Henderson, was instructed to bring the matter to the attention of the US Secretary of State. Henderson told General Alexander Haig that 'the temperature level was very, very high and the prediction was that there would be a seizure of the Falklands'. Haig ordered his Ambassador in Buenos Aires to urge that no force be used. It was to no avail. Eventually, more than twenty-four hours after Mrs Thatcher's personal message to the President, Ronald Reagan agreed to intervene.

At 6.30 pm, on Thursday, April 1, Reagan tried to call the Argentine President. But Galtieri refused to take the call. Al Haig was present in the Oval Office as Reagan tried to get through:

It was only two hours later, after considerable pressure and some threats from our side, that the call was received. Now, that call lasted about fifteen minutes as I recall. Using interpreters etc.

And during that call, President Reagan made it very, very clear that the use of force would be unacceptable to the United States. He offered good offices and the dispatch of the Vice-President to Buenos Aires to try to seek a peaceful solution. And during that call he never got a commitment from Galtieri not to use force. And so we left the experience very, very concerned that we were on the verge of conflict.

The fact that the President's call had failed to prevent an invasion was relayed to Mrs Thatcher, who received the message at 2.45 am in London on April 2, the day of the invasion. Only a few hours earlier the Prime Minister had decided with John Nott and Lord Carrington that troops be put on immediate notice for deployment to the South Atlantic along with the naval task force.

Political disaster threatened, but the Prime Minister was no doubt relieved to be informed that the naval task force assembling in British ports was at four hours notice to sail within the next forty-eight hours. Further south, Rear-Admiral John 'Sandy' Woodward was preparing to leave Gibraltar with a group of ships which would also be part of the British force. Mrs Thatcher's only hope of salvation now lay with the Royal Navy. Conversely, all the Royal Navy's hopes of a reprieve from the Defence Review lay with Mrs Thatcher and her ability to lead the country to a successful repossession of the Falkland Islands. The politician and the Admirals came together with a set purpose and a single-minded determination to achieve it. As Mrs Thatcher said later on television, 'Failure – the possibilities do not exist'.

6/INVASION

As the Argentine task force continued its slow journey towards the Malvinas, Rear-Admiral Carlos Busser announced to his men on board the landing ship *Cabo San Antonio* the historic purpose of their voyage. The need for secrecy had been so great that only the most senior officers had been aware of the destination. On April 1, however, there was no further need for secrecy. 6.30 pm had been set as the point of no return. That point had been crossed; no message from the Junta had been received ordering the ships to return to port. Task Force 40's mission was now unstoppable. The code-name for the operation was changed from *Rosario* to *Azul*, meaning 'blue', the colour of the national flag, and of the Virgin Mary's robe.

The storm which had delayed the invasion by a day had still not completely abated. The men of the task force were not allowed on deck; instead they crowded inside the assault ship's hold, alongside their armoured personnel carriers, and found places where they could.

Busser remembers that his announcement, made over the ship's tannoy and relayed to the rest of the task force, was greeted in the manner expected of loyal Argentine patriots:

Each Argentine wants the recuperation of the Malvinas from the moment they learn about it in Primary School. The Malvinas issue is not only in our minds, it's in our hearts. To the men who learnt at the time that they were on their way to recover the Malvinas it meant a great deal. I saw grown men, men with big moustaches, shed tears at that moment.

There was little time for emotion. The men set to work immediately they were told of their various dispositions and tasks. H-hour was set for 6.30 the following morning. The force had only twelve hours in which to prepare.

It was clear to the Argentine forces that the element of surprise which they considered so important had been lost. The Argentine Air Force representative in the Falklands reported that the Governor had issued a warning to the Islanders, and President Reagan's direct appeal against the use of force made it plain that an invasion was expected. Busser readjusted his plans accordingly, cancelling a direct flight to Stanley airport, and switching the main landing beach. The force of marines on the Islands was so small, however, that no other significant changes were considered necessary.

Although London had known that an invasion force was heading for the Falklands on the evening of March 31, no effort was made to inform the Islanders for a further twenty-four hours. At 3.30 pm local time, on April 1, Rex Hunt received a telegram from the Foreign Office:

It was couched in the normal diplomatic language and it's engraved on my heart. It read, 'WE HAVE APPARENTLY RELIABLE EVIDENCE THAT AN ARGENTINE TASK FORCE WILL ASSEMBLE OFF CAPE PEMBROKE' (that's just to the east of Stanley) 'EARLY TOMORROW MORNING 2ND APRIL STOP YOU WILL WISH TO MAKE YOUR DIS-POSITIONS ACCORDINGLY STOP'. That's all I had, and my communicator, Brian Wells, remarked, 'They might have said goodbye and the best of British.' So I made my dispositions accordingly.

The Governor immediately called Major Mike Norman, who had just arrived from Britain with the replacement Royal Marine detachment of forty-two men, and had taken over command from Major Gary Noot. The combined forces of the two detachments made up seventy-six Royal Marines; there were also nine sailors from HMS *Endurance* who had remained at Stanley to make room for a party of twenty-two marines sent to South Georgia with the Ice Patrol Ship. Rex Hunt was supposed to be able to call on the Falkland Islands' Defence Force as a reserve in times of crisis; on this occasion none, understandably enough, wanted to fight.

Major Norman could be forgiven for being sur-prised when he heard the news of impending military action. Having arrived two days before, on March 30, he had barely settled in:

My eyebrows disappeared into my hairline. I looked at Rex Hunt and Rex, who is a great one for coming out with immortal statements, said, 'Well it looks as if the buggers mean it this time, we've called their bluff for twenty years and it's you and I that have got to face it out.'

The Royal Marines had the night in which to prepare the defences of the Islands. Norman's orders were to 'defend the seat of Government'; this he did by fortifying a beach (the wrong one as it turned out), deploying a series of sections along the road from the airfield to Port Stanley to slow any Argentine advance by firing and with-drawing, and by concentrating the remainder of the force in Government House.

An earlier plan had pre-supposed that the Governor would be taken to a place of safety in the country, thus preventing Argentine access to a legitimate British negotiator. But Rex Hunt refused to leave his command post, as did his wife Mavis, who needed considerable persuasion before she could be made to retreat to a place of safety. The Governor armed himself with a pistol, and took refuge under a heavy desk in his office.

Major Mike Norman assembled his force in the NAAFI canteen and briefed them on their tasks. He ended with a sombre assessment of their chances:

I told them quite plainly, as I think there is only one way you can tell people: that we would fight until either the Governor told us to stop fighting or we were overrun, and being overrun meant us dying. And if that's what it came to, that's what would happen to the majority of us. They all knew that and they all accepted it.

At precisely the same time Rear-Admiral Busser was briefing his men, and making it plain to them that there should be no British casualties:

The whole plan had been conceived so that there was no bloodshed. Our idea was to carry out an operation that would confuse the defenders and render them unable to react. We wanted all our forces to attack at the same time in order to give the impression that we were in a superior position.

Busser's plan was to attack the Marine barracks at Moody Brook, the airfield, and Government House at the same time. At H-hour, 6.30 am, the Argentine forces landed and proceeded rapidly to their various objectives. Their arrival was seen by Marine Berry, a nineteen-year-old, who had volunteered to spend the night on Sapper Hill as a look-out. He reported by radio to Major Nor-man and Governor Hunt:

A rather panicky voice came over the radio, we had a Royal Marines radio in my room here in Government House, and Marine Berry said, 'There're upwards of 150 hostiles each side of me. What shall I do?', whereupon Major Norman gave good practical Marine advice and said, 'Keep your ruddy head down', which Marine Berry did . . .

Shortly after Berry's report, the occupants of Government House heard a series of bangs and firing at Moody Brook, the empty marine bar-racks. Almost immediately Government House itself became the object of attack. The Argentine commandos were using stun grenades, similar to those used by the British SAS during hostage operations: they make a tremendous noise, but do not kill. This was in line with the policy of

2 April 1982. Argentine Special Forces raise their flag over Stanley

avoiding British casualties, and of snatching the Governor as quickly as possible.

As the attack started the Royal Marines made no effort to limit Argentine casualties. They fired at everything and anything that moved in the vicinity of Government House. Three Argentine commandoes were wounded: one, Captain Giachino, died later of his wounds. Lieutenant Diego Garcia-Quiroga was one of those wounded in the attack:

I followed Captain Giachino out of the house, he was very close by, I saw him turn round and he shouted, 'They've shot me!' At that same moment they shot me too . . . time started to go very slowly at that point; I asked myself how it was that someone had been able to shoot me. I thought: 'Where did they shoot me from?' I really wanted to shoot the person who had shot me.

The violence of the Royal Marines' response halted the Argentine attack temporarily. There was a short lull in which the men could collect their thoughts. Mike Norman had to come to terms with his shock:

I was shaking from head to foot, like a piece of jelly. And I had to give myself a serious talking to. On the lines, 'Come on Norman, you knew it was going to come to this. You told everybody else it was going to come to this. Now get a grip on yourself. If you don't take charge, what do you expect your men to do?' And the other point I made quite clear to myself, if I stayed in this condition, I wouldn't be able to hit the wall, let alone any dark shape that appeared over it. And I then spoke to Chris Todd-Hunter and I remember saying to him something like, 'Are you married, Chris?' And he said, 'No. It's easier for me.'

The marines called out to one another, checking to see who had been harmed. None was. There were no British casualties. At that moment the Argentine forces called on the British Governor to surrender. Rex Hunt listened:

A very eerie loud hailer voice came over, Spanish, a thick Spanish accent. What he said was, 'Mister Hunt, you are a reasonable man, come out and surrender', whereupon one of our Royal Marines gave a typically lower deck reply . . . and whether our Argentine friend understood or not, I don't know, but he certainly got the message because the loud hailing stopped and the firing intensified.

But the position was hopeless for the small British force holed up inside the flimsy wooden building of Government House. Major Norman consulted with his colleague, Major Noot, and both men decided to approach the Governor for some straight talking. They found Hunt under his solid oak desk in his office and told him that the outlook was not good. The Argentine forces had a machine gun, which was far heavier than any of the British armament available to the marines. The Governor asked what this meant, and was told quite simply that 'they can knock the stuffing out of us, and we can't do a thing about it'. The decision was made to approach the invasion force to discuss a cease-fire.

After some to-ing and fro-ing, Rear-Admiral Busser was contacted and made his way to Government House with a white flag and two fellow unarmed officers:

I was amazed at the number of officers in the House; I think that almost half the British garrison was in the Governor's house at that moment. They asked me to go into the Governor's office where the Governor was. I explained the situation to him and the purpose of my visit.

Rex Hunt made it plain to Busser that he was not welcome in Port Stanley. The scene was reminiscent of a comic opera, as Mike Norman remembers:

You had these two completely differing characters, now stealing the scene. This tall elegant man, Busser, in battle fatigues and Sir Rex Hunt. Sir Rex Hunt couldn't be described as a big man. I suppose he must be about five foot six.

And he was in a pinstriped suit and he'd brushed himself down and in his brogues and he pulled himself up to his full height and squared his shoulders and looked at this tall man and said, before Busser could offer his hand or say anything else, he said, 'This is British territory. We don't want you here. You're not invited and I want you to go and take all your men with you.'

And I stood against my side of the room and I looked across at Major Gary Noot and raised an eyebrow and smiled because I thought well, we've tried everything else, so, you know, perhaps this will work!

But Busser would have none of this bluster, and calmly explained the situation in a prepared speech. He told Hunt that Argentina considered Britain to be the illegal occupant of the Islands, and that further fighting in the face of such overwhelming force would be pointless. As he made the point a force of amphibian vehicles trundled past Government House. The Governor needed little further persuasion:

I had a little pistol which the Royal Marines had given me during the night, and as Admiral Busser came in, I had a mad desire to take the pistol out of my drawer and shoot him, and I thought, 'You couldn't possibly do that.' I felt guilty immediately I had that thought, and he was very decent and polite, he complimented me on the professionalism and bravery of my troops but urged me to order them to lay down their arms otherwise I would be held responsible for any further casualties; I did point out to him that it was normally the people who started the shooting that were responsible, not the people who resisted, but I did take his point that he had brought an overwhelmingly superior force.

Rex Hunt had no option but to order the Royal Marines to surrender. At that moment the Falkland Islands ceased to be British sovereign territory. The following day, April 3, Argentine forces overwhelmed the twenty-two man Royal Marine party in South Georgia, and raised the blue and white national flag. Operation *Azul* was complete.

British humiliation: Major Mike Norman (below left) and his small party of Royal Marines were overwhelmed by the much larger Argentine invading force

7/DIPLOMACY

THE news of the successful capture of the Malvinas was received with predictable rapture in Buenos Aires. A deeply unpopular Government was transformed overnight into the beloved saviours of a nation. Only two days before the invasion crowds had been rioting in the streets of Buenos Aires; now the same people were demonstrating their joy. A mood of national euphoria prevailed. Politicians from all sides of the political spectrum and trades union leaders who had been in the vanguard of the street protests joined to applaud the Junta.

But from the moment of the invasion Argentina lost the initiative. The Junta's planning and decision-making process was unable to cope with the grave consequences of the invasion: the armed forces had made no contingency plans for the defence of the Malvinas and the Foreign Ministry had failed to brief its diplomats or to plan a campaign at the United Nations in defence of Argentina's aggression. The strong and, in the Argentine view, absurdly exaggerated British response to the South Georgia incident had brought forward plans for military action by some four months. The result was that the invasion of the Malvinas was undertaken recklessly with only vague and optimistic consideration for the future.

For this, the Minister for Foreign Affairs, Nicanor Costa Mendez, bore much responsibility. It was he, after all, who had advised the Junta that negotiations from a position of strength would begin after the invasion; and it was he who predicted that the United States would intervene to prevent any British military action.

Although both predictions turned out to be wrong, Costa Mendez had some justification in his belief that the United States, if not actively supporting Argentina, might intervene in a way which would benefit his country's cause.

He and the Junta remembered America's intervention at the United Nations in the Suez crisis in 1956, which forced Britain to conduct a military withdrawal, as an important historical precedent. Buenos Aires believed that American diplomats had indicated their willingness to follow a similar course over the Malvinas. Jeane Kirkpatrick, America's representative at the United Nations, was an old friend of the military dictatorship: her support in the matter seemed certain. She was also known to hold a strong influence over President Reagan, in whose Cabinet she sat. There were many other friends of the dictatorship in the United States' administration. Thomas Enders, the Under Secretary of State for Latin American Affairs, was a noted 'Latino' who had visited Buenos Aires only days before the invasion and indicated a 'hands off' approach to the issue. Vernon Walters, the polyglot former Deputy Director of the CIA, and Reagan's roving Ambassador-at-Large, had cultivated General Galtieri for some time. According to persistent rumours, he had advised Galtieri months before the invasion that the United States would remain neutral after the occupation of the Malvinas so long as no British casualties occurred. He is also alleged to have told the General that Britain 'would huff and puff and do nothing' in the event of Argentine aggression against the Islands.

There was, therefore, a direction in the Reagan administration's diplomacy which Sir Nicholas Henderson, the British Ambassador in Washington, later described as 'a degree of acquiescence in Argentine forward policy over the Falklands from the United States', and which – whether intended or not – encouraged the Argentine Junta in its aggression. This 'forward policy' quickly became apparent to British diplomats as they struggled to regain the initiative.

The first indications that the Special Relationship might not apply to Latin American affairs occurred five days before the invasion, on Sunday March 28. Lord Carrington had sent an urgent telegram to General Haig asking for American mediation in the dispute over the landings on South Georgia. Sir Nicholas Henderson received the State Department's response the next day, from Walter Stoessel, the Deputy Secretary of State:

He (Stoessel) took the line that the interests of the United States, and the policy of the US Government, would be one of neutrality as regards any conflict in the South Atlantic. And I took the view that issues like self-determination, which the Americans had pioneered as a matter of foreign policy, were at stake, and that if any ally of theirs was involved, a victim of aggression, they couldn't stay neutral, which led to considerable acrimony.

Stoessel made it plain that the United States did indeed wish to pursue a 'hands off' policy, and had no desire to become involved in what was regarded as an unnecessary piece of British trouble-making. Henderson passed the State Department's views to the Foreign Secretary in London. Lord Carrington was outraged. He summoned Edward Streator, the American Chargé d'Affaires, and made plain Her Majesty's Government's fury at America's neutralist stance.

Carrington's angry response was only partially effective, however. As events unfolded, Sir Anthony Parsons, Britain's Ambassador to the United Nations, discovered that he, too, could not count on American assistance in the Security Council.

On April 1 Parsons received news from the Foreign Office in London that an Argentine invasion of the Falklands was a certainty. Parsons was a distinguished diplomatist and linguist. His expertise lay in the Middle East. Fortuitously, however, he had a long experience of the Falklands dating from his previous assignment to the UN in the 1960s. On hearing the news of imminent invasion he went into action.

Parsons' first task was to call an emergency meeting of the fifteen-member Security Council in order to gain a statement (there was no time for a resolution) calling on both sides to refrain from the use of force.

I got the most extraordinary reactions, because the Falklands problem had never been in the Security Council before. It had only been pro-forma in the General Assembly. So really, except for Latin Americans and ourselves, very few people knew where the Islands were, what the dispute was about or anything. It took them completely by surprise. A lot of them thought I was pulling their legs, it was just some kind of elaborate 'Parsonian' joke.

One of my distinguished colleagues even went so far as to say that he knew our rules better than I did and that April Fool jokes ended at midday and it was now quarter to one and therefore I was off-side. So I had quite a lot of difficulty in persuading these people that I was actually serious.

Parsons succeeded in convincing his colleagues that he was not joking. The Security Council was convened, and the President, Kamanda Wa Kamanda of Zaire, read out a statement calling on both sides not to use force in any circumstances. Parsons immediately agreed to his request, and called on the Argentine Ambassador to do likewise. There was no reply.

Parsons' success had been achieved in the face of opposition from the United States. In an extraordinary move, Jeane Kirkpatrick had threatened to block the British call for an emergency session. Parsons responded by threatening to call an open vote on the matter in the Security Council, thus forcing America's lack of opposition to the likely Argentine aggression into the open. Kirkpatrick backed down, but her prevarication was an indication of things to come.

A further sign of the ambivalent attitude of

Sir Anthony Parsons. His skilful handling of the Security Council led to Britain's diplomatic victory at the UN

United States diplomats, if one was needed, occurred in Washington, the following evening on April 2. Fully aware that armed aggression had been used against British territory, a trio of senior American diplomats, Jeane Kirkpatrick, Walter Stoessel and Thomas Enders, dined with the Argentine Ambassador in Washington. Sir Nicholas Henderson was unable to hide his disgust when he met Jeane Kirkpatrick a few days later:

I suppose it wasn't very diplomatic. Certainly she didn't think so, because I said how would she think if I had dined at the Iranian Embassy the night they took the American hostages in Teheran?

Britain's difficulties with the United States failed to overshadow a diplomatic triumph at the United Nations which Sir Anthony Parsons achieved on Saturday, April 3. The successful passage of his proposed Resolution, 502, in the Security Council was a coup by which Britain stole the diplomatic high ground. It was not subsequently lost, despite many vicissitudes, throughout the duration of the conflict with Argentina.

As Parsons and his fellow British diplomats drafted the proposed resolution through the night before the debate on Saturday, they were aware of the fundamental importance of gaining UN support for the British position. It would help unify British public opinion behind Government action to bring about an Argentine withdrawal; it would encourage the support of the European Community for immediate sanctions against Argentina; and, most importantly, it would bring the full weight of the international community behind the United Kingdom.

In order not to upset the non-aligned countries, traditionally suspicious of anything which smacked of colonialism, Parsons avoided all question of sovereignty in his draft resolution. Instead he focussed on the fact that an act of aggression had taken place and force had been used to settle a political problem.

The Saturday emergency debate in the Security Council was a unique event. It was the time of the Cold War, and usually the outcome of such occasions was known in advance, with the super-powers taking up their predictable postures. This was different. For the first time in years the members of the Security Council actually listened to the arguments, deliberated, consulted with their home Governments and came to a conclusion as to how they should vote. Sir Anthony Parsons was fully aware that his speech to the Council could make or break world support for Britain.

Help for Britain's cause came from an unexpected quarter: the Argentine Foreign Minister. Nicanor Costa Mendez had rushed from Buenos Aires to be present at the debate. He arrived just before the start of proceedings and asked for a suspension, in order to brief the non-aligned delegations in private. He then spent twenty minutes haranguing the ambassadors about Argentina's claims on the Malvinas, and refused to answer any of their questions. It was not a good start for Argentina.

The British delegation opened the debate by tabling their resolution, in mandatory terms and in final form. It demanded an Argentine withdrawal, and called for negotiations. As the debate continued Sir Anthony Parsons was encouraged to see that the non-aligned countries were giving more weight to the fact that there had been an act of aggression, than to the fact that their governments had, in the past, subscribed to the Argentine view of Britain as an illegal colonial presence in the South Atlantic.

At one stage in the debate Dr Costa Mendez intervened to say that Article 2 of the UN Charter, which forbade the use of force between states, applied only to disputes which had arisen since 1945, the year when the Charter was adopted. Parsons and his team realised that this was a fatal error.

This was a long hop outside the leg-stump. Because most of the delegates round the table came from countries which were in the middle of long-standing territorial disputes, some of which went back to the nineteenth century. And I could feel the atmosphere turn against Argentina and towards me.

The debate came to its dramatic climax. The position of the Soviet Union was crucial to the British. As a Permanent Member of the Security Council, the Russian delegation had the right of veto. Parsons was unsure whether they would use it:

They were in two minds. Their instinct was to veto anything proposed by the British; at the same time, their other instinct was always to go along with the non-aligned majority. And I deliberately did not look in the direction of my Soviet colleague who sits in alphabetical order next to me when it came to the vote . . . In the event they abstained.

That, of course, I think to me, was the most dramatic moment and then of course we realised we had got ten votes and no veto. We'd got the Resolution.

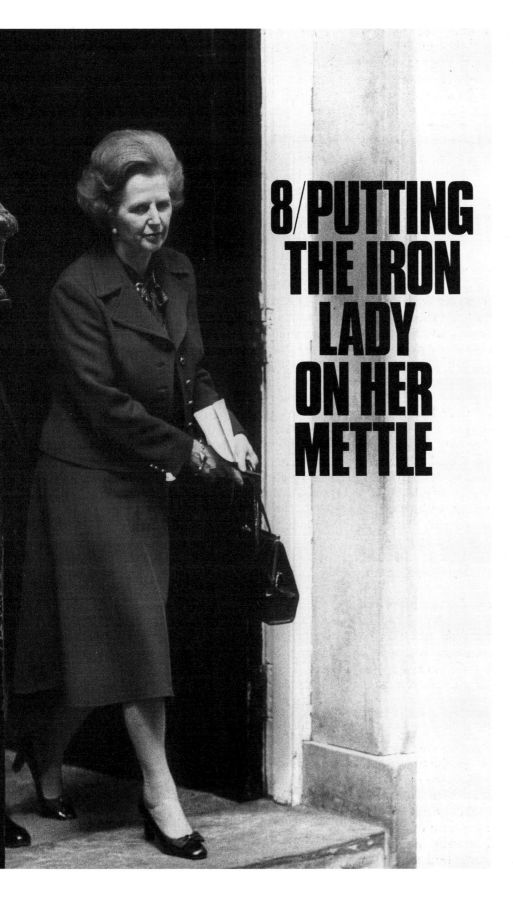

8/PUTTING THE IRON LADY ON HER METTLE

THE successful passage of Resolution 502 was welcome news to Mrs Thatcher's Government. It came at a time when the outlook appeared very bleak indeed. On Saturday April 3, as the Security Council met in New York, the House of Commons met in London in Emergency Session. Mrs Thatcher, unusually unsure of herself and nervous, opened the debate and announced to the world that '... for the first time for many years, British sovereign territory has been invaded by a foreign power'. The Prime Minister went on briefly to justify her Government's failure to prevent the invasion, and – her trump card – to announce that '... a large task force will sail as soon as all preparations are complete. HMS *Invincible* will be in the lead and will leave port on Monday'.

The Leader of the Opposition, Michael Foot, answered the Prime Minister. He was surprisingly supportive of the Government, making plain his detestation of the Argentine Junta, and his fundamental belief in the rights of the Falkland Islanders. His passionate belief in those rights overcame his latent pacifism, and he issued a challenge to the Prime Minister:

We are paramountly concerned about what we can do to protect those who rightly and naturally look to us for protection. So far, they have been betrayed. The responsibility for the betrayal rests with the Government. The Government must now prove by deeds – they will never be able to do it by words – that they are not responsible for the betrayal and cannot be faced with the charge.

From the other side of the House, Enoch Powell joined in Michael Foot's challenge to Mrs Thatcher for action, not words, to recover Britain's honour:

The Prime Minister, shortly after she came into office, received a soubriquet as the 'Iron Lady'. It arose in the context of remarks which she made about defence against the Soviet Union and its allies; but there was no reason to suppose that the Rt Hon Lady did not welcome and, indeed, take pride in that description. In the next week or two this House, the nation and the Rt Hon Lady herself will learn of what metal she is made.

Tony Benn recorded his impressions of the debate in his diary. As a fellow member of the left of the Labour Party he considered Michael Foot's speech 'very aggressive' and wrote that:

... the House was in the grip of jingoism, Silkin (Labour's Shadow Defence Secretary) and Nott made poor speeches. Nott trying to turn it into a party attack which didn't go down very well. I came away full of

Foreign and Commonwealth Office
London SW1A 2AH

PERSONAL   5 April 1982

Dear Margaret,

The Argentine invasion of the Falkland Islands has
led to strong criticism in Parliament and in the press of
the Government's policy. In my view, much of the
criticism is unfounded. But I have been responsible for
the conduct of that policy and I think it right that I
should resign. As you know, I have given long and careful thought to this. I warmly appreciate the kindness
and support which you showed me when we discussed this
matter on Saturday. But the fact remains that the
invasion of the Falkland Islands has been a humiliating
affront to this country.

We must now, as you said in the House of Commons, do
everything we can to uphold the right of the Islanders to
live in peace, to choose their own way of life and to determine
their own allegiance. I am sure that this is the right
course, and one which deserves the undivided support of
Parliament and of the country. But I have concluded with
regret that this support will more easily be maintained if
the Foreign Office is entrusted to someone else.

I have been privileged to be a member of this
Government and to be associated with its achievements over
the past three years. I need hardly say that the Government
will continue to have my active support. I am most grateful
to you personally for the unfailing confidence you have shown
in me.

(CARRINGTON)

The Rt Hon Margaret Thatcher MP

The Fall of a Foreign Secretary. Lord Carrington, whose career came to an end over a matter which had been 'no more than a pimple in the affairs of state'. His letter of resignation (right): 'To have to resign was very painful, but these things happen in political life'

gloom, because it's obvious that a huge fleet of forty or so warships will set sail for the Falklands and two weeks later they'll arrive, tell the Argentinians to go. Probably be attacked, and then there will be a battle.

The House of Commons reserved its anger for the Defence Secretary, John Nott, and for the Foreign Office. There were accusations of unilateral disarmament inviting aggression, and of appeasement. Richard Luce, the Minister of State for Foreign Affairs, was sitting on the Front Bench:

Sitting there was the most unpleasant experience I've ever had. I don't blame anyone for it. I mean, it was a terrible thing to have happened and I felt dreadful. I'm sure my colleagues in Government felt absolutely dreadful. It was a chance for the House of Commons to let off steam. It's not much fun though – being in the front line in those circumstances.

Two days later Richard Luce resigned, following the example of Lord Carrington, who, as a Peer, had been unable to take part in the debate in the House of Commons, and was thus isolated. John Nott, the proponent of the navy cuts, survived. Although many of his colleagues were disappointed by his speech in the debate, which

sought to justify the decision to withdraw *Endurance*, he himself remains proud of his performance:

In fact I have several times read the speech I made, and I commend those interested in the history of these events to read that speech. It reads extraordinarily well and I think I did about as well as could expected in the circumstances. There was bound to be a scapegoat, it was unlikely to be the Prime Minister in the debate. It was almost certainly going to be the Secretary of State for Defence. So I was expecting it and I took my medicine and it didn't depress me. It depressed everybody else!

When John Nott learnt that Lord Carrington had tendered his resignation to the Prime Minister he did likewise. But Mrs Thatcher rejected his offer, arguing that his was not the lead department in the crisis, and that it would be an unsuitable moment for the Defence Secretary to go, just when Britain was assembling a major fleet to redeem the Islands.

She did, however, accept the Foreign Secretary's resignation. Lord Carrington was adamant that he should go, not because he accepted personal responsibility for the Argentine invasion, but as a matter of honour. Britain had been humiliated, his Department held responsibility for affairs in the South Atlantic, therefore he should take the blame. It was an argument that Mrs Thatcher could not resist. 'If a person says it is a matter of honour then I am not at liberty to refuse,' she told a television interviewer on the day of the Foreign Secretary's departure. It was a bitter personal blow to Lord Carrington, but one which he took stoically:

I never thought for one moment that I would ever become Foreign Secretary, but it was the one thing in the world that I wanted to be, and when the Prime Minister appointed me of course it was a great honour, and for me a wonderful opportunity, and, to have to resign was very painful, but these things happen in political life. You have your ups and your downs, and you've just got to accept it, and if you're sure that what you're doing is the right thing, then you get on with it.

Carrington's resignation, and the rapid despatch of the task force, ensured Mrs Thatcher's survival in office for the time being. But she, and the country, were well aware that her future depended on the successful repossession of the Falkland Islands.

The Prime Minister and her colleagues set down to work with a unity of purpose and zeal for which Argentina had not bargained. There had been almost no dissension amongst Ministers when they were told of the decision to send the task force, at a meeting on the evening of April 2. Only John Biffen spoke out against the decision.

Mrs Thatcher was advised by two former Prime Ministers, Harold Macmillan and James Callaghan, to form a war cabinet, which could speed decision-making and liaise with the military. This she did four days after the invasion, on April 6. It was given the acronym OD(SA), made up of the initials of the Overseas Defence Committee, South Atlantic. Its political members consisted of the new Foreign Secretary, Francis Pym; John Nott, the Defence Secretary; Willie Whitelaw, the Deputy Prime Minister; and Cecil Parkinson, the Chairman of the Conservative Party. The Attorney General, Sir Michael Havers, was frequently co-opted onto the Committee in order to give legal advice about rules of engagement and international law.

At first sight the War Cabinet appeared an odd assortment of Ministers. Cecil Parkinson had no experience of battle, but was chosen for his ability to speak well on television. Francis Pym, a traditional Conservative, was by no means a Thatcherite, and owed his position to the Prime Minister's political vulnerability. He was regarded by the right as something of an appeaser, and readily took the Foreign Office line. John Nott's uneven temperament was generally considered unsuited to war. Only Willie Whitelaw seemed entirely appropriate: he had fought gallantly, like Francis Pym, in the Second World War; but, unlike Pym, he had a firm and steady relationship with Margaret Thatcher. Nevertheless the team worked well together, and their unity of purpose owed much to the presence on the committee of Admiral Sir Terence Lewin, the Chief of the Defence Staff.

The role of Chief of the Defence Staff had only recently been modified. In the past this most senior serving officer had been responsible only for reporting the consensus of views of the Chiefs of Staff, the heads of the three services. Now, however, he was the principle military adviser to the Government, and no longer had to follow the advice of colleagues. This change gave Lewin immense power and independence which he did not shirk. A confident man, easy to get on with, and able to explain the complexities of military planning without the jargon and acronyms that so often perplex civilians, he was ideally suited to the occasion.

When the conflict erupted Lewin had been on a visit to New Zealand. The Chief of the Defence Staff cut short his trip immediately, and on the long journey home pondered on what lay ahead. In 1956, during the Suez crisis, he had seen action in a destroyer. The indecision and lack of purpose in the Eden Government's dealings with the military had left a deep impression. He had no wish to let history repeat itself:

I wanted to get clear from the politicians exactly what it was they wanted to do. And I was determined to get an objective from the Government before anything started.
And when I got back to London, I was met by my staff and we had a briefing in the Ministry of Defence and we worked out an objective for Her Majesty's Government, which was to cause the withdrawal of the Argentinian forces from the Falklands and restore the British administration. And I went off to the first meeting of the War Cabinet at 9.30 armed with this.

The War Cabinet was happy to accept this objective, which was immediately passed on to the task force as it departed for the South Atlantic.

9/THE TASK FORCE DEPARTS

MANY of the men who received orders to head south in the British task force had no idea of the existence of the Falklands, let alone their geographical position in the world. When the news broke amongst the men on board HMS *Sheffield* there was, at first, considerable relief. The ship had been at sea for a long period, and the men, believing the Islands were somewhere to the north of the Outer Hebrides, thought they would be heading for home. Eddie Whitaker was a leading radio operator on board:

The Captain made an announcement early on the 2nd or 3rd; and he said that we've got to go. We're not going to go home, we're turning round and heading south and we're going to rendezvous with the rest of the task force at Ascension Island. And I'm sure I could hear an audible groan go through the ship. I mean, I was thinking about it, and it was just as if someone had knocked on your door and had said, 'Oh, hello, I've come to tell you you've won a million pounds on the pools.' And then you'd sat down, and you go, 'Oh, great.' And then he says, 'Oh, I'm sorry, it's your next-door neighbour.'

Sheffield was one of the first British group of eight ships to head south from Gibraltar as the vanguard of the larger task group which was being assembled. This small fleet had been taking part in the annual *Spring Train* exercises off Gibraltar, under the command of Rear Admiral John 'Sandy' Woodward. Woodward, the Flag Officer First Flotilla, was appointed Task Group Commander. He answered to Admiral Sir John Fieldhouse, Commander-in-Chief Fleet, who had overall command of the task force, and was based in Northwood, the Royal Navy's operational headquarters. The codename for the operation was promulgated at the same time: it was to be called *Corporate*.

The Royal Navy had seized the initiative. It was Admiral Sir Henry Leach who had advised the Prime Minister that a task force should be sent in the first place. The command structure now reflected the navy's dominance: Woodward reported to Admiral Sir John Fieldhouse, who reported in turn to Sir Henry Leach and to the Chief of the Defence Staff, Admiral Sir Terence Lewin.

The army, less anxious to be involved in the operation, did not press to participate. Although 5 Brigade, a newly created rapid reaction force, did exist for precisely such eventualities, it was not at first considered suitable for an amphibious operation because it was a parachute brigade.

The brigade's commander, Brigadier Tony Wilson, had hoped that his unit might be ordered to go south to reinforce the Falklands during the crisis over South Georgia. But now that was impossible:

Once we knew that the Islands had been invaded, I realised that any probability or indeed possibility of 5 Brigade moving instantly had gone out of the window. We were too late. We'd missed our chance. There was no way that we could go down. We had no aircraft that had the range to go from our nearest base, which happened to be Ascension Island at that time, to get down and return. We had no in-flight fuelling capability at that time. It hadn't come on line. It was projected, but we had no aircraft that could be refuelled in air. To parachute in would have been absolutely suicidal.

The operation, if it were to take place, would have to be amphibious: men would land from ships, as they had done on D-Day, thirty-eight years before. The Royal Marines were the men best suited to an amphibious operation: all their training had prepared them for this type of warfare. They were particularly used to the type of rough terrain and climate of the Falklands, having spent much time training in Norway. The fact that they came under overall naval command reinforced the view at the time that the operation was very much a one-service affair.

On April 2, 3 Commando Brigade, made up of three Royal Marine Commandos, 40, 42 and 45, was ordered to immediate notice, along with their brigade headquarters. They were commanded by Brigadier Julian Thompson. Thompson combined a deep knowledge of military history and strategy with a marine's physical strength and tenacity. When he received orders to prepare for departure and to join the amphibious assault ship HMS *Fearless* he had little doubt of what lay ahead:

Almost from the moment it happened, I was quite clear in my mind that there would be a war of some kind, unless the Argentines withdrew and I could see no reason why they should, because after all they were only 350 miles away from home, they had everything to lose by just pulling out without a fight and everything to gain by hanging on in the hope that we would give up and I'm sure that was their perception and therefore with that in mind, and bearing also in mind the situation at home and the people who were running it, I was quite clear in my mind there was going to be no compromise and that there would be a war.

Not everybody shared Brigadier Thompson's realism. There were references in the House of Commons to the Argentine President, General Galtieri, as a 'bargain basement Mussolini' which, in Thompson's view, belittled the ability and power of the Argentine forces. He was relieved, therefore, to find that the Commander-in-Chief shared his views:

Admiral Fieldhouse came up to me and said, 'I've just been briefing politicians and telling them this is going to be a serious and bloody business.' Now you might suppose that's rather a curious thing for me to be glad about but the reason I was, was that it indicated to me that at least the upper echelons of the services were approaching it seriously, and this was the message I was passing on to all my people, 'Don't underestimate the opposition', and indeed one of my staff who's a near-international standard rugger player was arguing with someone some days later, and I overheard him say, 'Look, I played rugger against the Pumas and I can tell you some of them are extremely tough.'

Planning for the operation began immediately. There was a great lack of intelligence about the Argentine forces, and information about the Falklands. In an amphibious operation it is essential, obviously, to know everything possible about the various beaches which might be considered for landings. One man was able to help: Major Ewen Southby-Tailyour. A genial, if unambitious, marine, he had all the knowledge that the navy and the marines craved.

Southby-Tailyour, a keen sailor, had spent a year in the Falklands as commander of the marine detachment in 1978. During that period he was asked by the Foreign Office to rethink the defence of Port Stanley and the Falkland Islands. This gave him the pleasant opportunity to reconnoitre all the beaches by yacht, and chart their suitability as landing places.

In late March 1982 Southby-Tailyour was filling in a brief hiatus with some academic studies.

Towards the end of March I went off to London to a course on 'Oil, Islam and the Middle East' at London University. And, on the second morning of the course – I hadn't actually made it back to the University, I have to admit, and the Adjutant telephoned looking for me. He spoke to me, but my voice was obviously so hung over that he didn't recognise it! And asked for a particular officer and I said, 'I've never heard of this chap, he doesn't live here.' He said, 'Oh well, what a pity. I was rather hoping he would know where Ewen Southby-Tailyour is.' I came clean, and I was caught. And he said, 'Well for God's sake, get back here. The Falkland Islands have been invaded.'

Southby-Tailyour rushed to get his charts, and then hurried on to join Brigadier Julian Thompson. The first stages of planning for the operation, before the hurried departure of the brigade, were taking place at Hamoaze House, in Plymouth, the Royal Marines HQ:

Julian Thompson met me and said, 'Right, you've got all your charts and stuff.'

And I said, 'Well, yes I have, but I'm damned if I'm going to let you look at them until you make me a promise.' Which isn't really the way perhaps majors should speak to brigadiers. But he was an old friend of mine. He'd sailed with me. I'd lent him my boat.

There was this hushed silence in the staff office, because all the staff officers were beavering away, and they didn't often hear their Brigadier spoken to in this manner.

And he said, 'What's the, what's the promise, Ewen?'
And I said, 'Quite simply that you take me with you.'
'Oh, no problem, you're coming. Now let's sit down.'

And that started three months or so of intense, exciting, exhilarating, terrifying, satisfying work.

The Chiefs of Staff soon realised that one commando brigade would not be sufficient to repossess the Islands, should diplomacy fail. On Sunday, April 3, they decided that the force be strengthened by the addition of the 3rd Battalion of the Parachute Regiment. This battalion was taking its turn as the 'Spearhead' force, at twenty-four hours readiness to go into action. It was more usually called out to emergencies in Northern Ireland.

3 Para, as the battalion was known, was part of 5 Brigade, Britain's new rapid reaction force. It was now taken out of 5 Brigade, and reassigned to Julian Thompson's command. Although the marines and the parachutists were tremendous rivals, the news of the order to proceed south with the task force was welcome. Professional soldiers train to fight, and this was an opportunity the men of the 3rd Parachute Battalion did not wish to miss, as Colour Sergeant Ian Bailey remembers:

We had people who were on courses, in Hong Kong, who were back at break-neck speed within three days, and back in the regiment, and, you know, signals were being sent, 'You're AWOL', and they said, 'No, I'm not, I'm back with my battalion.'

People on leave, people who didn't really have a job, who were in limbo, between jobs, were turning up and saying, 'Now do you need anybody to do this'. And, officers, senior officers, willing to be platoon commanders. Nobody wanted to miss this, if something did happen. This was perhaps the only time in your whole career you might do something that you've actually trained for.

The 44,000-ton cruise liner *Canberra* was taken up from the trade to help carry the 3,000 men of the Royal Marines and the Parachute Regiment south. Other merchant ships, ferries and tankers, were also requisitioned to transport provisions and service the task force.

The decision to commandeer the P&O flagship, *Canberra*, was an indication of the Government's determination to be seen to send a large number of troops on their way to the Falklands quickly. By good fortune, the cruise liner was on its way home to Southampton when the Falkland Islands were invaded. Surgeon Commander Rick Jolly was ordered to inspect the ship to find out how suitable it might be for his medical team, as it sailed to its home port. He flew to Gibraltar and joined the ship at sea:

We climbed these rope ladders, under the bemused gaze of all these passengers in their dinner jackets and in evening dresses, wondering what the hell was going on. And in order to allay their curiosity, they were told that we were Customs Rummage Officers boarding for the last leg of the voyage. Which kept them quiet a bit.

And shortly afterwards their suspicions started again and rumours began. So the Captain of the *Canberra*

decided to tell everybody what was happening, that *Canberra* had been taken up from trade, and was returning to Southampton to be converted as an amphibious asset, a troop carrier with hospital facilities. But the Prime Minister had not announced that fact then in the Houses of Parliament. So, as soon as he told the assembled crew, and everyone was very excited, the radio room suddenly and mysteriously became unserviceable, and there were no ship-to-shore telephone calls allowed.

Immediately the ship docked in Southampton and the passengers disembarked, work started on fitting out the luxury liner. Caviare and champagne were taken off, the dance floor was removed; in their place Rick Jolly's team arrived with an operating theatre, and soon the marines and parachutists began to board.

Mrs Thatcher had told the House of Commons on Saturday April 3 that a task force would depart on the following Monday. This was a political imperative. Such a short time was barely sufficient for the proper loading of ships; most left in considerable disarray, their stores loaded as they were delivered, rather than in an order necessary for fighting a war. But this did not matter; after some local difficulties, the United States agreed to allow the British to use their base on Ascension Island. Ascension is a United Kingdom possession close to the equator and about midway on the journey to the Falklands. The Americans leased their base from the British.

Ascension was to be the assembly point of the task force, where it could halt, be joined by the ships coming from Gibraltar, reorganise and store, and where the strategy for the repossession of the Islands could be established by the senior commanders.

On Monday April 5 the carriers *Invincible* and *Hermes* departed from Portsmouth watched by thousands cheering on the quayside, and by millions on television. The two ships, with their Harrier aircraft ranged on deck, and their lines of sailors standing to attention, presented a powerful image of sea power as they crept slowly out of harbour. It was a rare display for the British, who had for years been more used to seeing a retreat from Empire than watching gun-boats rallying to its defence.

Below left: Sea Harriers lined up on the deck of *Hermes* as she departs for the South Atlantic

Below: A new role for *Canberra*'s sun deck. Men of 3 Commando Brigade keep fit on their way south

The previous day, HMS *Conqueror*, the nuclear-powered submarine, had left her base in Faslane. There had been no cheering crowds and no publicity. Her orders were to proceed at top speed to the South Atlantic to join her two sister-ships, *Spartan* and *Splendid*. Commander Chris Wreford-Brown was in charge of *Conqueror*. In two weeks she would be on station in the South Atlantic, having travelled at an average speed of twenty-five knots.

During the remainder of the week more ships left from British ports. On Tuesday April 6 HMS *Fearless* departed with the commando brigade headquarters. On Good Friday April 9 *Canberra* steamed out of Southampton, with balloons and streamers flying, and the Band of the Royal Marines playing 'Don't Cry for Me, Argentina'. A long procession made up of aircraft carriers, tankers, two liners (the schools cruise ship *Uganda* was requisitioned as a hospital ship), assorted destroyers and frigates began to make its way south.

As the task force departed, the War Cabinet sat down to work out an overall strategy for the recapture of the Islands. The arrival of three British nuclear-powered submarines on station in the South Atlantic would enable Britain to impose a maritime exclusion zone around the Falklands. This was announced on April 7, to take effect from April 12. It applied only to Argentine warships and naval auxiliaries operating in an area 200 miles around the Falkland Islands. If such vessels were detected by a British submarine they were liable to be attacked and sunk.

The Chiefs of the Defence Staff, who advised the War Cabinet through Admiral Lewin, decided that South Georgia, 1,000 miles south of Port Stanley, should be recaptured before any operation to repossess the Falkland Islands began. Although the military wisdom for this was questionable, Lewin and Fieldhouse were convinced that the distant island should be the first objective. As Lewin put it:

All the pundits would say that you don't get diverted from the main aim. Something might go wrong, you would then have to reinforce failure, you would get sucked in and that would affect your ability to carry out the main aim.

But both John Fieldhouse and I felt that we could do this, quite simply, and it would be successful. Nothing much was happening militarily, and it was very important to get a military success, so that the politicians could have confidence in our ability to do what we said we could do.

The politicians welcomed the idea. An early success would also boost public confidence in the operation, and the War Cabinet agreed on April 7 that South Georgia be the first objective. The code-name for the operation, *Paraquet*, was promulgated. This was subsequently corrupted to *Paraquat*, the name of a weed killer.

With military preparations under way, the Prime Minister had time to attend to her political difficulties. On April 8, in a Written Answer to a Parliamentary Question in the House of Commons, Mrs Thatcher declared that: '... there should be a review of the way in which the Government departments concerned discharged their responsibilities in the period leading up to the Argentinian invasion.'

The announcement that there would be an inquiry into the loss of the Falklands was a deft political move. It soothed the opposition at a time when bi-partisan support was essential, and it gave the impression that the Government was not planning a cover-up.

Although the Conservative Government had considerable backing from the Labour Party and the public for the sending of the task force, the country was not united in its support of the action. Many resented the fact that the crisis had been allowed to occur in the first place, and others believed that the quick reliance on the possible use of force was premature. Although opposition came from all sides of the political spectrum, it tended to be most strongly expressed by the left. Tony Benn, in particular, argued against the use of force, and called for a peaceful solution to be found with the help of the United Nations. It was the question of British arms sales to Argentina, however, which aroused his greatest indignation:

This is the inconsistency of this very strong, nationalist, militarist position adopted by the Government. Namely that you have to show how tough you are, but at the same time, up to the very moment of the war and soon after a war you may resume arms sales.

Britain had indeed supplied two of Argentina's most modern destroyers, the Type 42 *Santissima Trinidad*, and the *Hercules*; but negotiations for the sale of these two ships had continued under both Conservative and Labour administrations. The destroyers were the main items in a long list of military hardware supplied by the United Kingdom, which included the bombs that were used by the Argentine Air Force to sink British ships later in the conflict.

10/THE MORNING AFTER

As the euphoria in Argentina died down, the Junta was faced with an uncertain outlook, and a paralysis of indecision. The news that the United Nations Security Council had passed Resolution 502, which called for the withdrawal of Argentine forces from the Malvinas, was a blow which General Galtieri sought to shrug off. On April 4 he rejected the UN's demands, stating that Argentina was not willing to renounce its historical rights to the Islands.

The news that the British would despatch a task force was a second blow. There were, quite simply, no plans for the defence of the Malvinas against a large British assault force.

General Benjamino Menendez had been appointed the Governor of the Malvinas some time before the invasion took place. On learning of his appointment from the President, he had asked whether plans were being made for a defence of the Islands, should the need arise. He was told that he need not worry himself about contingencies, that such matters would be decided by the Foreign Minister and the Junta, and that his role would be solely that of the civil administrator of the Islands. Menendez took this to mean that there were no plans for a war after the invasion, and that the Junta would be ready to negotiate with Britain.

A little later in the conversation with Galtieri, Menendez asked what sort of defence force he might expect to have in the Malvinas:

He told me that he was not planning to leave a garrison with more than five hundred men: very small. I asked: 'Are you planning to have a ship or a plane?'
He said: 'Maybe a coastguard, because the fishing will have to be controlled; maybe a plane, we will see. We have not thought of a military contingency, and if we do it will be in the hands of a colonel and it will depend on someone else. Its only object will be to maintain security, nothing else.'

Indeed, when the invasion of the Malvinas was successfully accomplished, Rear-Admiral Busser and his special forces swiftly departed, leaving a rump of inexperienced troops as a token force on the Islands. These were hastily reinforced when it was learned that a British force was being sent south. On April 6 the Junta sent the 8th Regiment to the Malvinas to occupy the west island. It was followed two days later by the 5th Marine Infantry Battalion, which was stationed in the region of Port Stanley.

Admiral Lombardo had also been told there were no plans for the subsequent defence of the

Islands, when he raised the question while planning for the invasion. This seemed so odd, even absurd, that he drew the startling conclusion that there was a conspiracy between the British and Argentine Governments, in which the Malvinas would be taken, and Britain would accept the invasion as a welcome *fait accompli*. Although successive British Governments had for years demonstrated a lack of interest in the Islands, there was no truth in Lombardo's theory. The Junta did not expect a British response, and therefore did not plan for one.

Only when the Argentine Government learned of the task force's departure were some preliminary operational measures taken. Admiral Lombardo was hurriedly appointed Commander of Operations in the South Atlantic and told to start planning. At that stage, however, there was little belief amongst the military that Britain would actually sail all the way to the Malvinas. Lombardo warned otherwise:

I said the English aren't going to allow a country like Argentina to give them a slap in the face, just like that. They're not going to turn the other cheek so we can give them another. So, they are going to respond. And, another experience, which I have gained from my life abroad, especially in Europe, is that the Europeans are serious, and when they say something, it's because they intend to do it . . . That's something that doesn't happen with us, the Argentinians.

Lombardo's grim warnings were not welcome to the Junta. Admiral Anaya, so famous for his aggressive stand on the issue of the Malvinas, suddenly remembered the effectiveness of the British nuclear-powered submarines. He ordered the Argentine fleet to remain in shallow waters for the duration. Lombardo had to fight to have this order countermanded.

The news of a British response was no more welcome to the Argentine Army. Many troops were already assigned to the defence of Argentina's southern border. Argentina had been threatening aggression against Chile for some time, and could not now leave the frontier undefended. The burden of defence of the Islands fell on untrained conscripts, many of whom had entered the army only a month or two before the invasion. The Argentine army itself had not fought for more than a century, and was more experienced in the art of civil oppression than of war.

The position was not entirely hopeless, however. The Argentine Air Force had numerical superiority over the British, and its more modern jets were flown by a cadre of highly professional fighter pilots. The Junta was aware of the British weakness in this area: the task force's lack of airborne early warning made it vulnerable to air attack, and would make unprotected landings extremely hazardous. But this advantage was compromised from the beginning by a lack of co-ordination between the three services, and by the incompetence of the Junta.

From the very start of Argentine operations on the Islands, planning for their defence was conducted in an inefficient and haphazard manner. One senior commander after another made the visit to the Malvinas, took a brief look at the cold and miserable weather in the terrain to be defended, discussed the matter with the Governor, and then hastily retreated to Buenos Aires. The command structure itself was unclear and confused. Senior officers acted on their own initiative without informing their colleagues or subordinates; few understood precisely who was in charge, or from whom they should be taking orders.

The Governor, General Menendez, had arrived in the Malvinas on the afternoon of April 4. He was under the impression that he was only to supervise the civil administration of the Islands. He was quickly disabused of this idea. The Junta informed him that, together with his duties as Governor, he would be responsible for the local defence of the Islands. The news filled him with foreboding:

I had many doubts and uncertainties: the UN resolution, the British announcement that it was sending a task force in order to repossess the Islands, the imminent arrival of nuclear submarines to guard the waters. These bits of information led to anxiety about the future, and it seemed that things were not going to develop according to plan.

Menendez was neither warlike in manner, nor martial in his bearing; he appeared to those whom he met, when he sought to administer the Islands, as courteous and intelligent, but not as a general ready to lead his troops into battle.

The Argentine Governor and his new administration went to great lengths to prevent any maltreatment of the Islanders. The occupying troops were threatened with the most severe penalties for any acts of violence; crimes against women were singled out for particularly harsh punish-

Port Stanley airport becomes the air base for Puerto Argentino

Argentine conscripts reinforce the Malvinas. Many had little training and were ill-prepared for the rigours of the local climate. Above right: A pint at the *Upland Goose*. Argentine soldiers toast their arrival in the Malvinas

ment. Perhaps as a result of these strict ordinances there were few outrages. The new Governor did his best not to alienate the local population which remained in the capital. Many had fled to friends or relatives in the 'camp', or countryside, but 500 to 600 Islanders remained.

On April 10 Admiral Lombardo arrived in the Malvinas to discuss the defence of the Islands with General Menendez. He told the Governor his plans: that Argentine forces should be concentrated into two or three key points, and that helicopters should be used for rapid responses to British attacks. Puerto Argentino (Port Stanley) and the settlement at Goose Green were chosen as places for reinforcement, where British attacks and landings were most likely. Lombardo was convinced that the British would be at their most vulnerable when landing, and he told Menendez that the combined Argentine forces should concentrate all their efforts on making an amphibious assault as difficult as possible. But his plans were vague, and depended on the ability of Menendez to move his forces rapidly about the Islands in helicopters. This was impossible. There were barely sufficient helicopters to move a battalion across the Islands, let alone a brigade.

Lombardo left the Malvinas on April 11. The next day Menendez was shocked to learn that an entire brigade was arriving at Stanley airfield. This was 10th Brigade, from Buenos Aires, led by Brigadier Joffre. The news came as a complete surprise to the beleaguered Menendez:

Everything happened very fast and there wasn't a well laid out plan, with logistic provisions and plans for moving the troops to the place where they should arrive and from there on to their positions. I can tell you, we had surprises.
    For instance, on April 11, a new brigade arrived with Brigadier Joffre in charge. He had received orders from the continent, but I knew nothing of his arrival.

It was impossible to make plans in such a chaotic atmosphere. From the beginning the problems of keeping the men warm in inhospitable conditions, and supplied with food and water, were enormous.

The men of 10th Brigade who arrived on April 11 had no time either to prepare for the ordeal ahead. General David Comini was in charge of the 3rd Mechanised Infantry Regiment, which was part of 10th Brigade:

The army was split in two: half the army knew what was going on, and were well prepared for this encounter, that is, the invasion. My regiment was in the other

Below: The new Governor of the Malvinas, General Menendez, briefs journalists in the room which only days before had been Rex Hunt's office

half of the army, and we were used when it was discovered that more British forces were on the way, so we didn't have any specialised training. We had been training for operations in general, but not particularly for the Malvinas Islands. The Malvinas terrain is rather unique, and I realise that it would have been preferable to spend some time in a similar region in Argentina, so as to be better trained and capable.

The position was much worse for conscripts of the class of '63. Born in 1963, they were called up in 1982. Jorge Eduardo Portal enlisted on March 18 to join the 9th Logistics Battalion from Comodoro Rivadavia:

I didn't have any field training. I learned how to load and unload the 9mm guns, and how to load anti-tank and anti-personnel bombs, when I was on the aeroplane flying to the Malvinas.

The weather in the Malvinas was something for which the men were also ill-equipped. Julio Omar Godoy was another conscript with 10th Brigade:

We took enough clothes with us to survive in the south of Argentina, where it's dry basically ... But what we hadn't bargained for was the amount of rain which would fall. Our clothes got wet, we had to take off our clothes and put dry ones on, we had to do this all the time. Towards the end of the conflict we couldn't do this, we had to stay in our wet clothes.

The rapid British decision to send the task force had thrown everything into disarray as the brigade's commander, Brigadier Joffre, admits: 'I think sadly, I don't want to say this, but I have to, we were forced to run behind the wave and not in front of it.'

On April 22, amid much publicity, General Galtieri visited the Malvinas. As a soldier, General Menendez credited him with a better understanding of the logistical difficulties and the necessary strategies to defend the Islands than that possessed by his naval and air force partners in the Junta. The two men had already paid their official visits to the Islands, two days previously, and had appeared to have very little idea of the difficulties of defending such a large area.

Menendez made it absolutely plain to Galtieri, as he had to Admiral Anaya and Brigadier Lami Dozo, that without sufficient heavy-lift helicopters, he would not be able to move the artillery and supplies necessary to keep a mobile force in battle. He further explained that it would be pointless reinforcing the Islands further without this logistical back-up that he so desperately needed. But the General didn't listen:

The result of all this was that General Galtieri sent a brigade even though we had told him that we would only accept it if he sent more helicopters, enough fuel, more food, etc. But that didn't arrive. The troops arrived, the rest didn't. We had to do what we could.

The unit singled out to reinforce the Islands was 3rd Brigade from Corrientes Province in the north of Argentina. Made up of conscripts from this sub-tropical area, it was ill-suited to the cold and wet of the Malvinas.

By the end of April there were some 13,000 Argentine troops stationed in the Malvinas. As there were insufficient helicopters to move them around the islands, it was decided to concentrate defences around Puerto Argentino (Port Stanley) and the vicinity. The only other significant garrison was located at Goose Green, sixty miles to the west of Stanley in East Falkland. Elsewhere small troops were posted to show the flag and keep a look-out. General Menendez ordered his men to dig in and wait for the arrival of the British.

Opposite: The Haig Shuttle

Above: Secretary of State Al Haig with Margaret Thatcher and Francis Pym at Downing Street. General Haig remains convinced that the British politicians were divided about the right response to Argentina's aggression. Below: With President Galtieri. Despite feeling he had much in common with the Argentine General, Haig never gained the trust of the Junta

11/SITTING ON THE FENCE

GENERAL Alexander Haig, the United States Secretary of State, was not popular with his colleagues in the White House. He was thought to have rather too obvious presidential ambitions, to be over-ready to seek the limelight, and to be keen to push President Reagan himself into the background. It was remembered that he had appeared to panic when the President was incapacitated by an assassination attempt in March 1981. He had also ignored constitutional niceties at the time, telling a press conference that he was 'in control' while the President was undergoing surgery.

The opportunity to mediate in the dispute between two US allies was something of a last chance for the General to prove himself to his colleagues, and to the people of the United States. If he achieved a peaceful settlement a Nobel Peace Prize and the White House beckoned; if he failed, oblivion.

On April 5 President Reagan accepted Haig's offer to act as an American intermediary in the dispute. The President had little understanding of the issue, and appeared perplexed when asked about it by the press. Haig's offer to mediate was welcome. It took the problematical dispute off his shoulders, and deflected any criticism of the United States' ambivalent response to British requests for support.

The President's difficulties had been compounded by the conflicting advice which he received from his Cabinet and aides in the White House. Ranged on one side were Jeane Kirkpatrick and her pro-Argentine friends in the State Department. On the other side were the 'Atlanticists', led by Caspar Weinberger, the Defence Secretary, and other members of the State Department who did not wish to see the United States' major European ally suffer a humiliating defeat.

Al Haig himself had to balance these two conflicting interests in his mediation effort. From the start, he sought to make it plain on which side the United States would come down should a negotiated settlement be impossible:

I can tell you from the outset, that the Argentine Government was informed, not only officially, through communication, but by me directly, that if this thing were not settled, it would be inevitable that we would side with Great Britain.

Even before Haig had started his mission the back-biting and sniping which was so common in the Reagan administration began. The Secretary

57

of State was offered an aeroplane without windows for his mission, a KC-135. He refused it, preferring an official jet with better communications and windows. The departure of the mission was delayed while the superior aeroplane was prised from a Congressional deputation. Haig was accused of 'grandstanding' in a series of stories leaked to the press by colleagues in the White House, to which he responded:

These little poison pen editorials would appear, that Haig was grabbing the headlines. Or that Haig wanted an aeroplane with windows instead of a flying submarine, and that I had seized control of this issue, and the Government.
It's not true, incidentally, because my discussions were with President Reagan and I think basically, although he was receiving conflicting advice (there were many channels for that advice, too many, including the United Nations Ambassador, Jeannie Kirkpatrick) that we should not get involved at all, he authorised my intermediary role, personally. And that's who I thought I should have the approval of.

On April 8 Al Haig arrived in London for talks with Mrs Thatcher and the War Cabinet. The Haig team included General Vernon 'Dick' Walters, and Thomas Enders, the Under Secretary of State for Latin American affairs. They found Mrs Thatcher in a defiant mood. Al Haig, however, detected a certain amount of disunity in the War Cabinet as it faced him across the table in Number Ten on his first visit:

I did not find a uniform enthusiasm for the kind of vigorous action which she advocated and executed. The exceptions would be my old friend Terry Lewin who was Chief of the Defence Staff and John Nott who was the Minister of Defence. There was clearly a degree of uncertainty in the Foreign Office . . . I have great respect for Mr Pym. And our communications and my personal experiences with him were only of the highest.

Mrs Thatcher was in robust form, readily ignoring any doubts which may have been emanating from the Foreign Office. It was plain to the American negotiators that she had little time for a compromise.
Haig and his team sought to gain the Prime Minister's agreement to a settlement in which Argentina withdrew its forces, in return for a negotiated transfer of sovereignty. What the Americans received in return was clear scepticism that any negotiation would be fruitful or worthwhile, and a determination to repossess the Islands, by whatever means necessary.

At one stage in the talks Thomas Enders attempted to explain to the Prime Minister that important United States interests, quite separate to those of the British, were at stake. He referred to the 'hemispheric policy' of containment of Marxism, and in particular to the danger of the Sandinistas in Nicaragua: Argentina's support for American policy in the area was crucial. These arguments received short shrift. The Prime Minister had little time for America's neutrality, and no time at all for any policy which might lead to appeasement, as Al Haig remembers:

I recall her rapping the table and referring to the position taken by Neville Chamberlain with respect to the invasion of Czechoslovakia, years before. In which she referred to Chamberlain saying, 'This distant land, these people about whom we know so little and with whom we have so few common interests.' And then she referred to the forty-five million casualties that emerged from World War Two.

The Prime Minister, in Churchillian mood, awed the men from the US State Department. While Thomas Enders had no great sympathy for the British position, he could not help but be impressed by Mrs Thatcher:

She was brilliant in these meetings. Dominant on her side. Better briefed than anybody else. Forceful in argument. Haig said to me, 'Now, I'll argue with her a little bit, but you argue with her a lot and then maybe after this, that she and I can go off and privately we'll reach some accommodation.'
That, of course, never happened.

The debâcle at Suez in 1956 cast its shadow over the proceedings. Many on the British side remembered Britain's humiliation at the hands of the United States, and feared a repetition when they learnt of America's assumed role as an 'honest broker' in the dispute. It was a considerable relief to Terry Lewin, therefore, when Al Haig made it plain where his interest lay:

He assured us that this would not be another Suez. And so we were reassured that we would have American support. I could see, and I'm sure the Prime Minister could, that they had to go through this period of sitting on the fence if they were to achieve a negotiated settlement.

Mrs Thatcher and her colleagues never once publicly criticised the Reagan administration for its neutral stance. The Prime Minister may have had little confidence in the prospects of a negotiated settlement, but she accepted the advice of her diplomats that Britain should be seen to be negotiating, while sending the task force south at

Caspar Weinberger. The US Defence Secretary was convinced that the Haig shuttle was 'a waste of time'. He ordered the Pentagon to do everything possible to aid Britain

speed. This twin-track policy of negotiation and military pressure enabled the British Government to retain popular support in the United States, and the diplomatic support of her other allies, while at the same time preparing for war.

Continuing good relations with the United States were essential for the progress of the task force. However much Mrs Thatcher may have been irritated by America's neutrality in the weeks after the invasion, she was well aware of the huge amount of military aid which Britain was receiving from the United States.

While Al Haig and the State Department pronounced America's neutrality, Caspar Weinberger and the Pentagon immediately came down on the side of the British. Partly as a result of the President's lack of authority, and partly because Washington conducts the business of government from several different centres, the two key departments were able to conduct policies totally at variance with each other.

Caspar Weinberger, an Anglophile and a long-term friend of the British, was ready and willing to help his NATO ally from the moment the Falklands were invaded.

I thought that this was a bold, naked aggression, that would not serve any favourable purpose in the world. That if it were allowed to succeed it would encourage others in other parts of the world. And that we should help as much as we could.
I talked to British Ambassadors here, and my counterparts in England, and when I found out that Mrs Thatcher was indeed going to take the Islands back, then we wanted to help even more. And we did.

The Pentagon was ordered to meet all British requests for military aid. Wideawake airfield at Ascension Island was made available. Above all, essential equipment was moved from the United States to the task force, via Ascension, with incredible speed, thanks to Weinberger's intervention:

The principal thing we did, was to take every request as it came in and turn it around within twenty-four hours. The request came in for the radios and they were on their way in eight hours. That was the kind of thing that was needed. And in order to accomplish that, it was necessary to eliminate thirty-one in-baskets or in-trays between the request and the time it would be acted upon.

Caspar Weinberger had little time for the Haig peace mission. Although he had agreed to the idea of the shuttle when the President raised the matter on April 5, he came to believe that it was a mistake:

I thought the shuttle mission was not only a waste of time but was basically very undesirable, because I don't think you should talk about or try to compromise or negotiate anything that basically is totally wrong and totally evil, a brutal aggression.

Al Haig, unsurprisingly, rejected Weinberger's charge that his mission was 'a waste of time':

Everyone benefits from hindsight, but I don't think it was a waste of time, either in Britain or certainly here in the United States, because the United States electorate was somewhat split on the issue. We'd always enjoyed the demeanour of an anti-colonialist power . . . But in Britain it was important to remember as well, that Mrs Thatcher was somewhat a lonely voice in the vigorous way in which she stood up to this aggression. And I can say that without a single reservation. And if you go back and look at your own press, in the early hours of the crisis, especially the opposition parties' demeanour with respect to the crisis, it was clear that she needed both the reality and the perception of attempting to solve this problem peacefully.

Ever since his shuttle mission, Haig has emphasised his belief that Mrs Thatcher was isolated and vulnerable, even within her own Cabinet. The Prime Minister was certainly politically vulnerable: her survival depended on a successful outcome of the crisis. But there is little evidence of disunity in the War Cabinet. Francis Pym, the Foreign Secretary, may have irritated the Prime Minister greatly by counselling caution, and by emphasising the need for Britain to be seen to be ready to negotiate. However much this annoyed the Prime Minister, it was advice which she heeded.

On the morning of Good Friday April 9 Al Haig boarded his aeroplane at Heathrow and set off on the long journey to Buenos Aires. He and his team had gauged the position of Mrs Thatcher and her Cabinet in London, and had little to offer the Junta, other than warnings of the British Prime Minister's resolve.

In the evening General Haig arrived in Buenos Aires. Whereas his reception in London had been low key, in the British manner, the people of Argentina laid on a massive demonstration of their country's support for the occupation of the Malvinas. Haig remembers:

It was in the evening after an eighteen-hour, very long flight with multiple refuelling stops. I only wish I'd had the Concorde for that occasion! When we arrived at the airport there were batteries and batteries of highly lit television cameras and flash bulbs, and a very sombre, grim Foreign Minister, Costa Mendez.

Automobile horns were blowing, flags were displayed on the route all the way into Buenos Aires. There was a surge of nationalism, both real and contrived, that obviously was set to be a *leitmotif* for the visit. And it was trumped up by the Government.

There was a strange contradiction in it all, at least to me in those early hours, as I looked at the eyes of the Argentine participants in these demonstrations. I could see a very nagging and worrisome demeanour in which there was fear, as well as nationalist fervour.

So worried was Haig by the manner of the demonstrators that he feared another Teheran. Immediately he arrived at the United States Embassy in Buenos Aires he issued instructions that non-essential staff should pack their bags and leave, and that the diplomats who stayed behind should ensure that their security was good enough to prevent a hostage crisis. These precautions were the first of a series of American decisions which outraged the Argentine Junta.

The first meetings were cordial enough. Al Haig and Leopoldo Galtieri, both Generals, took a shine to each other immediately:

General Galtieri was a very big, bearish, open sort of a fellow. And, I think the kind I'm accustomed to dealing with in the product of the military profession. He was a very likeable, a very handsome well-structured fellow who was warm, in the true Latin sense. As I walked in, he gave me a great hug. He said, 'Welcome, Generalee.'

Galtieri's expansive manner and capacity for whisky amazed the American delegation. They had been dealing only hours before with the very opposite in Mrs Thatcher. It was as if the two leaders represented their respective national stereotypes. The one, warm, expansive and emotional. The other, cold, restrained and determined.

The following morning, Saturday April 10, the Argentine negotiators treated the Americans to a long exposition of the history of the Malvinas dispute, going back to 1833 and Britain's 'seizure' of the Islands. Al Haig was taken aback to discover that there was a senior Argentine diplomat who had spent his entire career working on this single issue, an issue of which the American Secretary of State had only recently become aware. While the talks continued an enormous crowd assembled in the Plaza de Mayo outside the Casa Rosada, the Presidential palace, and started to shout and chant their support for the Junta.

The American delegation, having listened to the history of the dispute, put their proposed settlement on the table. It involved the withdrawal of Argentine forces, an interim administration of the Islands with international supervision, the possibility of some form of joint ownership, and a period for negotiations on the question of sovereignty. The Islanders would be allowed a say in any decision over their future. Haig, in his role as a military man, then outlined what he would do if he were in command of the British task force heading for the South Atlantic. Tom Enders believes this to have been unintentionally counter-productive:

He said that in fact he would come down with a certain type of expeditionary force. He would probably take the Georgian Islands first. He might then make a feint, in order to be able to land on one of the Islands and create a situation of uncertainty in the Islands. All of this he described in considerable detail.

He said, I think this is what the British are going to do. I will attempt to dissuade them from doing this if you can give us a basis on which to do that.

When subsequently in fact this did occur, members of the Argentine Junta accused General Haig of having acted on behalf of the British and in co-ordination with them, in order to bring this result out, and felt betrayed.

By lunch-time the crowd outside the Casa Rosada, the Presidential Palace, was nearly a million strong, and stretched for miles in all directions. General Galtieri asked the Secretary of State to step out onto the balcony with him to greet the crowd. Naturally enough, Haig refused.

The American negotiators put together a draft of their proposals which the Junta could study. They then withdrew to an ante-chamber, and waited as the Junta's Military Committee discussed the American ideas. The discussion went on for a considerable time. The United States team sat and watched as a stream of waiters plied back and forth with refreshments to keep the thirsty President and his colleagues going.

It soon became apparent to Tom Enders that negotiations could take place only after a large number of consultations with colleagues:

The Junta, we learned in the course of this, consisted not only of three members itself, but the Junta felt that it was representative of a larger body of senior officers in the Argentine armed forces, which, very early on in this process, it began to consult.

Whenever a difficult point came up, then in fact it (the Junta) would be talking to some fifty senior officers in the armed forces of Argentina. Talking to the head of the First Military District, for example. Trying to persuade him. So that enormous delays and reversals appeared.

General Haig with Nicanor Costa Mendez, the Argentine Foreign Minister, whom he found 'so clearly devious and tricky'

A further problem was that the Junta itself was split, with Admiral Anaya taking a predictably hard line, and the head of the Air Force, Brigadier Lami Dozo, counselling moderation.

Eventually the American team believed they had the Junta's agreement to a framework of proposals which they could now take to Britain for further discussion. Haig and his colleagues departed from the Casa Rosada by helicopter, the crowd outside being too dense and too emotional for a safe passage by car.

Nicanor Costa Mendez was at the international airport to see off the departing US Secretary of State. As the two men exchanged farewells Costa Mendez handed Haig an envelope and asked him to open it once he had boarded his aeroplane. As the jet roared into the air Haig read the letter. Its contents were a complete reversal of all that had been agreed. The American proposals were rejected, and in their place the Junta returned to its original demands: negotiations to proceed to a fixed timetable, with a specific date for the hand-over of sovereignty, and no account being taken of the Islanders' wishes. This, of course, would be quite unacceptable to the British. Al Haig was devastated:

They withdrew every concession that had been made in these excruciating hours of negotiation. And it led me to conclude, in that first round, that the Junta itself was not in control. And certainly that Galtieri was not in control.

At 5.40 am on Monday April 12 Al Haig's plane touched down in London. There were no senior officials to greet him at Heathrow; an indication of the Government's lack of faith in the outcome of the shuttle. Haig sensed that British public opinion did not welcome his initiative. He persevered, however, in his talks, putting the same proposals he had discussed with the Junta first to the Foreign Secretary, and then to the Prime Minister. Both emphasised that there could be no settlement without an Argentine withdrawal, and without the wishes of the Falkland Islanders being taken into account. To Tom Enders, the British appeared to have little interest in a settlement:

I think that already the effort appeared more far-fetched at that point. Although we continued to develop and elaborate proposals that we had, we were getting no effective input from the British side, which was, of course, quite prepared to express views on the draft we had, but was not prepared to commit to negotiate on the basis of those drafts; or to give us a position that could be used with the Argentines.

Late that evening, after a series of lengthy telephone calls with Dr Costa Mendez in Buenos Aires and Mrs Thatcher in Downing Street, Al Haig decided to return to Buenos Aires for one last effort to negotiate a peaceful settlement. He took with him a set of refined proposals, which made provision for withdrawal of Argentine forces, a timetable for negotiations with UN assistance, the removal of the British blockade, and consultation through a referendum of the Falkland Islanders. But the plan contained two insuperable stumbling blocks: the British Government would not accept a fixed timetable of negotiations ending with the hand-over of sovereignty; the Junta would not accept a referendum. Nevertheless, Haig persisted, knowing that his political future depended on the outcome.

On Thursday April 15 the Secretary of State reached Buenos Aires, having stopped off in Washington in order to brief the President. He arrived exhausted and jet-lagged in a country which was growing increasingly suspicious of American motives. The following morning he met General Galtieri and put to him his proposals. There followed three days of complex discussions in which both sides grew increasingly mistrustful of one another. Haig refused to outline the British position to the Junta; he knew that, were he to do so, the peace process would be at an end. The Junta resented this, suspecting him of collusion. On the other hand, the American team were continually frustrated by the Junta's inability to accept the determination of Mrs Thatcher to retake the Islands and the gravity of the British military threat.

The US Secretary of State held lengthy talks with his Argentine opposite number. By this stage he had little respect for Costa Mendez:

He was a very difficult counterpart, in every respect of the word, because he was so rational and reasonable in his demeanour and not an unintelligent man, but so clearly devious and tricky in his real performance ... I began to become very, very suspicious that if we were going to solve the problem, it would have to be around Costa Mendez and not through him, and that somehow we would have to get to the military leadership of Argentina ...

The lack of respect was mutual. Costa Mendez regarded Haig as obtuse. He believed that the Americans had little understanding of a complex historical problem and no appreciation of the importance of the Malvinas to Argentina.

On Saturday April 17 Al Haig succeeded in meeting the three members of the Junta together for the first time. It soon became clear to him that they were unable to understand the seriousness of British intentions. As usual, Admiral Anaya took the strongest line. Haig tried to convince Anaya that Great Britain would indeed fight, and would, in his view, prevail:

And then, Anaya said to me, 'Nothing would make me prouder than to have my young son, who is on the Malvinas, have his blood run through the soil of that land.'
And I said, 'Admiral, you've never seen the body bags with our young men coming home, and I think you'd better reassess that statement.'

Over the years, with some justification, the Military Government had come to the conclusion that Britain had no interest in the Malvinas, and would welcome the opportunity to hand the Islands to Argentina. No amount of persuasion was going to disabuse the Junta of this idea, as Enders recalls:

Haig said that he thought that the British would fight, if there were not a solution, and they would fight for the same reason that the Argentines had taken up arms: that they thought that they were right. That was over-powering. It was a matter of honour, and over-riding national interest. Anaya told Haig that he was a fool and that it was not possible.

The meeting ended in considerable acrimony, but the negotiations continued between teams from the two sides throughout that Saturday afternoon and evening, and on into the next day, Sunday April 18. On Sunday evening the Junta presented its proposals to Haig in a 'final' document. It stated that the rights of the Islanders would only be 'taken into account' in any solution, and that a final agreement should be reached by 31 December 1982. No mention was made of a compulsory transfer of sovereignty. Al Haig warned that these proposals were unlikely to be acceptable to Mrs Thatcher and her Cabinet, as they did not make provision for the wishes of the Islanders. The next morning, in a mood of some gloom, he announced that he would make the results available to the British Government, and that he would return to Washington to report to the President.

Late that evening Anaya insisted on the addition of a clause to the document which read:

As from 31 December 1982, and until such time as the agreement on the final status comes into force, the leadership of the Government and administration will be exercised by an official appointed by the Argentine Government.

Argentine commentators later called this the 'mad clause'. It sought to give Argentina the right to appoint a Governor without consulting the Islanders or the British. To all intents and purposes sovereignty would now be taken from the British, whatever the outcome of negotiations. Mrs Thatcher and her Government would, of course, never accept this.

As Haig boarded his aircraft to return to Washington he was, once again, handed a note by Costa Mendez to be read after take-off. When Haig opened it he read the 'mad clause', and a further sentence openly calling for the transfer of sovereignty by a set date:

It is absolutely essential and a *conditio sine qua non* that negotiations will have to conclude with a result on 31 December 1982. This result must include a recognition of Argentinian sovereignty over the Islands.

Haig's shuttle was at an end. In twelve days he had flown 32,965 miles, a negotiator's record, but without results. He had striven to achieve the impossible, and had failed. Any hopes he may have had of further political advancement were shattered:

I knew that the period ahead was going to be very, very rough. The vultures and the vampires had tasted the blood and they were going to move, as they did, with inevitable, relentless determination to get me out.

A few weeks later he told the President of his intention to resign, and on June 25 that year he left his post as Secretary of State.

The failure of the Haig shuttle did not bring with it the end of the diplomatic search for peace. But its lack of progress brought home to the British public the strong possibility of military conflict, and the extreme gravity of the situation. The military, for their part, had never been in doubt about the difficulties of the task ahead, and the need to plan for war, whatever the progress of negotiations. As the planning continued the sheer scale of the operation to repossess the Falklands became increasingly evident. Many senior officers in Britain and the United States doubted that it could be done.

12/DOUBTS AND FEARS

MILITARY analysts in the Pentagon watched the early progress of the British task force in a high state of alarm. It appeared to them that a major NATO ally was heading for a humilating defeat in the South Atlantic. To be assured of victory in similar circumstances, they calculated, the United States would need two or three carrier battle groups, a fleet of amphibious assault ships, and an armoured division. The British, they noted, could barely muster two small carriers, two amphibious assault ships, and a small group of destroyers and frigates. Most of the troops, barely a brigade of them, had to be carried in a requisitioned cruise liner.

The Pentagon was also concerned by the British lack of airborne early warning. Should an American task group go into battle far from the protection of its home bases, it would do so fully equipped with aircraft able to fly beyond the fleet and warn of the approach of hostile aircraft. Without this, the enemy would be capable of approaching within a few miles of its target before being detected. In earlier defence cuts the British Government had deprived the Navy of any aircraft carriers which could carry fixed-wing planes capable of providing early warning. This meant the task force sailed with inadequate air defences. Quite apart from the absence of early warning, the carriers could only carry a maximum of thirty-four Harrier aircraft, to defend against an estimated Argentine front-line force of 111 fighters and fighter bombers. The British task force, unable to detect the enemy air force, and outnumbered by three to one, was dangerously vulnerable.

The Pentagon was also anxious about the extremely long lines of communication. The Falklands, 8,000 miles from Britain, were too far, in American estimation, for the task force to be resupplied with the food, fuel and weapons necessary to keep an army in battle.

This advice was passed on to the Secretary of Defence, Caspar Weinberger:

The Pentagon's military assessment, the Joint Chiefs, all of the military advice was that an expedition to retake the Falklands was totally impractical and could not possibly succeed, that it was an enormous logistical task. You had to go some 7,500 miles, with only the Ascension Island in between for anything like a base, which was not at one point considered to be available to the British, although we made it available. And that in any event, it just couldn't be done, and that it would be better therefore to compromise, and to negotiate.

retaking of the Falklands. Almost immediately the task force departed doubts began to surface in the High Command. As news of Argentine reinforcements of the Islands was received, the number of British troops on their way south, 4,600 men in all, seemed absurdly small when pitted against a possible defending force of 13,000. The distance, and the lack of air superiority, increased the dangers and difficulties of the operation. The Chief of the General Staff, General Sir Edwin Bramall, was not happy with the situation:

I wouldn't have said that I was bubbling over with enthusiasm for the operation, because first of all I thought we needn't have got ourselves into this muddle. And I resented the casualties that I knew would be inevitable in order to recover from the mistakes we'd made.

Bramall was faced with the unexpected: the need for a risky and dangerous military operation had come out of the blue. He did not like the prospect which faced the British force:

I don't think there was any doubt in any of our minds that this was going to be a highly difficult operation. I mean, after all it was going to be undertaken 8,000 miles away, outside range of any of our air bases. So any air cover was dependent on floating platforms bobbing about in the bad weather in the South Atlantic. We were right under the lee of the Argentine air bases and well within their range.

The Chiefs of Staff recommended the immediate reinforcement of the task force. The War Cabinet agreed. On April 16 the 2nd Battalion of the Parachute regiment, 2 Para, was ordered to join the task force. The ferry *Norland* was fitted for battle, and the men departed south ten days later. The need for further aircraft was acknowledged and the 18,000 ton *Atlantic Conveyor* was requisitioned. She departed on April 25 carrying stores and helicopters, and was joined at Ascension by fourteen Harriers: eight of them RAF ground-attack versions of the aircraft. This brought the task force's total complement of jet interceptors and ground attack aircraft to thirty-four.

The men of 2 Para were delighted by the news that they, too, would be heading to the South Atlantic. Previously, they had been assigned, like 3 Para, to 5 Brigade, Britain's new rapid response force. Now, as their colleagues in the Parachute Regiment before them, they were detached from the Brigade, and reassigned to 3 Commando Brigade, under the command of Brigadier Julian Thompson. Thompson and his men were by now

Previous pages: Line ahead in the Atlantic. The ships of the first contingent of the task force, led by HMS *Andromeda*, sailing towards Ascension Island

Above: Admiral Sir John Fieldhouse (third from left), the Commander-in-Chief of the task force, with his staff at Fleet Headquarters, Northwood. On his right is Major-General Jeremy Moore, Commander Land Forces

It was advice which Caspar Weinberger preferred to ignore. He concentrated instead on making up the deficiencies in British equipment. But there was nothing, short of providing a carrier task force, that the Americans could do to give Britain the airborne early warning capacity it so desperately needed.

This lack of protection was no deterrent to the War Cabinet and the Royal Navy. From the beginning the Royal Navy's two senior Admirals, Sir Henry Leach and Sir Terence Lewin, had made it plain to the politicians that ships would be lost. Both men made their own private calculations of how many casualties could be expected, and concluded that six or eight warships would probably be sunk, but that the task force would get through.

The advice that severe losses could be expected was accepted with stoicism by the War Cabinet. Two members, Willie Whitelaw and Francis Pym, had seen action in the Second World War. The Attorney General, Sir Michael Havers, whose opinion was frequently sought, had served in the Royal Navy during that conflict. These men understood that in war losses were inevitable, and had to be accepted if an objective was to be reached. The Prime Minister was made aware of this, and did not demur.

Some of the Chiefs of the Defence Staff were less ready to accept the dangers implicit in the at Ascension Island, halfway on their journey to the South Atlantic. 2 Para had to move fast. Major Chris Keeble, the battalion's Second-in-Command, shared his men's keen determination to catch up with the Commando Brigade:

Here we were, an airborne force, trained to attack, trained to bring violence to the enemy and we might miss it. That was the great fear. And I was forever pressing the Captain of *Norland* to cut the corners and plot a straighter line on his chart to get us down to Ascension Island to catch up with the Royal Marines ... we were men, we were macho men. We had trained for years to go to war. And I'd be lying if I said that there wasn't a degree of enthusiasm for fighting.

Despite the reinforcements, Argentina's air superiority continued to worry the Chiefs of Staff. The Chief of the Defence Staff, Terry Lewin, regretted their lack of wholehearted support for the operation:

I think it's a pity to have that attitude. Once this campaign had started we had to succeed and you really had to put all doubts out of your mind. Because if the top commanders have doubts, then by goodness, they'll soon filter down to the chaps who actually had to do the fighting.

The doubts about lack of sufficient air defence *were* beginning to filter down to the commanders on board the ships of the task force. At their first planning meetings at the rendezvous point of Ascension Island it became clear that, despite the War Cabinet's clear sense of purpose, the military were not entirely sure whether their job was to recapture the entire Falkland Islands, or to establish a bridgehead with a *view* to their repossession.

The lack of a well-defined command structure within the task force at that moment also gave rise to some early anxieties and friction. Admiral Woodward, the Task Group Commander, was at this stage the most senior officer in the field, and appeared to have considerable authority over the amphibious forces heading south. In mid-April, as the ships stowed again for the second stage of their journey south, Woodward met with Royal Marines and his own Commodore, Amphibious Warfare, Mike Clapp, to discuss the campaign.

Major Ewen Southby-Tailyour was asked to attend the meeting, because of his specialist knowledge of the Falklands:

I think Admiral Woodward, to be fair, wanted or believed that he could starve the Argentinians out. And in many respects I probably helped him in that, ... because we had described there was very little water, there was no natural food, every ounce of food

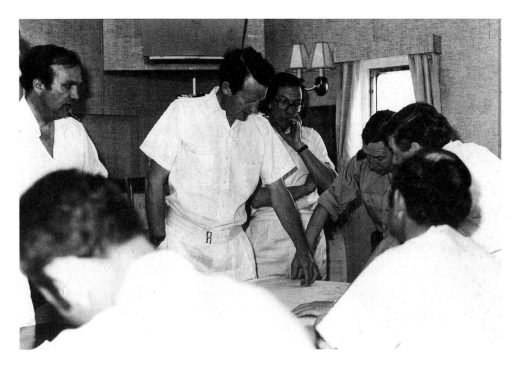

Rear-Admiral John 'Sandy' Woodward, Task Group Commander, discusses strategy on board HMS *Hermes*

that was eaten had to be brought in ... So I think maybe one of the plans, and of course it would have been a very nice plan, would have been to simply starve the guys out, and blockade them with our ships. But we, I think, felt that Admiral Woodward was a transmitter, not a receiver, to use that extraordinary military expression. And it didn't matter what we said, he had his views on how the thing would be done and it didn't accord with the amphibious warfare views.

Woodward proposed the establishment of a forward base on Lafonia, in East Falkland, where a landing strip could be built, and from where any subsequent operations to recapture the Islands could start, once air superiority had been achieved. This idea was greeted with disbelief by the Royal Marines. Lafonia was miles from the objective of Port Stanley, the base would take months to set up, there were no suitable landing beaches, and the campaign would inevitably be delayed through the southern winter. A heated debate followed, and the meeting broke up in disarray.

Lack of clarity of purpose and doubts about the feasibility of the operation, together with an ill-defined command structure, led to a vigorous and unproductive argument between the senior officers of the task force. The arrival at Ascension of the Commander-in-Chief, Admiral Fieldhouse, soon put matters straight. On April 17 Fieldhouse held a meeting with senior officers on board HMS *Hermes* and issued them with a firm set of objectives. He made it plain that fears of Argentine air superiority were not going to be allowed to hinder the task force's progress. Its purpose was to repossess the Falkland Islands. There was to be no blockade, and no waiting around during the South Atlantic winter. He further made it clear that the final decision about the nature and place of any landings rested with him, and that although Admiral Woodward was *primus inter pares*, he was not responsible for the conduct of the land campaign in the Falklands. Above all, he sought to emphasise the dangerous task ahead:

I think perhaps it wasn't the happiest of meetings because I became rather unexpectedly aware of the fact that there were those who were guilty of too much wishful thinking, and I was determined, if anything, to shift the balance in the opposite direction, so that they were prepared for the worst, and so I did my best to send them away from that meeting prepared to meet a horrible battle.

Fieldhouse warned the men that they faced the most difficult and demanding military operation since the Second World War.

The Commander-in-Chief flew back to Britain with a clear timetable which the military action would have follow. The imminent onset of winter in the South Atlantic, together with the limited length of time the ships of the task force could remain at sea, meant that landings would have to take place in the middle of May. They could not be delayed. The War Cabinet was made fully aware of this imperative: if there were to be a diplomatic resolution of the crisis, it would have to be achieved within one month. After the landings, repossession of the islands by the military would be the only remaining option.

The military imperative thus imposed its own timetable on Britain's programme of diplomatic negotiations. To some, like Tony Benn, it appeared that the act of sending the task force now meant that a military solution was inevitable:

Once you send a task force or military force, and give them a job to perform, then of course their tasks and problems become central to the political decisions that have to be taken. You can't leave a great fleet hovering around in the South Atlantic and so, as I pointed out in the House of Commons, the military take charge of the operation, even though they may have been told to go by their political chiefs.

On April 18, as the Haig shuttle collapsed, the first elements of the British carrier battle group started their journey south from Ascension. The chances of a peaceful solution were, by this stage, very slight indeed.

13/PARAQUAT

On April 20 the War Cabinet ordered the operation to retake South Georgia, code-named *Paraquat*, to go ahead. A small task force, made up of the destroyers *Antrim* and *Plymouth*, together with a tanker, *Tidespring*, and a group of marines and special forces, had already been detached from the main group and had sped south. As they approached South Georgia they were joined by HMS *Endurance*.

The nuclear-powered submarine, HMS *Conqueror* was also patrolling in the area, having arrived off South Georgia on April 19 with a party of men from the Special Boat Services, the naval equivalent of the SAS. These men were transferred to the *Antrim* task group, where they joined a group of SAS men.

The changeable and vicious weather conditions around South Georgia were new to the men in the small task group. They also had little knowledge of the area, and its dangers. After some argument with the more knowledgeable captain of the *Endurance*, Nick Barker, it was decided to land the group of SAS men on the Fortuna glacier, ten miles west of their objective: the Argentine bases at Grytviken and Leith. Their purpose was to observe the activities of the occupying force, and report back to the commander of the operation, Captain Brian Young, on board *Antrim*.

In traditional fashion, and to ensure a surprise, the SAS chose the most unlikely, and therefore the most difficult, approach to Leith and Grytviken. The Fortuna glacier, with its crevasses and rock runs, was inhospitable in the extreme; its dangers were compounded by the catabatic winds which often swept down the ice flow. These catabatic winds were sudden violent gusts in the opposite direction of the prevailing gales. They made flying conditions very hazardous.

Lieutenant-Commander Ian Stanley was *Antrim*'s Wessex 3 helicopter pilot. It was his responsibility to land the thirty-two men of the SAS team safely on the glacier, with two other troop-carrying Wessex 5 helicopters from the Royal Fleet Auxiliary, *Tidespring*. Although Stanley's Wessex 3 was not adapted to carry passengers, it was better equipped against the elements with electronic aids than those of his colleagues, and he led the way:

It was pretty turbulent and we really couldn't see an awful lot, and so I was relying on the instruments, with the rest of my crew helping me to maintain my position over the ground. And of course, I was the reference point, the hover reference point for the other two helicopters. And so we slowly moved our way up the glacier, over all the crevasses and found a suitable spot where we thought we could land them.

We all landed very gently, because you're never quite sure whether you're going to land on a snow bridge or not. In fact, I did, so I had to move over a little bit. I was just about to put my wheel through one, and one of the other aircraft had a similar problem. So we were fairly light on the wheels. We disembarked all the troops. And then staggered off back down the glacier.

The weather worsened that night. The helicopters were lashed to the decks of *Antrim* and *Tidespring*, and the aviators went below to join their colleagues in the warmth and shelter of their ships. As the ships rolled and pitched in the storm their thoughts were with the special forces, three thousand feet up on the glacier, moving across the ice to their recce position, suffering in weather conditions which soon became intolerable.

The SAS team were unable to move on the glacier which was criss-crossed by crevasses which were invisible in the blizzard. They dug in for the night, hacking a shallow depression out of the ice, and lay down and did their best to keep warm. The following morning, April 22, conditions were no better. John Hamilton, the commander of the special forces team, radioed Captain Brian Young. Hamilton advised that the men be taken off the glacier, and that a second landing be attempted later in a more hospitable location. Young agreed. Ian Stanley was then ordered to locate the team and bring them off the Fortuna glacier:

We flew around as best we could up there. It was quite exciting. Throughout the entire time wrestling with the airframe. Wind changing direction and lots of gusts and turbulence. But we couldn't find them, at all. The visibility was very, very poor. We must have been up there for at least an hour, and eventually I was starting getting a bit low on fuel. So I had to come back down off the glacier again.

Stanley returned to *Antrim*, refuelled, and decided with his colleagues in the two Wessex 5 helicopters to make a second attempt. The three aircraft formed up and flew towards the glacier. Fortunately the cloud base had lifted sufficiently to see to the top of the glacier.

At first the SAS men could not be found; in their white camouflage they were almost indistinguishable from the snowy background. After some time searching, a smoke flare was spotted, and the three helicopters moved immediately to its location, where they found the men. The air-

The Argentine submarine *Santa Fe* lies disabled at Grytviken, after being attacked by Royal Navy helicopters

craft landed, the exhausted and frozen men boarded, and the helicopters prepared to depart, led by Mike Tiddy, flying one of the Wessex 5s. Tiddy asked Stanley for clearance to take off:

I said, 'Yup, OK, away you go.' So he took off. And myself and the other pilot, Ian Georgeson, were watching him go off. And he flew quite nicely along the side of some rocks which were there, which were giving him a good visual reference. And then just flew straight into a snow squall. You could see it come in and hit him. And of course, as soon as he hit that, he'd lost all his visual references. He then turned left away from it and we just watched him quietly fly into the ground. Rotor blades hit first and he ended up on his side, skidding along through the snow.

The two remaining helicopters flew to the site of the crash. When they landed they were relieved to discover only one man had been slightly injured, hitting his nose against a piece of metal. It was a remarkable escape. The men in the crashed helicopter climbed out, divided into two teams, and boarded Stanley and Georgeson's aircraft.

Stanley ordered Ian Georgeson to stay close and follow him off the glacier. They slowly lifted off and moved gingerly down the glacier. Stanley came to an ice-ridge:

As I went over the ridge, poor old Ian lost sight of me. So he was then suddenly lost, without any references. He quite rightly stopped moving forwards and started coming down very gently. The only trouble was, he had a little bit of sideways drift on, which he couldn't pick up, and, of course, when the aircraft hit, it rolled over on its side. My second pilot was watching behind. He had his head out of the door, watching them following us off and he actually saw him go in.

Loaded down with men, Stanley had no choice but to head back to *Antrim*. Two troop-carrying helicopters were now lost, and with them possibly sixteen men. The situation was bleak indeed. Having landed and disembarked his passengers, Stanley headed out once more over the glacier in an effort to find the second crashed helicopter. During this search, in zero visibility, the pilot of the second crashed helicopter made contact on the emergency frequency. He told Ian Stanley that all the men were unharmed and that they were sheltering in one of the helicopter's inflatable emergency rubber boats:

And there was only guy who was slightly hurt, and it was the same chap that had been in the first aircraft that had crashed. He'd been put in the same seat, and hit a very similar piece of metal! Poor chap. So he was not well pleased about that.

Ian Stanley returned to *Antrim* and reported that he had heard from the men on the glacier.

The news of the loss of two helicopters was transmitted to the Chief of the Defence Staff in London. Terry Lewin was in his office at the Ministry of Defence with John Nott. He advised the Defence Secretary that the Prime Minister should be told of the disaster:

He and I went over to No 10, and she was sitting on one side of the Cabinet table with Robert Armstrong, Secretary to the Cabinet, and John Nott and I sat on the other side. And I explained what had happened. This first military action of the Falklands campaign had ended in disaster. She sat there silent, and I could see passing behind her eyes, 'What on earth have I let myself in for? Is this the way these military people are going to conduct this whole operation?' I tried to calm her down and say, 'Look, the weather was very bad, these sort of things happen in war. This isn't going to upset the operation. We shall still continue and it'll be successful.'

It was a very bad moment. On board *Antrim* Stanley pondered what to do. The weather conditions remained atrocious, night was fast approaching, and the men in their inflatable on the glacier were unlikely to survive another night. The *Antrim* task force had only one remaining helicopter, his own

Wessex 3, which was designed for anti-submarine work, and had little room for carrying men. Nevertheless, he decided to make one final rescue attempt, in the hope that a miracle might happen. It did:

I think we were about 500 to 600 feet above the top of the mountains. And I don't know what it was, but suddenly there was a hole in the clouds and I was looking at a little red dinghy, sitting there on the ice. And we took the opportunity to just dive straight down through the hole, and landed alongside. We were no sooner down on the ground, when cloud cover closed over again, and we were back into the turbulence and low visibility. It was quite dreadful.

Stanley had planned on making two trips, because he doubted that his Wessex could carry sixteen men. But it was immediately apparent that only one mission could be flown back to the ship. There was no choice but to cram all the men on board:

Here were people with arms sticking out of the windows. And we had to leave their kit, which was a pity. But they kept their personal weapons and we managed to get them all in. And then we took off from there. The aircraft did jolly well.

The helicopter staggered back to *Antrim*, where it made a controlled crash landing on the rear deck. The entire SAS team was safe and sound, with no serious casualties. The news was greeted with tremendous relief in London. Ian Stanley was later awarded the DSO for his skill and courage.

South Georgia, however, had not been retaken. *Antrim*'s task force had lost two helicopters, and a second effort to land the party of SBS men had also ended in near-disaster when their Gemini inflatables failed to work. Surprise had also been lost, as on April 23 the small task force was spotted by an Argentine C130 Hercules aircraft on its way to drop supplies to the occupying forces.

Remedial action had to be taken fast. Captain John Coward, in command of HMS *Brilliant*, the Royal Navy's most up-to-date Type 22 destroyer, equipped with two Lynx helicopters, was ordered to reinforce the *Antrim* group immediately. *Brilliant* was already far south with a small task group, made up of *Sheffield*, *Glasgow*, *Coventry*, the frigate *Arrow*, and a Royal Fleet Auxiliary, *Appleleaf*. The ships had been instructed to make headway as fast as possible during the Haig shuttle.

Captain Coward pressed his ship forward through the South Atlantic storms:

We pushed the new Type 22 frigate faster than we thought was safe, and it proved what an exceptional sea-boat it was, and went very fast into the weather. And then at dawn when we arrived off South Georgia, rather worried about icebergs and that sort of thing, we couldn't see South Georgia because it was locked in mist. And the very first thing we heard was reports of a submarine off the coast.

News of the approach of the Argentine submarine *Santa Fe* was intercepted by signals intelligence and passed to the task force on April 24. Its arrival compounded the anxieties of Captain Brian Young, on board *Antrim*. Ian Stanley, having recovered from the rigours of the Fortuna glacier, was ordered to find and destroy the enemy boat. On the morning of April 25 he took off in his Wessex and set out to look for the *Santa Fe*. It was presumed, correctly, that the submarine had landed men at Grytviken, and was now heading back out to sea, where it would be a great danger to the assembled British ships. Stanley's observer, Chris Parry, soon spotted a suspicious object on the helicopter's radar. It turned out to be the *Santa Fe*:

We ran in and used a technique which I got taught a long time ago, when I first learnt to fly: just by looking at the aircraft and deciding what the throw forward would be. Chris Parry in the back, was doing much more scientific calculations, but I think we more or less came to the same conclusion at the same time. And I said, 'Drop', and luckily enough the two depth charges went off alongside the submarine, lifting its stern out

Captain Alfredo Astiz signs the surrender document after the battle for South Georgia. Astiz, notorious for his part in the dirty war, was taken back to Britain to face possible criminal charges, but was later returned to Argentina

of the water. And it started careening around the place and then headed off back to Grytviken.

As it limped back to harbour other helicopters from the task force delivered the *coup de grâce*. The *Santa Fe*, one of Argentina's two new submarines, purchased from Germany in 1976, was out of action.

The time for reconnaissance was over. An attack had to be made, as all surprise was now lost completely. The three naval ships of the task force, *Antrim*, *Plymouth* and *Brilliant* began to bombard the enemy. Captain Coward, on board *Brilliant*, was impressed by the spectacle:

The ships formed up in line ahead, rather like the old Gaumont British News. And started shelling the coast. I remember thinking that it was the most extraordinary event to be witnessing, after all these years. British guns echoing off the mountains of South Georgia – and it was certainly a very stirring sound and sight. And after the bombardment, then the marines moved in.

The bombardment, designed more to impress than to injure, was enough to convince the Argentine garrison that resistance would be pointless. When the assault force of Royal Marines and assorted special forces landed at Grytviken, the occupiers offered to surrender without a fight. The next morning, April 26, Captain Astiz agreed to surrender his garrison at Leith. South Georgia was recaptured.

The task group commander transmitted the news of the successful recapture of the island to London. The fact that there had been no British casualties after the initial difficulties was a tremendous boost to the military. Terry Lewin had spent some time building up Mrs Thatcher's trust in the armed forces:

She'd had nothing to do with defence ... She didn't know who we were, what we were capable of. So, we had to win her confidence before she would believe what we had to say. I think we did this, because one Saturday morning when she was on her way to Chequers, I went with her in the car and we stopped off at Northwood (the task force's operational headquarters). On the way, I was able to go through the personalities of all the senior people, all of whom I'd known for many years. What they'd done and what sort of chaps they were. And when we got there, we went down to the tunnel and she was briefed by Wing-Commanders, Second Officer Wrens, Majors, that sort of level, and they were absolutely first-class. They were very professional. They knew their job. They told her how far the planning had got, how the operation was going. And I think she really began to get a confidence from those people.

Then, of course, South Georgia convinced her that we could deliver. And from then on she was completely on our side, accepted advice and was tremendously supportive.

So relieved was the Prime Minister by the news of the repossession of South Georgia, after all the vicissitudes on the Fortuna Glacier, that she led the Defence Secretary, John Nott, out of Number Ten and stood by him, beaming, while he read the Task Group Commander's announcement of the recapture of South Georgia. When Nott had finished the statement, the press and television formed up in line and bombarded him, and the Prime Minister, with questions. She turned on the media, and in a famous outburst, imperiously told them, 'Just rejoice at the news ... rejoice!' She then led a rather sheepish Nott back into Number Ten.

Mrs Thatcher's emotion was understandable: she had been waiting in a state of considerable tension for news of the operation. After the first set-backs an easy victory in South Georgia had seemed unlikely. An early defeat would have been a disaster militarily, politically, and diplomatically. That had now been avoided. The public, however, had been unaware of the early difficulties, and to many the Prime Minister's outburst appeared inappropriate, and reeked of jingoism and old-fashioned imperialism.

The news of the British recapture of South Georgia was also surprisingly welcome in Buenos Aires. As Admiral Lombardo remembers, the Junta hoped that British honour would now be satisfied:

Someone in the Government said, well, this is what the English needed to do to begin to really discuss the matter politically, because having taken South Georgia, they already had a military success to present to the British people and also had their influence over the south, over the Antarctic, assured. They now had a possession with which they could maintain their relations, both physical and political, with the Antarctic. So now they were going to begin serious negotiations.

It was an attitude typical of the air of unreality which pervaded the Junta at the time. The action in South Georgia did nothing to further the chances of a diplomatic settlement; rather, it convinced many in Britain of the relative ease with which a military solution could be imposed. Only the shock of heavy British casualties would dampen this unjustifed optimism and bring home to the public the reality of war.

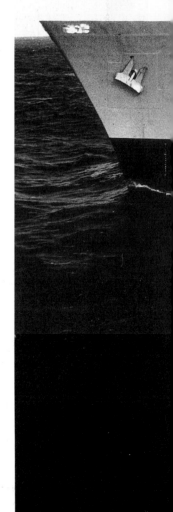

A Sea Harrier takes off from the deck of HMS *Invincible*. The British Harrier force, heavily outnumbered by Argentine jets, was placed in the front-line of the task force's air defences

14/CLEARING THE DECKS FOR WAR

O N April 18 a vanguard of nine ships of the British carrier battle group left Ascension and headed for the Falkland Islands. Led by the carriers *Hermes* and *Invincible*, the group was scheduled to enter the maritime exclusion zone around the Falklands, 3,500 miles south, on April 29. The remaining ships of the task force and the men of 3 Commando Brigade followed.

The news of the failure of the Haig shuttle forced the men of the task force to come to terms with the prospect of conflict. Before the departure from Ascension many had believed that the crisis would blow over, and that a political resolution would be found. Steve Newland, a corporal in the Royal Marines, was one of them:

Although we'd trained for war, you never really expected to do it, because politicians are very, very wary about unleashing the power ... But as soon as we left Ascension, we knew it was for real then.

As the task force came closer to the Falklands by the day, and the weather changed from balmy tropics to the cold grey of the South Atlantic, any lingering hopes of peace quickly evaporated. Sailors now took up their positions with real urgency when action stations were called; the paras and marines put even greater effort into the daily routine of fitness training and weapons' firing; and they started to think about their spiritual welfare. David Cooper, 2 Para's Padre, found that numbers at his services on board *Norland* increased:

I wouldn't want to be cynical about that: I was providing some form, I like to think anyway, of spiritual consolation and, if soldiers felt the need of it at any time, I was happy that they availed themselves of it. But you know, some made comments about ultimate insurance and so on, but that was what I was there for!

The military commanders in London also had to adjust to the fact that their men would soon be fighting and dying. The prospect of battle was not one which they welcomed.

British intelligence about the capacity of the Argentine fighting forces was extremely poor at the time of the invasion. Task force planners were often reduced to rummaging in libraries, and looking through *Jane's Fighting Ships*, to find out what they could about their opponents. As time passed, however, more information was received. The British had the ability to break most of Argentina's military and diplomatic codes; intercepted signals were the primary source of intelligence throughout the conflict.

Information from allies was also useful: the United States supplied much material, including details of recent joint training exercises with the Argentine Marines in Patagonia. As the conflict progressed, the United States also provided limited satellite surveillance information to the British forces. The French, too, were forthcoming about the Exocet-carrying Super-Etendards which they had supplied to the Argentine Navy.

As the intelligence picture became more detailed, the concerns of the military increased. Admiral Fieldhouse, the Commander-in-Chief of the task force, realised that it would be hazardous to send down a single commando brigade, albeit with two additional battalions of parachutists, to confront a garrison of up to 13,000 men, protected by a large air force. Although many of the defenders were conscripts, Fieldhouse was aware of the maxim that an attacking force should have numerical superiority over defenders if it is to gain its objective. The preferred ratio, the Admiral knew, was about three attackers to every one defender. In this case the British were heading for a conflict in which the ratio was reversed.

If the force going south could not be increased at this late stage, a large reserve following behind was now essential. It would be in a position to relieve the vanguard of marines and parachutists, act as a garrison and, should the worst come to the worst, step in when the going got tough. A reserve would also be necessary if the Argentine forces were to retreat to Port Stanley and then settle down for a siege throughout the winter.

The problem was that the British army had very little in reserve to send down after the first wave of troops had departed with the task force. 5 Infantry Brigade, which would normally respond to this sort of demand, had already been plundered. Two parachute battalions had been taken from it and assigned to 3 Commando Brigade. All that was left was a rump of a battalion of Gurkhas and an inadequately equipped headquarters' staff. Tony Wilson, 5 Brigade's commanding officer, was worried that his force had been emasculated:

There was the nagging worry that two thirds of the fighting strength of the brigade had gone south and it left not just a truncated brigade, but a brigade which at that point, really was no longer an effective fighting force.

General Bramall, the Chief of the General Staff, shared Wilson's concern. He was aware that if landings on the Falklands went ahead, a reserve would indeed be required; but none was readily available. 5 Brigade had been the fat into which the Treasury's knife had cut. Now, deprived of two battalions, and with an ill-equipped headquarters' staff, it was in no condition to go south. It took some argument before Admiral Fieldhouse could persuade the Army that a reserve brigade should be prepared.

Bramall eventually agreed to take the necessary steps to reconstitute 5 Brigade. Two battalions to replace the parachutists were sought and found: the 2nd Battalion Scots Guards, and the 1st Battalion Welsh Guards. On April 22 they were packed off to Sennybridge in Wales, where the terrain is somewhat similar to the Falklands, for two weeks' training with the Gurkhas. The brigade, whose communications equipment and artillery was severely lacking, had to be resupplied hastily. The operation had all the hallmarks of a last-minute rush, as Field Marshal Lord Bramall now agrees:

The reason it wasn't well done, was because we'd had, as you always had, up to the Falklands, in the period '79, '80, '81, a series of financial cuts and therefore this tended to actually affect the logistic backing, and the headquarters and so on, of 5 Brigade. It was very much a sort of a framework force which would have needed a period of tension to build it up.

In this case there was no period of tension and no time in which the framework could be built up. The condition of the two Guards' battalions also caused some concern. The Welsh Guards had recently finished service in Northern Ireland, and had been on ceremonial duties in London: hardly a recipe for soldiering in the harsh environment of the Falklands. There was also a difference in attitude. The Guards tended to take a more traditional view than their counterparts in the Royal Marines and the Parachute Regiment. Brigadier Wilson, charged with reforming his brigade, was aware of this:

In no way were the Guards battalions, you know, unable to soldier. They were bloody good soldiers and extremely well led and they'd do anything you told them to do. But on the other hand, they hadn't been brought up on, shall we say, the lean hungry tradition of people like the paras and the commandos, who month after month had been living off very little over very rough terrain.

Wilson's difficulties were compounded by a dire shortage of equipment. There were problems

continued on page 81

The conquest of the
Malvinas. An Argentine
Marine of the Amphibious
Vehicles Battalion waving
his unit's flag after the
occupation of Port Stanley

The Hunters and the Hunted

Left: HMS *Conqueror*, the nuclear-powered submarine which single-handedly defeated the Argentine navy. After the sinking of the *Belgrano* no Argentine naval ship dared challenge the Royal Navy in open seas again

Below: The stricken *General Belgrano* sinks, her bow blown clean away by the impact of HMS *Conqueror*'s torpedoes. 323 of her crew died, the largest number of men to be killed in a single incident in the Falklands War. The elderly cruiser was sailing *away* from the task force, well outside the total exclusion zone, at the time she was torpedoed

Right: A-4 Skyhawks of the Argentine Air Force take off from their base in the south of Argentina. They were a potent threat to the task force, which was inadequately defended against air attack

Below: HMS *Coventry* sinking in Falkland Sound after an air attack on 25 May, Argentina's National Day. Eleven British ships were hit in 'bomb alley', but only three were sunk. The others were saved by the failure of the bombs to explode

Left: An RAF Harrier returns to HMS *Hermes* after a Combat Air Patrol. Although the Harrier was superior to anything in Argentina's armoury, it was not sufficient to give the task force the air superiority it so desperately needed

Above: HMS *Plymouth* in San Carlos Water after bombing by a Mirage Dagger on 8 June. A Sea King helicopter hovers ov Plymouth's starboard side while HMS *Avenger* stand by to render assistance

Below: Beach-head at San Carlos. The British landings were unopposed, and there was great political pressure to move out and win a quick victory

Right: Break-out from the beach-head: the start of the long march to Port Stanley

Right: With the onset of the southern winter, weather conditions deteriorated rapidly. Fighting took place in freezing cold, wet and windy conditions

Below: Council of War. Brigadier Julian Thompson, Commander of 3 Commando Brigade (centre), and Major-General Jeremy Moore, Commander Land Forces (right), discuss tactics before the final battle for Stanley

Below: Damage control parties fight the fires on board the Royal Fleet Auxiliary *Sir Galahad* at Fitzroy on 8 June. 'They ran into port, but they didn't get the troops on shore, and they were caught' (Lord Lewin)

Below right: A ward on board the hospital ship *Uganda* with Welsh Guardsmen injured and burned following the Argentine attack on *Sir Galahad*

Right: Men of 2 Para bury their dead after the battle for Goose Green. 'It didn't surprise me to see a number of soldiers, very hard men in some cases, with tears streaming down their faces' (David Cooper, Padre of 2 Para)

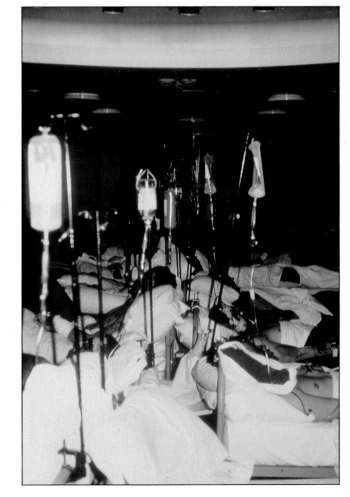

Left: The Royal Marines who surrendered at Government House on 2 April raise the Union flag once again after the Argentine surrender

Below left: Sir Rex Hunt with the Islanders whose rights he so strongly defended

with everything from communications equipment to the men's boots. Although all the brigade's requests for supplies were honoured, there was no time to check the new material during the exercises at Sennybridge.

The exercises themselves did not augur well for the future. The battalions had not worked together before and teamwork was difficult. It would obviously take some time before they were a fit fighting unit. But, as events in the South Atlantic progressed, and it became increasingly unlikely that a diplomatic solution would be found, the decision not merely to prepare 5 Brigade, but to send it south, became inevitable.

Another major difficulty for the military at that time was the presence in the South Atlantic of the Argentine aircraft carrier, the *25 de Mayo*. The Chiefs of Staff were keen for it to be sunk at the earliest opportunity. The politicians, however, were reluctant. Terry Lewin tried to persuade the War Cabinet of the gravity of the threat:

She was equipped with Skyhawk aircraft with a range of 250 miles. So, virtually, she had a gun with 250 miles range. It's very difficult to get politicians to understand that she really only had to come out of Buenos Aires, and out of territorial waters, and we were worried.

On April 22, the day that 5 Brigade started training, the submarine *Splendid* was ordered to locate and then trail the *25 de Mayo*.

When the War Cabinet became aware of this, they instructed the submarine to withdraw. Even Mrs Thatcher agreed, somewhat reluctantly, that the rules of engagement should not be changed to allow an attack at this stage. Francis Pym, the Foreign Secretary, was in Washington to discuss the outcome of the Haig shuttle. It was considered insensitive to have a British submarine ready to sink the Argentine ship during delicate negotiations with the Americans. *Splendid* was duly ordered to turn back. When she did so she was close enough to the carrier to detect its radar emissions. To many senior commanders, the sinking of the carrier was the *sine qua non* of a successful repossession of the Falklands. On this occasion, however, the political imperative took priority over the military necessity. It was the last contact a British submarine would have with the Argentine carrier.

Four days later, on April 26, Argentine Air Force planes spotted the spearhead of the task force advancing toward the Malvinas. Captain Guillermo Martinez was flying a Skyhawk on a routine reconnaissance patrol with his squadron leader, Lieutenant-Commander Manzotti:

About thirty or forty minutes after take-off, as we were flying over the Atlantic Ocean towards the Islands . . . I spotted, to our north, a light, then others slightly separated from each other. Since my squadron leader had ordered us not to communicate via the radio, I didn't use the radio and didn't tell him about what I'd seen. So I started to wonder what those lights might really have been. When we reached our base, landed, and I asked my squadron leader if he had seen those lights, he said to me, 'Don't you realise that was the British fleet?'

The approach of the British fleet was confirmed by several other reconnaissance missions of an Argentine Air Force Boeing 707. The Junta was now in no doubt about the seriousness of British intentions, but it had neither the will, nor the political strength to withdraw its forces from the Islands.

On Wednesday April 28, the leading elements of the task force were closing on the Falkland Islands. The two aircraft carriers *Hermes* and *Invincible* were accompanied by the destroyers *Broadsword*, *Sheffield*, *Coventry* and *Glasgow*, and the frigates *Alacrity*, *Yarmouth* and *Arrow*. Three fleet auxiliaries accompanied the group. The ships were at battle stations, all too aware of the danger posed by the air threat, and in particular, by the Argentine Navy's Exocet-equipped Super-Etendards. Intelligence reports had also warned of the presence of an Argentine submarine, the *San Luis*, in the area.

Admiral Woodward, on board *Hermes*, now refined his strategy for an attack on Argentine positions and assessed the threat which he faced. He knew that the submarines *Splendid* and *Spartan* were cruising in their patrol areas or 'boxes' in the South Atlantic, still vainly looking for the Argentine aircraft carrier, *25 de Mayo*. Woodward shared London's concerns about Argentine air superiority and the threat of the carrier. In order to neutralise both, he had devised his own deception plan to draw out the Argentine forces. The hope was that they would be destroyed early in the battle for the Falklands.

Although the amphibious forces had barely left Ascension, and a British landing was not planned for another three weeks, Woodward wished to create the impression of a large and slow-moving amphibious force as his ships sailed towards the

Overleaf: The British Chiefs of Staff grouped around the conference table in Whitehall. In the foreground (right) General Sir Edwin Bramall, Chief of the General Staff; (left) Admiral Sir Terence Lewin, Chief of the Defence Staff; (behind him) Admiral Sir Henry Leach, Chief of the Naval Staff and Sir Michael Beetham, Chief of the Air Staff

Falklands. He hoped to do this by releasing clouds of aluminium 'chaff' whenever an Argentine reconnaissance plane approached. Reflected on the plane's radar, the aluminium gave the impression of a ship. The deception was successful. As the task force approached the Falklands, Admiral Lombardo and his colleagues were under the strong impression that a landing was about to take place.

The Argentine High Command ordered Rear-Admiral Gualter Allara, the fleet commander, to transfer his command from naval headquarters in Puerto Belgrano to the *25 de Mayo*. The carrier was cruising not far out to sea, in shallow water off the Argentine mainland. Allara had discussed his strategy with Admiral Lombardo, and the two men had decided to hold back from any offensive action, until the British intentions became clearer.

On the same day John Nott announced to the House of Commons the establishment of a total exclusion zone. He told the House that it would take effect from April 30. Nott declared that any ship or aircraft found operating within a radius of 200 miles around the Falkland Islands in support of the illegal Argentine occupation, would be liable to attack. The Defence Secretary also stressed Britain's right to take additional measures in self-defence, under Article 51 of the United Nations' Charter.

In Washington, General Haig put his final proposals for a diplomatic solution, little changed from those of his abortive shuttle, to Britain and Argentina. Britain remained silent, waiting for an Argentine response. It came quickly, the following day, April 29, in the form of a curt rejection. As conflict loomed, Nicanor Costa Mendez told the BBC 'The Falklands can result in a Vietnam for Great Britain. The place is located 10,000 miles from London, and is very difficult for the British to defend.' With similar difficulties in mind, the Chiefs of Staff in Britain finally confirmed that the newly reconstituted 5 Brigade would be sent south, subject to the War Cabinet's approval.

On April 30 President Reagan announced that the United States would end its neutrality and come down on the side of Britain. For the first time, Reagan announced unequivocally that he believed Argentina to have been the aggressor. The decks were now cleared for British military action. Diplomatically, support for Britain remained strong in the United Nations. Militarily, the vanguard of the task force was closing on the

Falklands, ready to impose the total exclusion zone.

Amphibious forces were following behind the battle group more slowly. Landings were not planned for another three weeks. In the interim period, special forces inserted on the Islands by helicopters from Admiral Woodward's task force were ordered to gather as much intelligence as they could about the disposition of Argentine forces, and the nature of any chosen landing site. It was also hoped, wrongly as it turned out, that three weeks would give sufficient time for the Argentine air threat to be neutralised.

In Argentina, the High Command ordered Rear-Admiral Allara to lead his fleet out to the high seas. The plan was to divide Allara's naval force into three groups and to carry out naval actions against the expected British landings in a pincer movement from the north and south. In the north the *25 de Mayo*, two destroyers, and a separate group of three frigates; in the south, the elderly cruiser *General Belgrano*, and two destroyers.

Admiral Lombardo had devised the plan. He was acutely aware of the threat posed by the British nuclear-powered submarines. At the same time he wished to put the naval forces under his command to good use. The compromise solution was to operate the forces close to the Argentine mainland, where they could seek shelter from submarines in shallow water. They could then attack stragglers *outside* the well-defended main body of the task force. Lombardo was also well aware that the British forces would be most vulnerable when landing:

We were waiting for that decision day, the day of the landings, not to attack the ships when they were landing, but to try to disrupt the operation by surrounding it and attacking stragglers, transports, any ships which were outside the area of specific combat which was going to be the landing zone.

On April 29 the Argentine task groups took up their positions in the mistaken belief that a British landing force was approaching the Islands. The aircraft carrier, together with its accompanying destroyers and frigates, assembled just outside the exclusion zone to the north-west of the Islands.

In the south, the *General Belgrano*, with its escort of two Exocet-carrying destroyers, approached eastwards to within 260 miles of the Falklands. Captain Hector Bonzo was in command of the elderly cruiser. Argentina had purchased the ship

HMS *Hermes* with Harriers and Sea King helicopters on the flight deck. Right: *Hermes* at sea, a view of the crowded main hangar beneath the flight deck, with Royal Marines lining up for a weapons check

from the United States in 1951. *Belgrano* was equipped with five turrets, each with three 152mm guns with a range of 1,800 metres. In the age of the Exocet, with its thirty-mile range, such armament, though powerful, was obsolete. Her two accompanying destroyers, the *Hipolito Bouchard* and the *Piedra Buena*, both equipped with Exocet, were smaller, but much more dangerous.

The *Belgrano* had been at sea, with 1,093 men on board, since April 16, patrolling the southern approaches to the Falklands to prevent any British reinforcements coming from the Pacific. On Thursday, April 29, Bonzo received specific instructions from Admiral Allara:

Our mission was to approach the English fleet together with the other ships in the task group ... We were not to go to attack and confront the English task force, because that would have been suicide. Our position was, in the event of damaged ships or ships in bad condition moving to the south, that the *Belgrano* would be there to stop them, or at least to try to prevent an escape to the south.

To the north the *25 de Mayo* and her escorts were detailed to be the main attacking force. *Belgrano*'s role was to take part in the action as an aggressive back-stop.

On the British side Woodward set May 1 as the target date for the first attacks. Air raids on Stanley airfield would be followed by naval bombardment. He hoped that such action would draw a strong response from the enemy and force the carrier into the open. After several requests the War Cabinet agreed, on April 30, to allow the rules of engagement to be changed to authorise an attack on the *25 de Mayo* outside the total exclusion zone.

Woodward, to his chagrin, was not in command of the three nuclear-powered submarines then operating in the South Atlantic. These were controlled by the Flag Officer Submarines, Admiral Peter Herbert, based in Northwood. As the British received intelligence of the movements of the Argentine task force, the submarines were alerted and ordered to seek out the enemy. On Thursday, April 29, the nuclear-powered submarine, HMS *Conqueror*, had been told to intercept and shadow the *Belgrano*. Intelligence received in Britain had indicated her possible whereabouts. But neither of the other two submarines in the north, *Spartan* and *Splendid*, had any idea of the exact whereabouts of the carrier *25 de Mayo* and her accompanying task group.

A 'chaff' launcher is prepared for firing. After launch, 'chaff' rockets explode or 'bloom' into a cloud of aluminium fragments which confuse the enemy's radar

On Friday, April 30, the task force, now reinforced by the arrival of *Brilliant* from South Georgia, penetrated the total exclusion zone, two hundred miles north of the Falklands. The crews on board listened in tense silence as their captains addressed them. In *Hermes* Captain Middleton warned his men that May 1 was going to be 'the big day', and urged them, over the ship's tannoy, to be courageous: 'If at any time you feel you are unable to carry out your duty, remember that nothing you do should bring discredit upon your family, or on the Royal Navy.'

As it turned out, every man on board did his duty.

Later that evening Admiral Woodward was alerted by Northwood to a signals intercept confirming that an Argentine pincer attack was developing, and that he was now being approached to the north by the Argentine aircraft carrier, and to the south by the cruiser *Belgrano*. He was also aware of the presence of the Argentine submarine *San Luis* to the south-west. The task force was now under considerable threat.

AT 4.40 am on Saturday May 1, a Vulcan bomber dropped twenty-one 1,000-pound bombs on Port Stanley airfield. Hostilities had begun. The bomber's 7,000-mile round-trip flight from Wideawake was an extraordinary achievement, necessitating seven in-flight refuellings during the sixteen-hour journey. The operation, code-named *Black Buck*, was not, however, an outstanding military success. The Vulcan made its final approach at 300 feet to avoid Argentine radar, and dropped its stick of bombs diagonally across the runway. Only one hit the tarmac, which was quickly repaired by the local forces.

The raid, however, came as a complete surprise to the Argentine defending forces. Commodore Hugo Mayorano was on duty at the airport:

It was about 4.40 am on May 1, when our radar detected a plane. When hostilities first broke out we didn't know if these were our own planes or those of the enemy. So we decided to consult a radar station in Puerto Argentino, which had a wider range, to find out if more Argentinian planes were really on the way bringing supplies and equipment. While we were consulting this radar station the Vulcan dropped twenty-one 500-kilogramme bombs over the runway. Only one side of the runway was hit by these bombs . . . the rest of the bombs were scattered around the airport.

Mayorano felt the stunning concussion of the bombs' shock waves as they exploded. All the windows in the control tower were smashed, and fires started. Three men were killed.

Once the Vulcan had completed its bombing mission its crew transmitted the single code-word *Superfuse* to the task force. The bomber's mission was accomplished. Now Woodward's attacks could begin. At 8 am, Stanley time, twelve Harriers were launched from *Hermes* to attack Stanley and Goose Green airfields. They were joined by six Harriers from *Invincible*. Within the hour the aircraft returned to the carriers having attacked their objectives. Brian Hanrahan, the BBC reporter with the task force, asked for permission to report that all twelve Harriers had returned safely. This was refused. Instead he was allowed to use the famous phrase 'I counted them all out, and I counted them all back'.

Once again, however, the raid was not a complete success. Although no Harriers were shot down, the British pilots encountered extremely stiff opposition from the Argentine defenders. The surprise which had benefited the Vulcan attack had been lost, and the jets had to run a gauntlet of anti-aircraft fire and surface-to-air

missiles. It was only extreme good fortune that prevented the loss of a plane. Having put so much lead into the sky, the Argentine anti-aircraft crews were convinced at the time that they had successfully shot down at least one Harrier. Later they reluctantly accepted British reports that there were, in fact, no losses. Commodore Mayorano was certain that the strength and power of the defences took the British by surprise:

Although we might not have known exactly whether one, two, three or however many planes were downed, our low-level anti-aircraft strategy was working very well, because they then changed their attack tactics, which meant that they were unable to destroy the runway. This is quite clear, because up until the last day of the conflict our planes were still using the air base.

It would have been foolhardy to risk the loss of precious Harriers in further low-level attacks on the airfield. From then on bombing raids were carried out from well above the range of the Argentine defences.

During the attacks General Menendez was busy co-ordinating the Argentine response and communicating with the mainland. Shortly after the Harrier bombing raid on the airfields at Stanley and Goose Green, Menendez was informed by an officer that Admiral Woodward was calling him on the radio:

On my way to the radio receiving station I met the commander in charge of that section. He said: 'Where are you going, sir?' and I said, 'They tell me that Woodward wants to talk to me.' He said, 'Yes, he wants to send a helicopter so that we can go to the *Hermes* and surrender. My reply was that he should send the helicopter with the little Prince Andrew for us to deal with.' I looked at him and he said, 'Did I do wrong?' I said, 'I wouldn't have said that but if you said it then we don't need another reply. We cannot talk about surrender today. We have to fight.'

Only minutes after the Harrier attacks on Stanley airfield, the next stage of Woodward's attack on the Islands began. The destroyer *Glamorgan*, together with the Type 21 frigates *Alacrity* and *Arrow*, approached Port Stanley to bombard the airfield and other selected targets. Andrew Johnstone-Burt was a young Sub-Lieutenant on board *Alacrity*:

It was in daylight and we closed the coast, quite rapidly with *Glamorgan* and another Type 21 (*Arrow*), the three of us in close formation. Being of pretty much insignificance in the command team, I was on the gun direction platform above the bridge with the smaller calibre weapons with a bird's eye view. We hoisted the battle ensign, and with that came a great sense of excitement, people were keen to start the first action; but also in retrospect, a great feeling of naivety. We were about a mile off the coast, and took up our position and started the bombardment. Some twenty minutes into the bombardment all eyes were concentrated on how effective our bombardment was, rather than perhaps what we should have been doing, which was looking out for enemy aircraft.

In the south of Argentina, at the San Julian air base, Major Norberto Dimeglio, the Squadron Leader of a group of Israeli-built Mirage jets, was on alert. After the news of the Vulcan raid on the Malvinas, Dimeglio and two colleagues were ordered to a high state of readiness: they boarded their planes, warmed up their engines and waited for the order to attack. It came at two o'clock in the afternoon. Three ships had been seen approaching the Puerto Argentino area.

We took off armed with two bombs and the 30mm cannon which the Mirage carries. We approached the Islands without any problems, and began our descent to approach the area where the ships were at very low altitude.

Without the benefit of airborne early warning, the ships were unable to detect the approaching aircraft. Johnstone-Burt and his men were taken by surprise, as were the crew of *Glamorgan* and *Arrow*:

The aircraft swooped down onto us. He had a clear beam-on view: side view of the whole ship, in broad daylight. And we on the upper deck had a perfect picture of it, and we were alarmed to see that our main gun hadn't acquired the target, hadn't come round to point at it, nor had our missiles. The Ops Room was completely unaware of this attack.
The aircraft closed rapidly and it dropped two bombs. One early and one late. They scissored the ship. I was above the bridge and I turned around to one of my colleagues, about ten yards away, and the 1000-pound bomb passed between us, and just grazed one of the boats that was on the boat deck.
The other bomb blew up underneath the ship, and damaged one of our main engines. There was a complete sense of shock. I had ordered the seventeen-year-old boy on the Oerlikon to engage the aircraft as he was coming in. He had failed to do anything. He was struck with fear. And we all knew that we had got away with it. And there was a sudden feeling of relief in the sense that we'd been bloodied for want of a better word, and that we had to concentrate on what we were doing and not get distracted by the excitement of it.

Alacrity had a narrow escape. So did her sister ship, *Arrow*, and the destroyer *Glamorgan*. As Dimeglio and his two fellow Mirage pilots turned for home they strafed *Arrow* with cannon. The pilots were mistakenly confident that they had hit

such easy targets with their bombs, but they were correct in thinking that their cannon fire had found its target. Dimeglio's attack caused the first British injury in the task force. Able Seaman Ian Britnell on board *Arrow* was slightly wounded by a splinter. The three Mirages made their escape:

Then came the tensest moment, as we headed back to the mainland. I radioed to find out what had happened to my two companions, and I felt a great emotion when I heard that they had both got out without a problem.

The attack was a salutary lesson to the British. It was abundantly clear to even the most junior officer, like Andrew Johnstone-Burt, that the task force lacked sufficient air cover:

Admitting that I had limited warfare experience, or knowledge, it struck me between the eyes that we didn't have much defence against the air threat. It was a worry that these aircraft couldn't be detected.

The lack of early warning to alert the task force was also of concern to more senior officers. Captain Coward, in command of *Brilliant*, had the benefit of the modern Seawolf close-range missile defence on his ship, but was still aware of the problem: 'There was obviously a glaring gap in our entire defences, which was proper organic air cover.'

Most of the Royal Navy's ships were equipped with the Sea Dart missile, a long-range surface-to-air missile, which was capable of hitting planes flying at high altitude, but was unable to destroy low targets. As Argentina was also equipped with the same Sea Dart by the British before the war, her pilots knew how to counter it: whenever they attacked the task force they made their final approaches skimming over the sea at wave-top level.

The British did have the advantage in air-to-air combat. The United States had hastened the supply to the task force of their latest Sidewinder air-to-air missile, the AIM 9L. Once launched, the missile, which weighed only 186 pounds, could accelerate to speeds of up to 1,980 mph in pursuit of the enemy, its heat-seeking homing device locking on to the hot gases of the target's jet engine. The combination of these missiles and the nimble Harrier was deadly, as the Argentine pilots soon found out. On May 1 the Argentinians flew about thirty combat missions, using Mirages, Skyhawks, and their elderly Canberra bombers. The Harriers, firing their Sidewinders, succeeded in shooting down three jets as they flew over the

Falklands. Andrew Johnstone-Burt was able to witness the Harrier's superiority in air-to-air combat from his vantage point on board *Alacrity*:

A Harrier on station above us was being tailed by a Mirage. The greater speed of the Mirage enabled it to get in behind the Harrier. The Harrier did a most impressive manoeuvre where it came up vertically and then slotted in astern of the Mirage and released a Sidewinder. It was just above our heads when the aircraft blew up. There was immediate elation from everyone on the upper deck: cheers, and in a sense, a sort of relief. And it was only later that we realised what was going on, and that there was a man who'd just been blown up inside that aircraft.

Commodore Oscar Aranda co-ordinated the Argentine air attacks from Puerto Argentino:

Those are some of the saddest memories I have about the war. We followed the air battle on our campaign chart as if we were watching something on television. We traced the positions of our planes, and those of the enemy planes. Since we have a small air force we practically knew all the pilots of those planes personally. So when one of our planes was shot down or lost, we had to remove one of the pins, taking off a little model plane. That simple act of removing one of the pins marked the loss of one of our colleagues. This was really very difficult to accept, and for the first few days, especially May 1, when we had a lot of casualties, one after the other, it was a shock which we found difficult to come to terms with.

The Argentine problems in the air were compounded by the distance of the Islands from the mainland bases, and poor communications. General Menendez quickly came to appreciate the difficulties:

Because we hadn't extended the runway in Puerto Argentino (Port Stanley) we were unable to have high performance planes there. We had to make all our requests for air support to the mainland; the planes then had to fly a 600-mile round trip ... in order to avoid being detected they had to fly very low. There were too many penalties and complications to pay in order to arrive on time and be able to fight back. Therefore the air combat didn't materialise at the right times, and when it did conditions were very disadvantageous to our force.

After May 1 the Argentine Air Force made no attempt to engage the enemy in air-to-air combat. It had quickly learned that its advantage lay in surprise low-level attacks on task force ships. It was hopeless to wait around and engage the enemy in dog fights.

The British, too, had learned some important lessons on the first day of battle over the Falklands. The Harriers took care to approach Stanley at a higher and safer level, and close bombardment of the shore henceforth took place at nighttime, or under the protection of the two available Seawolf destroyers: the Type 22s, *Broadsword* and *Brilliant*.

May 1 ended with both sides claiming victory. The British had carried out successful raids and bombardment of the enemy without casualties. Harriers had downed three enemy aircraft, and a fourth was shot down in error by friendly fire. Despite the close call with *Alacrity*, *Arrow* and *Glamorgan*, all the ships of the task force had survived the first day's fighting.

The Argentine High Command was also encouraged by the day's combat. It was clear that the British had not succeeded in destroying the airfield, despite the effort put into the attacks on it. It was also evident that the enemy was unable to repulse high-speed low-level bombing attacks, and had, as a result, been unable to achieve air superiority. Above all, the Argentine military were under the impression that their forces had successfully repelled a large British landing force. It was this mistaken belief that amphibious forces were standing by to land which led inevitably to the loss of the *Belgrano* the following day.

The runway at Port Stanley airfield. Despite several British attacks, only one bomb found its target. The crater can be seen near the end of the runway. Argentine aircraft continued flying to Stanley until the last day of the war

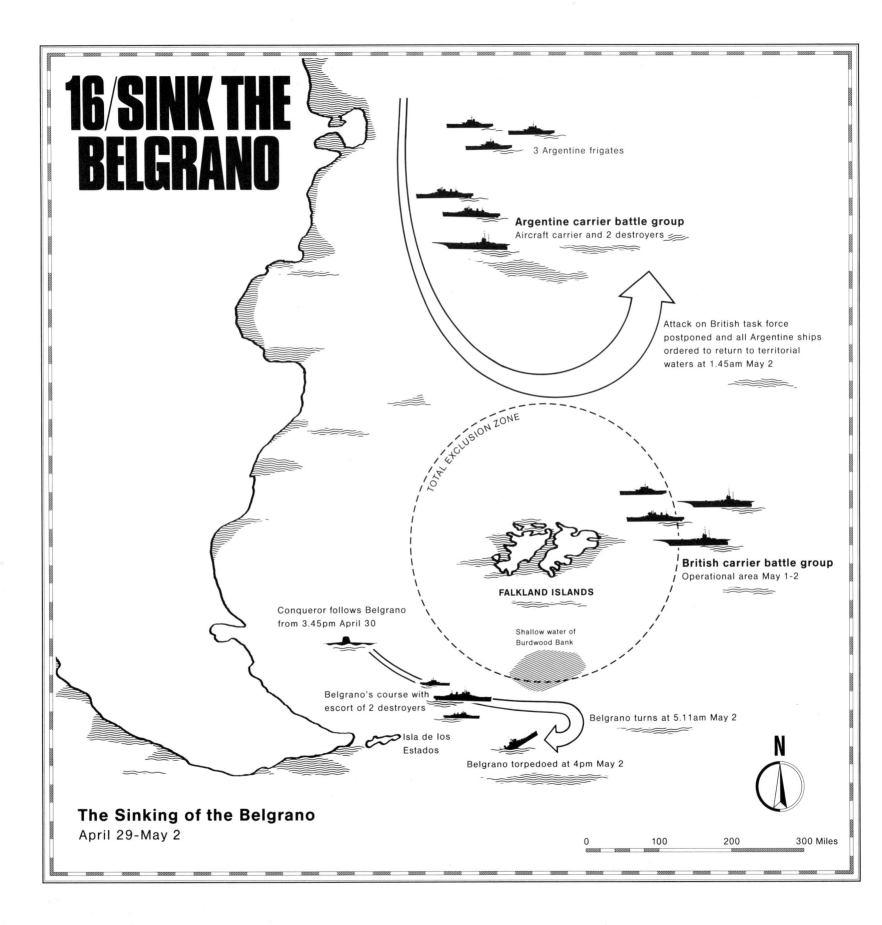

16/SINK THE BELGRANO

3 Argentine frigates

Argentine carrier battle group
Aircraft carrier and 2 destroyers

Attack on British task force
postponed and all Argentine ships
ordered to return to territorial
waters at 1.45am May 2

TOTAL EXCLUSION ZONE

British carrier battle group
Operational area May 1-2

FALKLAND ISLANDS

Shallow water of
Burdwood Bank

Conqueror follows Belgrano
from 3.45pm April 30

Belgrano's course with
escort of 2 destroyers

Belgrano turns at 5.11am May 2

Isla de los
Estados

Belgrano torpedoed at 4pm May 2

N

The Sinking of the Belgrano
April 29-May 2

0   100   200   300 Miles

THE sinking of the *General Belgrano* was, and remains, the single most controversial event in the Falklands War. For a time, after the conflict, it took centre-stage in British political life as politicians fought to conceal or reveal the minutiae of the cruiser's course before it was sunk, and the precise nature of the orders to HMS *Conqueror*'s Commander, Christopher Wreford-Brown.

During the war, and for some time afterwards, much remained secret about the decision to sink the *Belgrano*. Now that a decade has passed, almost all that there is to know about this episode in the conflict has been released to the public or been quarried out by persistent questions in the House of Commons. But a judgement about the rights and wrongs of the sinking remains difficult. To the Argentine military it was a political act which had little to do with the strategy of the war. To the British it was a purely military action, essential for the preservation of the task force.

On April 29 Christopher Wreford-Brown, an utterly efficient, no-nonsense naval commander, arrived on station off the south-west of the Falkland Islands. *Conqueror* had finished its mission to South Georgia, where her satellite-receiving aerial on the boat's mast had been badly damaged by heavy waves. Despite the best efforts of the submarine's radio experts to repair the mast, Wreford-Brown's communications with naval headquarters at Northwood remained extremely difficult. He could send signals with ease, but could only receive them intermittently. That evening Wreford-Brown managed to receive a message from Northwood ordering *Conqueror* to patrol an area outside the total exclusion zone, to the south-west of the Falkland Islands, between the shallow water of the Burdwood Bank, and Los Estados Island off the Argentine coast. British intelligence had established the rough position of the three Argentine task groups: *Belgrano* and her two escorts in the south, and the carrier *25 de Mayo* with two destroyers, together with another group of three frigates in the north. Wreford-Brown was ordered to find and trail the *Belgrano* and to sink her if she entered the total exclusion zone. In the north the submarine *Splendid* was instructed to find the carrier; she searched without success.

Wreford-Brown was much more successful. In the far south Atlantic acoustic conditions are extremely good. Few ships were sailing in the waters to the south of the Falklands, and in the cold, still sea the threshing of propellers was soon heard by the submarine's sonar. On the morning of April 30 Wreford-Brown ordered *Conqueror* to dive and follow the bearing of the contact. The submarine travelled fast; she was deep under water to avoid detection. The next day Wreford-Brown confirmed the contact:

The following morning (May 1), returning to periscope depth in daylight, we found the surface was extremely calm and visibility was excellent. Nothing in sight, although overnight the contact had been getting louder. We went deep and continued to run in, and then later that morning we came to periscope depth and when I looked through my periscope, I saw four contacts. The one that had been making the noise was a tanker, the *Rosales*, and that was refuelling the three warships, the *Belgrano*, and her two destroyer escorts, the *Hipolito Bouchard* and the *Piedra Buena*.

As the *Belgrano* refuelled on its way towards the task force, on the edge of the exclusion zone, the first British air raids on Port Stanley airfield were taking place.

Admiral Lombardo, at naval headquarters in Buenos Aires, received news of the attacks:

All I had to tell Admiral Allara on board *25 de Mayo* was to act freely, because I thought the English were sticking to their operation, their main operation which was the landing. So the only information I had to give Allara was to tell him, 'go on, off you go', that was all I had to tell him. He was stationed with the fleet which had been divided several days before into three groups approaching the Malvinas. When I told him that the English had commenced the landing and that he could act freely, there was nothing else for him to think about. So he ordered his three ships, his three groups, more or less to proceed to the east to the ships that they were to fight.

Lombardo transmitted his orders to Allara on board the carrier. These, too, were intercepted by the British and passed on to Admiral Woodward, together with new information about the whereabouts of the *25 de Mayo*. She was now reported to be closing on the task force with her escort of two destroyers, some 100 miles to the north-west of the total exclusion zone. *Splendid* continued to seek her, but in vain.

In the south *Belgrano* continued on her course, heading east, just outside the exclusion zone. The crew on board were quite unaware that they were being trailed by HMS *Conqueror*. Later that afternoon Captain Bonzo summoned the ship's officers together:

I told them that we were in rather an uncomfortable situation, given the considerable differences between the forces which might confront each other. I explained to them what my feelings were. Bear in mind that the cruiser is a small community of a thousand men who have to be fed, not only materially, but spiritually as well, since it was the first war that Argentina was facing in a hundred years. So we had to search for everything that we had learned throughout our careers, in order to get the best out of every man.

On board *Conqueror*, Wreford-Brown watched *Belgrano* through the periscope as she finished refuelling, lined up in formation with her two destroyers, and set off in a south-easterly direction. The Argentine task group zig-zagged at twelve or thirteen knots.

That afternoon Wreford-Brown signalled Northwood that he was on the trail of the *Belgrano* task group. His rules of engagement were quite explicit: he could only attack Argentine warships if they entered the total exclusion zone. The submarine had little alternative but to follow the ships as they meandered towards the British task force.

Wreford-Brown ordered *Conqueror* to dive, so as not to be detected by the *Belgrano*, and then tracked the three ships using his sonar:

We trailed them moving south-east and then east, keeping well outside the exclusion zone for the rest of the day and all that night. I had quite a lot of time to actually contemplate what the next manoeuvre might be. I had no doubt that I was in a right sort of position to actually attack them when required. And it occurred to me from the military aspects of it all that it was sensible if they were neutralised to prevent them being a risk to our own task force. However, until they entered the exclusion zone, there was nothing I could do except send regular reports, which is what I did.

To the north the Argentine carrier group was actively searching for the British fleet. At regular intervals through the afternoon and evening of May 1, Tracker surveillance aircraft were launched from the deck of *25 de Mayo* to seek out the enemy. Commander Benito Rotolo was a Skyhawk pilot on board:

We were almost 400 miles out to sea, and with the help of our scout planes we detected the position of the British forces, some 300 miles to our east. This was May 1, around 1700 hours. The Trackers trailed the British fleet until we were able to make our advance and prepare to attack.

At midnight on May 1, Admiral Allara ordered six of his A-4 Skyhawks to prepare for a strike against the British fleet at dawn. Rotolo and his colleagues were briefed on the mission, and donned their flying gear:

The carrier was at attack stations and our destroyers were well distributed. We had hoped the encounter would meet with success. In fact, at least on our carrier, there was considerable excitement and expectation. It seemed like an adventure to us . . .

Thirty minutes later a Sea Harrier, flying from *Hermes*, approached the Argentine task group and detected five ships: the carrier and her four escorts. When the Harrier closed on the force, the destroyer *Hercules*, using her British-built air-defences, spotted the incursion and illuminated the Harrier with her Sea Dart missile system's radar. The Harrier beat a hasty retreat, and reported back to *Hermes* that the enemy was now forty-five miles north of the total exclusion zone, and 190 miles from the task group.

The British were in an extremely dangerous position: to the south, the *Belgrano* was approaching slowly but steadily, with two Exocet-destroyers, little more than 200 miles away. She, at least, was being trailed by a British submarine, and could be neutralised if necessary. A much greater threat was developing to the north-west. The carrier group, under orders to attack, was positively identified heading towards the British task force. The men on board the *25 de Mayo* were confident of their superiority, as Commander Rotolo recalls:

We set out professionally analysing our options, and one thing that encouraged us was that we had the advantage of having a carrier with a wide exploration range of about 500 miles in front of us, and we were able to attack at a wider range than the Harriers.

It was an advantage which had long concerned the British Chiefs of Staff and which explained their strong desire to sink the carrier at the earliest possible opportunity. That opportunity had been lost for political reasons, during the final days of negotiations in late April. Now, as the carrier approached, its position finally identified by the Harrier, no submarine was close enough to destroy it. *Splendid* was 150 miles to the south, too far away to be effective.

Just as the task force seemed at its most vulnerable, circumstances combined to turn events in Britain's favour. Late on May 1 Admiral Lombardo, in his operational HQ at Puerto Belgrano, realised that he had been mistaken, and that no British landings were taking place. He decided that the full-scale attack on the task force should be postponed immediately. Shortly after one o'clock in the morning of May 2, he sent a signal to the *25 de Mayo* warning Allara that there were no landings, that the British task force was not hampered by the need to protect amphibious ships and was at liberty to attack where it wished.

Quite coincidentally, fifteen minutes later, at 1.30 am, the Peruvian President, Belaunde Terry, contacted President Galtieri on the telephone, and offered his services as a mediator between Argentina and Britain. The outbreak of hostilities the previous day had increased diplomatic pressure on both countries to find a peaceful solution. Aware of this pressure, Galtieri accepted.

Ignorant of the renewed peace effort, Admiral Allara was making his own assessment of the *25 de Mayo*'s situation in the light of Lombardo's message. The carrier was at battle stations, and Benito Rotolo and his fellow pilots remained on the alert:

We were half-dressed in our flight gear; we couldn't sleep because we were very close to the British fleet, almost 140 miles away, and they had detected us with their Harrier. Our battle stations siren kept going off, so we had to keep getting up and running to our combat positions; it was a tough night.

A change in the weather early in the morning of May 2 finally made an air attack on the British impossible:

Because the wind dropped, the South Atlantic was completely calm; still as oil, as we say. This complicated our dawn take-off because bomb attacks are always complicated by in-flight refuelling, and the lack of wind would have meant that our planes' flying range would have to be reduced, which would have put the carrier within the Harriers' attacking range.

Admiral Allara could not risk his carrier. At 1.45 am he signalled Lombardo that he was unable to attack and that he would order the fleet back to its original position: the two groups in the north were to retreat close to the mainland, and the *Belgrano* group in the south was to go back to a waiting position.

The *Belgrano* had been making slow but steady progress to her position about 180 miles due south of the British task force, east of the Falkland Islands. Deliberately, she had not entered the total exclusion zone. *Conqueror*, deep under water, was still following the Argentine cruiser. At 2.50 am Captain Bonzo received the signal ordering him to turn back. It took some time before it was decoded:

Captain Hector Bonzo, commander of the Argentine cruiser, *General Belgrano*

The order was received to return towards a waiting station, not towards the mainland as has been said so many times, and not towards port as has been said on so many other occasions, but to a waiting circle, of which we already had many allocated to us in the South Atlantic.

Bonzo's waiting circle was an area directly to the west, just off the Isla de los Estados. Although the attack on the British had been called off for the time being, it had not been cancelled.

On board the *25 de Mayo* Benito Rotolo's disappointment was tempered by his understanding that there would be another chance to get at the enemy the next day:

At about two or three in the morning it was decided that, having taken the initiative, we would retreat 100 miles and wait between twelve and twenty-four hours, by which time it was forecast that there would be sufficient wind for the planes. The next day the fleet decided it would fly its planes for as long as possible, then follow up the attack with the destroyer's missiles, thereby engaging the British in a war of attrition.

On board *Hermes* Admiral Woodward was unaware of the order to the Argentine fleet instructing it to return to waiting areas off the coast. He was alarmed by the state of affairs, as he saw it, in the early morning of May 2. The carrier strike force was apparently approaching him unimpeded. In the south the second claw of the pincer also appeared to be closing. Only *Conqueror* was in a position to take action.

Woodward was doubly concerned. He also feared that Wreford-Brown might soon lose the cruiser. After studying his charts, the Admiral concluded the Argentine ships in the south were heading for the Burdwood Bank, an area of shallow water south of the Falklands. As a submariner himself, he knew that Wreford-Brown would be unable to operate safely in shallows, and risked losing the *Belgrano*.

Although the Admiral was aware that the rules of engagement forbade it, and knew too that he was not in command of the submarines in the South Atlantic, he decided to take action into his own hands. At 4.10 am he sent an order to Wreford-Brown, via Northwood's satellite link, ordering *Conqueror* to sink the *Belgrano*. Admiral Herbert, the Flag Officer Submarines, intercepted the signal when it arrived in London, and removed it from the transmission net. But Woodward's peremptory action convinced the Commander-in-Chief, Admiral Fieldhouse, that a change in the rules of engagement was now essential.

An hour after Woodward sent his signal to *Conqueror*, *Belgrano* and her escorts began to turn in a large arc, and set off in a westerly direction towards their holding position, away from the British task force and the Burdwood Bank. Captain Bonzo, like Commander Rotolo on board the carrier, believed his orders were not a cancellation of the operation, but a postponement:

My final objective was the waiting zone. I supposed, because the order telling me to change course gave no details, that we would go to the waiting zone before repeating the pincer movement at the most opportune moment, when the inequality between the Argentine and British forces was a little more balanced . . .

On board *Conqueror* Chris Wreford-Brown noticed the change of course on his sonar, and came to periscope depth to see what was happening. Looking through the viewfinder he saw clearly that the three ships were now heading in the opposite direction, on a heading 270 degrees west, steering towards the Argentine mainland at fourteen knots.

As *Belgrano* was turning, the Chief of the Defence Staff, Admiral Lewin, arrived at Northwood. It was 9.15 am British Standard Time on Sunday May 2. Admiral Fieldhouse was there to meet him:

I immediately got hold of Admiral Lewin and said, 'I need approval, urgently, to attack the *Belgrano*, and if we don't have that urgent approval, if we don't have that approval quickly, we may well lose her,' and he said, 'Is there time to spare?' and I said, 'None,' and he said, 'Well, you'd better tell the Prime Minister.'

Lewin quickly appreciated the situation as it appeared to the British. He was, at that time, unaware of the change of course. It appeared that the Argentine forces were engaged in a pincer movement and now, as Woodward warned, there was the added fear that the submarine could lose *Belgrano* in shallow water. The orders to the Argentine ships reversing the instructions to attack had not been decoded, and the British were unaware that the operation had been called off and that the *Belgrano* was, in fact, reversing her course. Under the incorrect impression that a full-scale attack was still developing, Lewin, together with the Commander-in-Chief, Admiral Fieldhouse, decided to request an immediate change in the rules of engagement allowing *Conqueror* to sink *Belgrano*.

The Prime Minister was spending the weekend at Chequers where she was due to have Sunday lunch with the War Cabinet. Conveniently, Chequers is only a few miles from Northwood, and the two Admirals were able to discuss the situation and brief the naval staff before leaving to meet Mrs Thatcher. They instructed that a signal be sent to Wreford-Brown ordering him to take no action until the rules of engagement were changed, and then left to meet the Prime Minister.

It was a fine May day, and Mrs Thatcher greeted the Admirals in the garden. Other members of the War Cabinet were inside the Prime Minister's country residence. As they walked indoors the three quickly got down to business. The Prime Minister had been unaware that *Conqueror* was in touch with *Belgrano*; there had been no opportunity to report the fact to her the day before. Lewin now told her all he knew:

I got hold of the Prime Minister and said, 'Look, Prime Minister, *Conqueror*'s in touch with *Belgrano*. She can't attack because the rules of engagement don't allow it. We would like to change the rules of engagement to give all submarines freedom to attack Argentinian warships.'
And so she said, 'Is it urgent?'
And we said, 'Well, we want to do it as soon as possible because the *Conqueror* may lose contact.'
So we assembled the members of the War Cabinet in a side room. We had a little discussion, standing up, and approval was given. Fieldhouse went off and telephoned Northwood and the signal was sent.

The Chief of the Defence Staff, Sir Terence Lewin, outside Fleet Headquarters at Northwood. Lewin was convinced that the *Belgrano* posed a substantial threat to the task force, and asked Mrs Thatcher for permission to sink the cruiser

As the secure line between Chequers and Northwood was not working, Fieldhouse had agreed a pre-arranged code to use on the open line to his staff at naval headquarters. In the excitement of the moment he forgot it, and blurted out the identity of the ships involved. Fortunately for him, the Argentine Navy was not listening.

The decision taken, the Admirals sat down to lunch with the War Cabinet. The local time was 1.30 pm. In the Northwood bunker, the Flag Officer Submarines, Admiral Herbert, transmitted the change in the rules of engagement to *Conqueror* and the other submarines in the South Atlantic. They were now allowed to attack Argentine naval ships outside the total exclusion zone.

The signal, as was usual, was sent via an American defence satellite. As the system was shared with US signals traffic, messages took some time to get through to their destination. In addition *Conqueror*'s wireless mast was damaged, which made the reception of messages extremely difficult. To make matters worse, Herbert's signal releasing *Conqueror* to attack was garbled when the submarine received it for the first time. Wreford-Brown, understandably, was reluctant to take action until he was certain of his orders. He decided to wait until he had received the signal clearly before taking action. In the meantime he sent a signal to Northwood informing Admiral Herbert of the *Belgrano* group's change of course. This was received at 3.50 pm, British time. Admiral Herbert did not consider the change of course relevant to the change in the rules of engagement, and did not pass the news on to the Commander-in-Chief at Chequers.

In Washington that Sunday, the Foreign Secretary, Francis Pym, sat down for a discussion of a possible diplomatic settlement with General Haig. He was unaware of the goings-on at Chequers, in England, that morning. Now that the United States had come down on the side of the British, Pym was eager to discuss American diplomatic support with his opposite number. Haig, for his part, had refined his own proposals and was in touch with President Belaunde Terry of Peru. The Peruvian President was ready to put them forward to both sides, with few changes. Al Haig considered, correctly, that a negotiator from a Latin American country would be more acceptable to the Argentinians. This new initiative was still at a very tentative stage, as Francis Pym understood:

On that day, there was no flesh on the Peruvian proposals whatsover. They were outlines and ideas as Al Haig himself told me at my meeting with him, which would have to be worked out further.

The two men discussed the different options for three hours. At midday, local time, Pym broke off the talks in order to have an early lunch before travelling to New York, to discuss the possibility of UN peace moves. He did not tell London of the Peruvian initiative.

At the same time that Pym broke off his talks with Haig, Wreford-Brown finally received a clear version of Northwood's signal releasing him to attack *Belgrano*. Half an hour later he sent a message back to Herbert telling him of his intention to attack:

I was then about seven miles or so astern of the group, because while I'd been at periscope I'd been going slowly and they'd been moving slowly ahead. I'd decided earlier, two things. One, that I'd conduct the attack using the Mark 8, straight-running diesel torpedo, that's fired in a salvo, because I knew if I got in the right position, that would actually damage the warships, whereas I wasn't so sure about our other torpedo. I'd also decided that I would actually attack the *Belgrano* rather than her escorts. Although we'd been told the escorts had got Exocets, I wasn't totally sure that the *Belgrano* hadn't got them. She was the larger target and she also had the Task Group Commander (Captain Bonzo) on board. So all those reasons made me think she was the better target to go for.

Having received the attack signal Wreford-Brown ordered the ship to action stations. His aim was to get into position about 1400 yards to the south of *Belgrano*'s bow, on the opposite side to the cruiser's two escorts. They were to the north, defending her from possible attacks from the Falklands area. This manoeuvre took two and a half hours. Although *Conqueror* went deep and ran in fast, she had to rise to periscope level periodically to check the position of the *Belgrano* group. Every time this was done, the submarine lost ground.

While *Conqueror* was manoeuvring for the attack, the Peruvian initiative appeared to be gaining pace. Francis Pym, hurrying to board his aircraft at Washington National Airport to go to New York, was called to the phone to talk to Al Haig. The US Secretary of State re-emphasised the importance of the Peruvian mediation. Pym answered that he would 'leave no stone unturned' in his search for peace, and quickly left to board his plane. An hour later, President Belaunde announced a positive response to his proposals from both sides in the conflict, and said that he would issue a press statement later that day.

The Peruvian President had been encouraged in the belief that the British welcomed his proposals after speaking to General Haig that afternoon. In fact Pym had barely considered the Peruvian plan, and had not informed the War Cabinet of its existence. As they made no provision for the wishes of the Islanders, they were unlikely to be accepted by London.

One hour after Pym's phone conversation with Haig, at 4 pm in the South Atlantic, Wreford-Brown was in a position to launch his attack:

I gave the order to fire three Mark 8 torpedoes. We heard them clearly run, through the hull and also on one of our sonar sets. And after some fifty odd seconds or so, we heard a noise like one striking, and I recall asking whether that was a hit. We heard it also on the sonar set, and I was looking through the periscope at the time and very shortly afterwards I distinctly remember seeing an orange ball and a puff of smoke from the middle of the cruiser, and a little bit later a further puff of smoke from for'ard.

Charles Foy was a radio operator on board *Conqueror*:

I remember, we were sitting there, and then we heard the order to fire the torpedoes. Heard the three go. And then we were all looking at our watches, waiting to hear the explosions, if any. And it was about a minute or so later, we heard two very clear explosions. And there was a heck of a cheer. And the first lieutenant came on the net and told everybody to shut up! And then we were going fast and deep, and clearing the area.

In the age of electronic warfare *Conqueror* had attacked and destroyed a Second World War cruiser using Second World War torpedoes. Captain Bonzo was on his way to the bridge when they hit:

It was the afternoon of May 2, at 1600 hours, 1601 to be more precise, at least by my watch, when we heard the explosion of the torpedo amidships. We realised later that it had been amidships. What we felt then was a great shudder, as if the ship were going up in the air, its progress slowed, and immediately three seconds later, a second explosion. When I got to the bridge, I was informed straight away that twenty metres forward had disappeared. The second torpedo had cut the bow off the ship.

The fatal torpedo was the first one, which had hit amidships. It pierced the outer skin of the ship, and exploded in the engine compartment. The force of the explosion, bottled up inside the compartment, smashed through the armoured ceiling plates, and escaped upwards through two decks. The first deck contained two mess rooms; the second, a relaxation area. Both were crowded with men. Few survived. According to Captain Bonzo 270 men died in these first moments. Many others were burned:

Those who witnessed the advance of the heat wave described to me how they saw the destruction advancing in many different ways. Some spoke of a fire ball which was coming towards them, others of a heat which surrounded them as if it were a room full of steam. The fact is that the explosive heat wave passed through many people.

On board *Conqueror* Wreford-Brown considered whether he should make a second attack on the two destroyers escorting *Belgrano*. After hearing explosions from their depth charges, he thought better of it, and ordered his men to make a quick getaway. Half an hour later, about seven miles from the stricken cruiser, *Conqueror* surfaced to periscope depth and signalled Northwood that the attack had been successfully carried out. Mrs Thatcher and the War Cabinet were informed of the news.

Meanwhile, in the *Belgrano*, Captain Bonzo had to come to terms with the destruction of his ship:

Immediately after the explosions there was a total silence on the ship. I'd say that silence is the most cursed thing that can be heard on a ship. Because we sailors feel at ease when we hear the sounds of the engines and ventilators. When there's silence it is because something is wrong. At that moment it wasn't just quiet. It was total silence; silence combined with total darkness.

The *Belgrano* was listing at a rate of about one degree a minute. Outside the wind was up, and the heavy sea was becoming rougher by the minute. The cold was intense. The stern compartments flooded, and the ship began to go down. At 4.20 pm the crew gathered at their various assembly points and launched the ship's life rafts. The injured were carried up on deck. Those in greatest pain were given morphine by medical orderlies.

At 4.30 pm Bonzo gave the order to abandon ship, 'the most tragic cursed order that a Captain can ever have to give in all his professional career'. Men jumped onto the rafts in the heavy swell of the freezing South Atlantic and clambered aboard as best they could. Some of the inflatables were blown towards the broken ship's bows, where they were punctured by the jagged steel. Those on board had to jump out and swim to other rafts further down the ship.

Ten minutes later all the surviving ship's crew had abandoned the sinking cruiser. Bonzo thought he was the only man left on board, when he heard a voice behind him:

It was one of the ship's non-commissioned officers, who was shouting at me, trying to make himself heard above the wind, the water which was splashing, the oil which was flooding us with fumes; a voice of encouragement to his Captain, a voice of help, to keep him company. I ordered him to jump into the water immediately, but he wouldn't. I asked him to help me launch the raft, and we did it between the two of us, after promising him that I was going to follow him. He made the sign of the cross and jumped over the starboard side. After that I also made the sign of the cross and jumped into the water. I swam fifty metres, and many arms of my crew members were waiting to help me into the raft. I fell exhausted into the bottom of the raft. It was 1700 hours, a petty officer who was in the raft informed me: 'Captain, sir, the ship is sinking.'

Bonzo and his companions watched as the cruiser slid beneath the waves. That night the weather worsened, and a terrific storm blew up. The life-rafts were separated from each other by the force of the wind and the waves. Because the *Belgrano* had rafts for a full complement of 1,500 men, 400 more than the ship was carrying, some were only partially full. Lacking the physical warmth of a fully laden raft, men on board the empty rafts died of exposure. On those which were more fully laden, like Bonzo's, the sailors helped each other keep warm:

The men attended to the wounded, taking care of the burned, warming their foreheads or wrists with a bag of urine which was collected from the crew members, a sort of hot water bottle which helped those who were in great pain, had a deep wound or a first degree burn.

The men on the rafts were left to survive the night as best they could. The two escort destroyers, fearing their own destruction, had left the scene of action immediately the attack took place.

323 men died in the sinking of the *Belgrano*, the largest number to be killed in a single incident in the Falklands conflict. When the Argentine High Command first learned of the sinking it was feared that many more – possibly the entire ship's crew – had gone down with the ship. The news had a profound impact on the Junta. At seven in the evening, Galtieri, Anaya and Lami-Doso had gathered at the Presidential Palace, the Casa Rosada, to discuss the Peruvian peace plan. The Foreign Minister, Nicanor Costa Mendez, was also present. The men's mood was cheerful. They believed that their forces had successfully repulsed an attempted invasion of the Malvinas, and

that Britain would now be ready to concede a settlement more favourable to Argentina.

After an hour of discussion Admiral Anaya was called out of the room. He returned a few minutes later, his pale and stern face even grimmer than usual, and broke the news of the sinking to his shocked colleagues. They decided immediately to suspend all negotiations. The Peruvian plan was dead.

The news that the *Belgrano* had been torpedoed had a powerful and immediate effect on the strategy of the Argentine Navy. When the carrier strike force received the signal telling of the sinking it was sailing westward and waiting for better flying conditions. Commander Benito Rotolo was still hoping to attack:

We were waiting for the wind, about 250 miles from the British fleet, which we were still tracking, when we found out about the sinking of the *Belgrano*. This obviously influenced the decision-making of those directing our operations, and once again the threat became real. We were well aware that a nuclear submarine, with its great destructive capacity, could sink a fleet of our size in a day or two, especially since we were so far from the coast. So the High Command decided to save our fleet for a later date, and in the event the attack never took place.

The *25 de Mayo*, her escorts, and all the Argentine naval ships on the high seas, rushed straight for the protection of shallow waters, and for the remainder of the conflict the Argentine Navy remained within the safety of the twelve-mile territorial limit. In a single stroke the Royal Navy had rendered the enemy fleet useless. It was a graphic demonstration of the awesome power of the nuclear-powered submarine.

If *Belgrano* had not been sunk, and the pincer attack had taken place, the course of the war may have been different, as Benito Rotolo argues:

Looking back on it after so many years, and having talked about it so much with colleagues and British naval officers who were also in the conflict, I think that night could have been a decisive one, as much for us as for them. The fact is that, had we entered into combat, we might have lost more units, but we could have damaged the British fleet, sunk some of their capital ships, and this surely would have altered the course of the war.

The news of the sinking stunned the world. For the first time, despite the fact that the outbreak of hostilities had occurred the previous day, it was realised that Britain and Argentina were fighting a bloody war over the Falklands. Diplomatic support for Britain's position did not wane, however. The UN continued to press for Argentina's acceptance of Resolution 502; the United States remained firm in its support of Britain; and the European Community, despite some wavering by the Italians and Irish, stood by the economic and military sanctions it had imposed after the invasion.

The sinking of the *Belgrano* became a *cause célèbre* after the war. The allegation was made that the cruiser was sunk, not for military reasons, but to put an end to the Peruvian peace plan and the chance of a peaceful settlement. Now that the full story is known, it can be seen that such allegations are baseless. The War Cabinet was unaware of the Peruvian plan when the decision was made to sink the *Belgrano*. It has also been argued that, since the *Belgrano* was heading away from the task force, she posed no threat: her sinking, therefore, could only have been politically motivated. The evidence for this is more equivocal. The cruiser was heading to a holding position; the pincer attack had been postponed, not cancelled. The British were unaware of the order to the Argentine task groups instructing them to withdraw. The only signals intercepts available indicated that an attack was still being prepared. Nevertheless, *Belgrano*'s change of course was known to Northwood, and the fact that the threat of an attack was diminishing was also appreciated on board the task force. The War Cabinet, however, was not told of the change of course.

The Government's behaviour after the sinking gave the strong impression of a cover-up. From the beginning facts were withheld, the record was altered, Ministers avoided the truth in their answers to Parliament, and Mrs Thatcher herself gave the erroneous impression that the *Belgrano* was heading towards the task force. Only two days after the sinking John Nott announced to the House of Commons that the *Belgrano* 'was close to the total exclusion zone and was closing on elements of our task force'. This statement was based on what he had been told by Northwood. It was an inaccurate account of events which the Government never sought to correct. Indeed, once given, it became the party line from which all the lies and cover-ups proceeded.

It is difficult to understand the reasons for the Government's long adherence to an untruthful account of the events of the sinking. The most plausible explanation is that, because *Belgrano* was torpedoed outside the total exclusion zone, the sinking may have been questionable under international law, and certainly appeared to be dishonourable. Far better then, from the Government's point of view, to promulgate the myth that the cruiser was heading towards the task force and was moving in and out of the exclusion zone.

Admiral Lombardo has always argued that the decision to sink the fleet's most venerable cruiser was not motivated by military necessity:

It was a warship which was sailing in a war and the enemy had every right to attack it. However, it's my conviction, that the sinking of the *Belgrano* was a political action and not a military action. I think that both Governments, the Argentinian Government and Her Majesty's Government, after the first few days in April, no longer wanted to stop the war machine. And part of that unwillingness to stop was the sinking of the *Belgrano* to give a demonstration of will to continue and carry out the military operations.

Lord Lewin utterly rejects Lombardo's accusation that it was a political act:

That's absolute tripe. Unless you say it's a political decision that we shall undertake warlike operations against the Argentinians. Now let's just look at what happened on the day before the *Belgrano* was sunk, which was the day the exclusion zone came into force, and the day that, as far as the British were concerned, the war really started. At 4.30 in the morning, a Vulcan dropped twenty-one 1,000-pound bombs across the runway. And the Harriers then came in and attacked the airfield installations. The Argentinians replied with an air attack with Canberras and Mirage and Skyhawks in the afternoon. They near-missed *Glamorgan* with a 1,000-pound bomb on either side of the quarter deck. The whole of the Argentinian Navy was at sea, with the object of intercepting and attacking the task force. All that happened on May 1. So, when we sank the *Belgrano* on May 2, it seemed to be quite a reasonable thing to do when she was at sea and in a position to attack our ships.

On the morning of May 3 Captain Bonzo and his crew in the *Belgrano*'s life raft watched as the sun rose above the bitterly cold South Atlantic. The storm of the previous night had abated, but a strong wind was still pushing the rafts towards the Antarctic and away from the mainland. At midday the sailors, to the Captain's great relief, heard the sound of an aircraft:

Just at that moment I realised that there were other rafts at sea in addition to my own. In order to give encouragement to each of the rafts in the sea, the aircraft began to dive above each of the rafts that were around there, which we had been unable to see. And so, by countless dives by the aircraft, that blessed aircraft, I realised that many others had also survived the night.

Captain Bonzo and his men were picked up by an Argentine patrol boat and taken ashore. To this day the Captain of the *Belgrano* cannot understand why the commander of HMS *Conqueror* attacked his venerable cruiser, rather than the two Exocet-armed destroyers travelling with him; he is also mystified by the delay in the attack:

The submarine *Conqueror* had been following me since the morning of Saturday May 1, when I was going east, getting closer to the English fleet every minute, yet the submarine did not make the attack. I changed course to the west at six o'clock in the morning of May 2, I sailed the whole morning and part of the afternoon on a clear course to the west, and four o'clock in the afternoon the attack occurred. When I was going towards the enemy forces they let me in, when I went away they attacked.

The reasons for the delay in the attack are now known: *Conqueror* was under orders to attack only if the cruiser entered the total exclusion zone. As *Belgrano* skirted it for some time without entering, the attack was delayed. A change in the rules of engagement was necessary to allow the attack to go ahead outside the zone; when the change was authorised its transmission to *Conqueror*'s submarine was slowed by the failure of the submarine's communication links. By that late stage the cruiser had turned and was heading west. But Bonzo's nagging doubt is a valid one. It must have been clear to the task force, and to naval HQ at Northwood, that the attack was diminishing. The *Belgrano* was sunk, less because of the immediate threat she posed, and more to establish the domination of the high seas so vital for the task force.

After the sinking of the *Belgrano* on May 2 Britain's military position appeared strong. South Georgia had been retaken, Stanley airfield bombed, and the Argentine Air Force engaged, all without the loss of a single British life. There was a mood of confidence, if not over-confidence, at home in Britain, and aboard the ships of the task force. When the news of the heavy Argentine loss of life on board *Belgrano* reached the United Kingdom, however, any triumphalism which might have been felt quickly abated. Even the *Sun* newspaper changed its headline 'GOTCHA' to the more tame 'DID 1200 ARGIES DROWN?'. The reality of war in the South Atlantic, which so many had never taken seriously, now hit home. Two days later it struck harder. On May 4 the Argentine Navy demonstrated that, although its ships were forced to flee, its aircraft could still operate with deadly potency.

17/EXOCET

MS *Sheffield* burns after being hit by an Exocet. The ship was filled with acrid black smoke seconds after impact. Although the warhead did not explode, the missile's burning fuel was sufficient to turn *Sheffield*'s interior into an inferno

ON the same day that the *Belgrano* was torpedoed and sunk, Captain Jorge Colombo, leader of the 2nd Naval Attack Squadron, took off in his Super Etendard, armed with an Exocet, and flew towards the British task force. His flight was one element in the combined attack on the task force, which involved the *25 de Mayo* carrier force in the north, and the *Belgrano* group in the south. Flying with him was a second Super Etendard, also armed with Exocet. Colombo had a clear knowledge of the location of the task force. Details of its position had been signalled from the Tracker aircraft operating from *25 de Mayo*. His mission was to launch two Exocets at major units in the British fleet.

Colombo himself had ordered that the valuable missiles should only be released if conditions were perfect. This time things went wrong. His plane's in-flight refuelling system failed. Having met up with a C130 Hercules tanker close to the Malvinas, Colombo found that he was unable to take on the necessary fuel to be certain of completing the mission and aborted the action. Two days later, as dawn broke on May 4, Lieutenant-Commander Augusto Bedacarratz and Sub-Lieutenant Armando Mayora prepared for a second attack. This time they would be successful.

Only a month before, Captain Colombo had received a top secret signal from the naval High Command. He was warned of the possibility of an invasion of the Malvinas, and ordered to make the recently purchased Exocet missile ready as soon as possible. The squadron had set to work. The Super Etendards, together with the air-launched AM 39 Exocet missiles, had only just arrived in Argentina. Five missiles had been delivered by the French in 1982, and a team from France was expected on April 17 to complete the technical procedures to make the system work. Because of EEC sanctions, however, the French team never arrived. The squadron had to find out how to work out the complex, computer-controlled firing system for itself. Captain Colombo took charge:

We had to make the system operative knowing very little about it, and we were not in a good enough position at that stage to make it work. So we all set to work together: officers, petty officers, together with civilians from the command base at Espora. The job involved working day and night to put the system into operation. In approximately two weeks we were able to find the missile's maximum range if operated in the best conditions. It was a hard job, and we had to make use of all the technical knowledge we had at the time, using our imagination and professional know-how.

The squadron also exercised with the two British-designed destroyers, the *Santissima Trinidad* and the *Hercules*. This enabled them to calculate the limited early-warning capacity of the British, and the range of the Sea Dart missile – the backbone of the task force's anti-aircraft and anti-missile defences. In order to extend the Super Etendard's limited range Colombo joined with the Argentine Air Force to develop in-flight refuelling from a converted Hercules. A Neptune anti-submarine aircraft was also commandeered to help find the British task force. By May 1 the system was up and running.

At 8.50 pm on May 3 the task force, operating approximately 100 miles east of the Falkland Islands, detected an unidentified aircraft seventy miles to the south, flying in the area of the sinking of the *Belgrano*. Although *Hermes* scrambled two Harriers, nothing was found. The British presumed that the radar contact was a Neptune aircraft on a search and rescue mission.

The plane was indeed a Neptune, but it was not carrying out a rescue operation. Its purpose was to locate the task force while giving the appearance of looking for *Belgrano* survivors. That night the co-ordinates of the task force's position were passed to the 2nd Attack Squadron. Bedacarratz and Mayora prepared for their attack.

The next morning, May 4, at 6.22, all hands in the task force were called to action stations in expectation of an Argentine air attack. After an hour and a half of waiting, at 8.05, the men were ordered to stand down and resume defence stations. As nothing had materialised, the task force's air-raid readiness was reduced.

Just as the men of the task force were standing down, Bedacarratz and Mayora were carrying out their pre-flight checks. Flying conditions were near-perfect, the weather slightly overcast and calm. The squadron had continued to receive updates of the position of the task force through the night. At 8.45 am the two Super Etendards took off and headed for the target. A Neptune reconnaissance plane remained airborne, transmitting the position of the British to the two pilots. The co-ordinates were entered into the aircraft's navigational system, which in turn guided the planes to the target.

The task force was prepared for retaliation after the sinking of the *Belgrano*. Although intelligence had suggested wrongly that the Super Etendard was unlikely to be modified to refuel in the air, and could not, therefore, reach the task force, some form of air attack was expected. Admiral Woodward arranged his ships in layers in order to give maximum protection to the two carriers, without which the whole mission would be impossible. Furthest out, he placed a picket line of Type 42 destroyers, *Coventry*, *Glasgow* and *Sheffield*, all armed with Sea Dart. Next he positioned three frigates, *Alacrity*, *Arrow* and *Yarmouth*, and one destroyer, *Glamorgan*, in line; behind them he put a missile barrier of three supply ships; and finally behind them, the two carriers, each guarded by a Seawolf 'point defence' destroyer, *Brilliant* and *Broadsword*.

After refuelling from the Hercules tanker aircraft 100 nautical miles out from Rio Grande, the two Super Etendards dived and flew on, skimming the flat sea at top speed. At 10.56 am (13.56 task-force time) the aircraft climbed to 120 feet, detected three blips of the three picket ships on their radar screens, and returned to sea level. Once the targets were acquired and the co-ordinates passed to the Exocet guidance computers, the Etendards climbed again, launched their missiles and turned for home at top speed. It was a clean and simple operation, little different from the many training exercises in the weeks beforehand.

The ships of the task force had four minutes in which to react and take what limited evasive action they could. *Glasgow*'s operations room, more alert than others, quickly detected the radar emissions of the Exocet missiles as they sped at 650 miles per hour towards their targets, and alerted *Invincible*, the task force's air defence control ship. But *Invincible*, having received many false alarms over the previous days, at first dismissed the warning and refused to pass it on to the other ships in the task force. Thus only *Glasgow* was in a position to take defensive action, turning to face the missile (in order to present a slimmer and more difficult target) and firing aluminium chaff to confuse its radar.

On board *Sheffield* the approach of the missiles went unnoticed until it was too late. One Exocet, possibly confused by *Glasgow*'s chaff, flew past the three picket ships and landed harmlessly in the sea. The other hit *Sheffield* amidships, pierced the ship about six feet above the water level, and partially exploded inside two large compartments. The warhead itself did not explode. Only the missile's fuel burst into flames, but that was

enough to disable the ship for ever. In twenty seconds the whole of the working area of the ship was smothered in acrid and pungent smoke.

Eddie Whitaker, a radio operator on board *Sheffield*, was answering a call of nature when the missile struck:

I was just coming out of the cubicle and there was this almighty bang, and I can only compare it to having a metal tin put over your head and someone banging it with a hammer. It was just like a sudden vibration. And it didn't last long, and it didn't throw the ship off course. It was just this sudden vibration, all the lights went out.

John Strange, an engine room artificer, had just finished his lunch and was working in the machinery space on one of the ship's diesel generators:

As I turned round to the starboard side of the ship to put the rags I had in a bin, there was a massive bang on the starboard side of the ship. And that was the last thing I remembered. I came round. I'd obviously been knocked unconscious, and I was lying on the plates, some seconds, maybe minutes later. Not a great deal of time, because otherwise I wouldn't have got out of it. There were no lights on, a lot of smoke and a lot of flames in the compartment. And I'd been hit with some shrapnel because I had blood on me, in various places, and there was blood running out of me. I didn't realise at that stage that I'd had any burns.

John Strange made for the exit hatch, but it had been bent out of all recognition by the impact of the missile. He was trapped:

I decided to make for the emergency hatch, which was over on the portside of the ship. As I turned round, I was met by a similar problem of a bank of flames. But I could see the other side of the compartment. So I knew that if I got through these flames, that I would probably be alright. So I put my hands up over my face to cover my eyes and face and I just ran through the flames to the emergency hatch. I had a ladder to climb up, one deck, to lift the hatch. And as I was climbing up the rungs, all the skin had fallen off my hands and fingers and was just hanging limp. But I didn't really have time to pay any attention to that. There was no pain. Obviously the burns were below nerve level and I didn't feel any pain from it. And I climbed up the ladder and I pushed up on the hatch. Fortunately during the explosion a lot of the clips, which hold the hatch down, had been blown open, so I had only two clips left to get off before opening the hatch. I got out and made my way for'ard, and there I was met by members of the ship's company who helped me forward to a smoke free zone at the time.
I was left lying in a small cabin for some time and I could see the blood running from me on to the carpet of the cabin. I realised I was fairly badly injured but I didn't realise how bad at the time.

The crew of HMS *Sheffield* with their Captain, Sam Salt, shortly before the invasion of the Falklands

As the fire spread through the stricken ship the wounded were carried out on deck. John Strange was shaking uncontrollably in the cold air. A medical orderly injected him with morphine, and he passed out. He had 44 per cent burns, as well as shrapnel wounds. His was a lucky escape. Twenty men died, a further twenty-four were injured. The remainder of the ship's crew, 242 men, escaped unharmed.

Even though the Exocet's warhead had not exploded, the fire started by the unused fuel spread uncontrollably through the rear of the ship. Dense black smoke from rubber-covered cable made fire-fighting difficult, and as the ship's main water supply had been broken, little could be done to dowse the fire. Eddie Whitaker, trying to raise *Hermes* on a portable radio set, watched as men attempted in vain to save the ship:

I actually looked down the side of the ship and I saw some blokes dangling buckets on a rope into the sea for water. It's unbelievable, but they were. It was obvious nothing could be done. Time sped by, and so it was about half past five when the Captain decided to abandon ship.

The Captain, Sam Salt, realised that he could not save *Sheffield*. By this stage the metal decks of the ship were becoming unbearably hot; soon men would be unable to walk on them without burning their feet. The ship's superstructure was steaming, and the paint starting to peel off; the area around the site of the missile's penetration was glowing red and white. Flames and smoke continued to pour out of the gaping hole smashed in the ship's side, as well as billowing through the ship's funnel. Captain Salt donned a smoke hood and went back down into the ship for a final inspection. He saw that the whole centre section was aflame. He knew then that the decision to abandon ship was the right one.

Men scrambled from the *Sheffield* to *Arrow* which, in the calm weather, was able to draw up close to the burning destroyer. The wounded, including John Strange, were then taken by helicopter to *Hermes*. *Sheffield* herself was taken under tow, but sunk a few days later.

Back at the Rio Grande air base the Commander of the 2nd Naval Attack Squadron, Captain Colombo, and his colleagues waited anxiously for news of their mission:

Initially we didn't know if our sortie had been successful or not. We had a lot of doubts, even though the missiles had been launched from such a good position. We had to wait until the BBC announced it, immediately after it was reported by the British Government.

The news of the sinking was deeply shocking to the British Government, the armed forces and the public. All the lingering fears about the lack of air cover resurfaced. The optimism generated by the first military action was replaced by deep gloom. Other bad news further dampened the nation's spirits. On the same day that *Sheffield* was hit a Harrier was shot down over the Falklands, two others collided in mid-air, and a second Vulcan raid on Stanley airfield – this time flown at high altitude to avoid the Argentine defences – had missed its target. The bombs fell clear of the runway.

The loss of British lives brought home to the men on the ships of the task force the fact that they, too, could die. The news rippled through the fleet and reached the *Canberra* and *Norland*, heading more slowly south behind the carrier battle group. Corporal Ian Bailey was in one of *Canberra*'s bars when he heard that *Sheffield* had been hit:

There was a bingo night on in one of the bars, and most of the battalion was there. It had just finished and the RSM came in and said that the *Sheffield* had been sunk. Everything went quiet. You know, you're talking about a warship here being hit with a tremendous amount of firepower and obviously quite a considerable amount of death. And we're sitting on some luxury liner and all that we've got is fifteen or twenty blokes outside with weapons to guard us. And that's it. We've got none of the technology that they had.

Men coped with the tension as best they could. Surgeon-Commander Rick Jolly was encouraged to find that some sought a release in humour:

Some of the naval party, particularly floating around in a huge white hull like *Canberra*, found the possibility of being hit by an Exocet, launched in this spectacular way by the Argentinian naval air arm, rather difficult to grasp. The bar bills were quite high that night. It was my first introduction to the humour in real adversity of the Royal Marines, when my Sergeant-Major said as we gazed at the sunset, 'I spy with my little eye something beginning with E and you've got six seconds to answer, Sir!' And, it allowed us to laugh, but when you repeated that joke to some of the naval friends, they got very serious indeed, and questioned us as to how it was possible to make a joke about a situation like that. But, of course, it was humour which is a coping process, rearing its wonderful head, as it did on many occasions during the campaign.

In London the Chief of the Defence Staff, Admiral Sir Terence Lewin, broke the news to Mrs Thatcher and the War Cabinet. The Prime Minister was deeply shocked and upset. She did

Super Etendards of the Second Naval Attack Squadron on the runway at their base in Argentina after the war. Below: the painted silhouettes of HMS *Sheffield* and HMS *Invincible* on the aircraft which sank *Sheffield*. The Argentine armed forces remain convinced to this day that they hit the British carrier

Right: A casualty from HMS *Sheffield* arrives on HMS *Hermes* for treatment. The sinking of the *Sheffield* brought home to the task force, and the British people, the vulnerability of the fleet to air attack

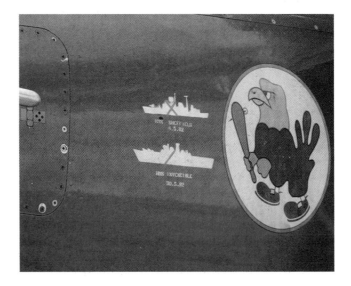

not hide her feelings. After a tearful interlude she quickly returned to the business of running the War Cabinet. Mrs Thatcher and her colleagues had been told to expect casualties by Terry Lewin and, despite the emotion of the moment, they did not allow it to obstruct the business in hand. Lewin told them of a particularly difficult convoy to Malta in which he had taken part in the Second World War. The date of the sinking of *Sheffield* happened, coincidentally, to fall on the anniversary of that convoy. The Chief of the Defence Staff related how nine out of fourteen ships had been sunk, including an aircraft carrier and a cruiser, and yet the mission had been successful. The convoy had got through, and Malta had been saved.

Privately, Lewin was slightly relieved that a British ship had been lost:

I was certain this was going to happen at some time, a ship was going to be hit. And I felt there was perhaps too much euphoria, that all this was going to be too easy ... Now we had warned them, in briefing them, that because of the risks of air attack from fighter bomber aircraft, with really inadequate air defence, we might lose up to six destroyers and frigates and maybe one major unit. A major troop ship or even maybe one of the carriers hit. We thought if a carrier was hit by a bomb it could probably carry on. But we'd warned the War Cabinet to expect losses to that extent. So the War Cabinet were very robust, after the initial shock.

Although the War Cabinet received the news with fortitude, the full Cabinet, reflecting the vagaries of British public opinion, showed slightly less resolve. Francis Pym, whom many had regarded as at best an irrelevance, and at worst a man intent on placing 'tedious obstacles on the path to glory', was now perceived as the man of the hour. Pym, often to the intense irritation of the Prime Minister, had doggedly pursued his own agenda: the pursuit of a diplomatic settlement. Despite her irritation, Mrs Thatcher never stopped the Foreign Secretary in his search. Although she may not have liked it, she understood the need for Britain to be seen to be negotiating.

Three days after the sinking of the *Sheffield* Francis Pym, having returned to London from Washington, briefed the House of Commons on those proposals put forward in the Peruvian plan which Britain would find acceptable. He declared that the United Kingdom was ready, after an Argentine withdrawal, to accept an interim administration of the Islands conducted by third parties and that a change of sovereignty was possible, 'without prejudice to our principles or the wishes of the Islanders'. After the loss of British life in HMS *Sheffield* the Prime Minister needed some persuading to accept the possibility of a transfer of sovereignty. But she did accede to it, provided, as usual, the wishes of the Islanders were taken into account.

Now that the Peruvian plan had been rejected by Argentina, the focus of attention shifted once more to the United Nations, where the Secretary-General, Javier Perez de Cuellar, offered to mediate. This mediation was accepted by Argentina and the United Kingdom. It fitted in well with Francis Pym's plans. The Foreign Secretary was determined that Britain should be seen to be reasonable as the country pursued its military goals.

While Britain maintained diplomatic pressure, the decision to reinforce the military with the 5th Infantry Brigade was announced. On June 12, amidst scenes of patriotic rejoicing, the requisitioned liner, *Queen Elizabeth 2*, departed from England with 3,500 troops of the Welsh and Scots Guards aboard. Major-General Jeremy Moore, the Commander Land Forces, also travelled with the brigade. He planned to take overall command of the campaign when they arrived in the Falklands.

The decision to send 5 Brigade had been delayed for some time. After the loss of *Sheffield* had demonstrated so forcibly Britain's lack of air cover in the South Atlantic, it was considered even more essential to have a reserve ready to step in, if the campaign got into early difficulties. The exact purpose of 5 Brigade when it arrived in the Falklands was unclear, however. Its transit would take nearly three weeks. In that period General Moore, isolated from the battlefield on the luxury liner, had to work out a strategy for recapturing the Islands, once his men were ashore.

In London a period of tense and anxious waiting began. The task force, now operating well away from the Falklands by day, for fear of bombing and missile raids, was waiting for the arrival of the first wave of amphibious troops on board *Norland* and *Canberra*. Only then could the landings take place. It was also realised that the Argentine Air Force was refusing to be lured out for combat before the amphibious assault. There was now no chance that the enemy planes would be destroyed in air-to-air combat in time. The assault on the Falklands would have to be undertaken in extremely dangerous conditions. The risks were very high.

18/BACK IN THE UNITED NATIONS

Mrs Thatcher and her colleagues in the War Cabinet were under no illusions about the nature and extent of the military aid which they were receiving from the Pentagon. They were aware, too, that the United States was in a position to prevent ultimate humiliation. If the worst came to the worst, and the British carriers were sunk, American help would be of paramount importance. Ten years after the crisis, Caspar Weinberger is now prepared to admit how far the United States would go:

If the request had been for a carrier, we would have responded to that. There were a number of ways you could do it. It could have remained as part of one of the American carrier groups. Or it could have been transferred temporarily. And obviously that would have been something that would have attracted a reasonable amount of attention. So we would have had to have a number of deep philosophical considerations of what was the best way to do it. But as far as doing it, yes, we were prepared to do it.

Weinberger's deep commitment to the British cause reflected a prevailing mood in the United States, which was little dented by the sinking of the *Belgrano*. Sir Anthony Parsons, Britain's Ambassador to the United Nations, found himself a celebrity in the streets of Manhattan:

Amongst the majority of American public opinion, there was a feeling that there had been aggression, that Britain was the closest friend and ally of the United States in the world and that Britain had to be supported. I found myself, to my astonishment really, walking to and from my apartment, to the United Nations and back, and doing my shopping, because my wife was away. I was astonished to find myself being slapped on the back and my hand pumped by complete strangers in the street and I never had any hostile reaction from anybody throughout that time.

Although Britain was the United States' closest ally, the support from the American public did not come unasked. The task of working for it fell to Sir Nicholas Henderson, the British Ambassador in Washington. He appeared on countless television shows arguing with retired admirals and generals matters of military strategy:

It was rather disturbing of course to be in a studio and then confronted with somebody of admiral stature or higher, or great military expert, to be told what you're doing can't work. You realise Britain is going to go down the drain. You're 8,000 miles away down the high seas in the South Atlantic. You're going to be sunk. And I had to say, this is not true, the British Navy hasn't sailed the high seas for 500 years to find itself unable to deal with a problem like this; of course it can.

Sir Nicholas had to ensure that the many centres of power in Washington were kept in line. This meant frequent trips to Capitol Hill for lunches with senators, and visits to reassure the wavering State Department and the confused White House. Although the United States had pledged support for the British, occasionally Henderson would be contacted by an agitated senator:

I remember travelling between one place and another, in my car, in which I had a telephone of course, and some senator getting on to me, *à propos* of a ship being sunk, and saying 'this blood-letting has got to stop. Would you tell your Government straight away, from me, this can't go on'.

Both Sir Nicholas Henderson and Sir Anthony Parsons were convinced of the importance of Britain's twin-track policy of negotiation and military force. They were certain that, so long as Britain gave the appearance of being reasonable, they could hold American and world opinion on the United Kingdom's side. Henderson made it the main theme of his telegrams to London:

If we were to get America on our side and then hold American opinion with us, we had at all times to show that if there could be a negotiated settlement on reasonable terms, we were ready for it. We weren't seeking blood. We weren't seeking to crush Argentina as such. That was essential because that is what the Americans believed the outcome should be, that neither side should be losers. Aggression should be shown to have failed, but nobody should be victimised. There shouldn't be colossal bloodshed. So it was terribly important to give the impression in America that we were always ready to be reasonable. And I think with some difficulty we succeeded in doing that.

When the mediation shifted to the United Nations, after the sinking of *Belgrano* and *Sheffield*, Sir Anthony Parsons was determined that the British position at the United Nations be as accommodating as possible, and that it should be seen to be so. To the Argentinians, however, disillusioned with the diplomatic process, the British desire to continue with the mediation smacked of humbug. In Buenos Aires it was perceived as a delaying tactic, during which the British could prepare for their assault on the Malvinas. The Deputy Foreign Minister, Enrique Ros, was Argentina's principal negotiator at the UN:

There was no trust in the British Government in Buenos Aires at the time. They thought it was a gimmick, in order to give a cover to the military operation that was taking place. The Island was already being bombed by British forces. So they thought that it was not the best time to be negotiating under duress.

Dismissing the Argentine doubts, the UN Secretary-General began two weeks of intense negotiation. The two sides in the conflict never met. Javier Perez de Cuellar summoned each delegation in turn, sometimes two or three times a day, in an effort to find common ground. Slowly an elaborate treaty involving a temporary withdrawal of forces, an interim UN administration with Islander representation, and a timetable for further negotiations, was hammered out.

So complex was the British draft that Parsons considered it essential to return to Britain to discuss it with the War Cabinet. Sir Nicholas Henderson agreed to return to London with him to emphasise the need for reasonableness if American support was to be maintained.

On Sunday May 16 the diplomats arrived at Chequers to brief the Prime Minister on the British proposals, and to win her agreement to them. The British position at this stage represented a considerable shift. It was now accepted that the central question was not Britain's claim to sovereignty – that was negotiable – but the Islanders' right to self-determination, which was not. The United Kingdom agreed to the mutual withdrawal of forces to 150 miles from the Islands, an interim UN administration, and Argentine representation in the administration of the Falklands. There was a commitment to end negotiations on a final agreement by 31 December 1982.

The meeting at Chequers with the Prime Minister was tense and dramatic. She, dominant in the War Cabinet, confronted two diplomats who urged compromise and negotiation. Domestically neither was needed; the Prime Minister had the support of her party, and of public opinion. At the same time she shared the right's latent mistrust of the 'appeasement-minded' Foreign Office.

Parsons went in to bat for the Foreign Office: his was a bravura performance. Once, when the Prime Minister became agitated, he paused, sat back and smiled. Mrs Thatcher asked him why he was smiling, to which he is reported to have replied, 'Because you amuse me, Prime Minister.' Few dared to speak to the Premier in this way, but Parsons' command of the situation and natural rapport with Mrs Thatcher allowed him to get away with it. The tension was defused.

The meeting was highly organised, with about twenty people around the main table: politicians

The Security Council at the UN. As the crisis developed British diplomats were determined that the United Kingdom should appear willing and ready to negotiate a peaceful settlement. Only then, they argued, could Britain retain the support of the Security Council and officials, and a large number of advisers sitting behind. The Prime Minister was in the chair, facing Sir Anthony Parsons. Every single nuance of the complex set of proposals was examined in minute detail. When this stage had been completed the Prime Minister did not withdraw, as was usual in such situations. To Sir Nicholas Henderson's astonishment, she insisted on remaining with the officials:

We were all pretty tired and the general line had been agreed, and I assumed therefore that we officials would be left to get on with working out the drafting of it. But not at all. Mrs Thatcher insisted on going through it line for line and I was astonished by her energy and her stamina. She just went on and on and on, determined to pay attention to every detail.

Anthony Parsons stressed that the important issue was not sovereignty but self-determination, under Article 73 of the United Nations Charter. Britain's position, he argued, was to accept that there was a legitimate dispute over the title to the Islands, but not over the Islanders' right to choose their destiny. Mrs Thatcher accepted this principle, and it was enshrined in Britain's final proposals to the Secretary-General. This, for a right-wing Prime Minister intent on a military solution to recover sovereignty, was a considerable compromise, and one which she only accepted reluctantly. For Parsons it was something of a victory:

I must confess that at the end of that meeting, I was surprised that the Government was prepared to go as far as it was prepared to go. I was in very little doubt that there were members of the Conservative Party on what one might call the right wing who would regard this as a sell-out. Still, there it was. These proposals were agreed.

The following Monday Parsons took the morning Concorde flight to New York with the single draft of the British proposals. It was full of crossings-out and balloons containing redrafted sections. There had been no time to type it out in fair form. Within hours, Parsons had put the proposals before Perez de Cuellar:

He looked at them with astonishment, and said 'Is this really what you are prepared to agree to?' And I said, 'Yes, this has been gone through by the War Cabinet and everybody's agreed it and this is what we will accept.'
    I went on to say that the negotiating had been going on so long, that we were not prepared to put up with a long delay. That we were giving Argentina forty-eight hours to respond. We didn't consider this to be unjustifiable at all, because everybody had negotiated so closely, that it was only the matter of a change of a few words or a sentence or two here and there. And we reckoned that was plenty of time.

Parsons was aware that a settlement had to be either accepted or rejected fast. Britain could delay little longer if the military option was to be used. The War Cabinet had reminded him forcibly of the dangers, both political and military, of a prolonged wait in the South Atlantic.

The Secretary-General agreed with Parsons' request for an answer within forty-eight hours, and passed the British proposals to the Argentine delegation, which in turn sent them to Buenos Aires. When the Foreign Minister, Nicanor Costa Mendez, and his colleagues studied the British position they saw little change. Although the British proposals did indeed represent a considerable shift on the question of sovereignty, the insistence on the right of the Islanders to self-determination was a stumbling block which could not be overcome. The Argentine diplomats were fully aware that the Islanders would never accept a transfer of sovereignty. They further believed that the principle of self-determination in the case of the Malvinas was misapplied. The inhabitants were illegal settlers, in their view much like the Israeli occupants of the West Bank in Palestine, and therefore had no inherent right to self-determination.

When the Junta saw the proposals, its members agreed with the diplomats. Anything other than draft proposals of the means by which sovereignty would be transferred to Argentina was unacceptable to them. The Military Government's political survival depended on the full and permanent reconquest of the Malvinas. A compromise on sovereignty would mean oblivion for General Galtieri and his colleagues. The British proposals were rejected.

On May 18 the UN Secretary-General, Javier Perez de Cuellar rang Sir Anthony Parsons at 11.00 pm:

He said that he had received the Argentine reply, but it was in Spanish and he hadn't got anybody to translate it, and could I wait until the following morning to receive it? I said no I couldn't, because with the five-hour time gap, that would mean that we would lose a whole day. So I said could I come down that night and could he get one of his staff who was also a Peruvian, his Chief of Staff, to translate the document as we went along. And he said yes. I suppose I got down there about midnight. Now, as soon as he and his colleagues began reading out the Argentine reply to me, I realised that it was a rejection. Because at no point did

Tony Benn MP, a determined opponent of the use of armed force to resolve the problem, addresses an anti-war rally in Trafalgar Square

it address the articles in our draft. I mean it didn't say, 'I agree to article one, we don't agree to article two, we want to amend article three, etc, etc.' It just amounted to a kind of flood of negative rhetoric. I remember it was rather dramatic. We sat in silence, the Secretary-General and I, when he had finished the translation. And I said to him, words to this effect, 'Well, Javier, that is a rejection, you would agree with that? It's absolute.' And then I said, 'That as a result of this, a lot of young men who are alive today, are not going to be alive for very much longer' ... And we parted, both extremely gloomily.

On May 20 the Prime Minister announced the outcome of the negotiations at the United Nations to the House of Commons. Mrs Thatcher explained Britain's final proposals in some detail, and told the House that the Government had rejected the Argentine counter-proposals outright. Tony Benn was in the Chamber at the time, and like many of his fellow MPs on both sides of the House, declared his astonishment that the British Government had gone so far:

The proposals involve the abandonment of the substance of sovereignty, which is the right to have troops on one's territory and to control its administration. By publishing this document the Government have published their readiness to abandon, in substance, British sovereignty over the islands ... If such an offer had been made at any time over the past twenty years there would have been no invasion of the Falkland Islands.

Benn had captured the absurd paradox of the conflict: by military action Argentina had pushed Britain to a position which, before the conflict, could have solved the problem. Now, however, the Junta was utterly dependent on the fruits of its aggression for political survival. To yield in any way to the British was impossible.

The publication of the final British position was a canny political move. It showed the world just how far Britain, the aggrieved party, was prepared to go to remedy the situation, but it was done in the knowledge that the proposals had been rejected by Argentina. Had the Junta come close to accepting the British position, the War Cabinet would have been in much greater difficulty. International pressure, particularly from the United States, on Mrs Thatcher and her Government to accept a messy compromise would have been impossible to ignore, yet would have been politically and militarily damaging. Argentina, by its intransigence, had played into British hands. The military solution could now be imposed in the knowledge that the diplomatic battle had been won.

19/ LANDINGS

he North Sea ferry
Norland straddled by
bombs on 21 May, the first
day of the landings. The
amphibious force
commanders had been
assured that landings
would only take place after
air superiority had been
achieved. This never
happened

EARLY on a calm and foggy morning on May 21, the British landing force, including supply ships, two ferries and the cruise liner *Canberra*, slowly approached San Carlos Water in East Falkland. The British landings, code-named Operation *Sutton*, were under way. Barry Norman, a Company Sergeant Major with the 2nd Parachute Battalion, was on board the car ferry *Norland* as it eased its way into Falkland Sound:

We woke on the morning with our regimental march being blasted over the ship's tannoy. Although we hadn't had any physical orders at that stage, as soon as the battle march came over the tannoy and it was loud, the whole ship vibrated with it, we thought, 'Bloody hell, something's happening here.' And then during that day we got our orders and we were moving in.

Below decks, in the holds and companionways of their ships, the Royal Marines and Parachutists of 3 Commando Brigade, their faces blackened by combat paint, their bodies bent under the great weight of their kit, gathered nervously. They had little idea of what to expect. Intelligence from special forces indicated that there would be few Argentine forces to oppose the landings, but this was no certainty.

The choice of San Carlos, fifty miles as the crow flies from Port Stanley, for the D-Day-style landings, had been made on May 10 on board *Fearless* at Ascension, after much discussion and some bitter argument amongst the task force's senior commanders. Each service, quite naturally, wanted the best advantage for its own forces. Ewen Southby-Tailyour, with his detailed knowledge of the waters and bays of the Falklands, acted as an adviser to the Royal Marines:

The Navy always want one set of attributes from a landing site. The Royal Marines always want another. And as luck would have it, of course, they are almost always diametrically opposed. We want to be as close to our objective as possible, that usually means that the naval ships will be too close for comfort, from bombardment, aerial or otherwise, because they've got to anchor or remain reasonably static while they're unloaded.

As each landing site was mooted, the Navy, understandably, demanded the best possible protection from the air threat, enemy artillery and submarines. This meant, in turn, placing the amphibious force some distance from Port Stanley. The Royal Marines and the Army, on the other hand, wanted to be as close as possible to Stanley to avoid the difficulty of a long march.

San Carlos was the compromise: a long and sheltered snake's tongue of water on the west side of East Falkland, it was a perfect natural harbour with calm waters and the benefit of sandy coves suitable for landing craft. Its narrow inlet to two large anchorages made submarine attack unlikely; the hills on either side of the water offered a confined space with protection from air attack; and its distance from the enemy put the British landing forces out of range of hostile artillery. There were disadvantages: the surrounding hills and confined location made it difficult for the navy's radar to spot incoming Argentine aircraft, and it was far from the main objective. 3 Commando Brigade, and any reinforcements, would have to travel at least eighty-six miles, if they wanted to take the fight to the Argentine force dug in around Port Stanley. The choice was a difficult one but, according to Ewen Southby-Tailyour, probably the right one:

Even the Navy had opposing views, whether you're a submariner or whether you're Fleet Air Arm, on what makes a good landing place. I think in the end, San Carlos represented everything that was best, or everything that was least worst to both sides. Of course then, Brigadier Thompson assumed that we were going to be able to close on Stanley quite quickly using helicopters. If we knew we were going to have to march across East Falkland, then perhaps San Carlos may not have been the choice.

On May 21 nineteen ships of all shapes and sizes made their way slowly towards San Carlos under the protection of a thick blanket of fog. Twelve of the ships made up the amphibious landing force, including the three requisitioned civilian ships: *Canberra*, *Norland* and *Europic Ferry*. The remainder were naval destroyers and frigates acting as escorts. Commodore Mike Clapp, from the Royal Navy, was in command of the amphibious operation; Brigadier Julian Thompson, from the Royal Marines, was responsible for the land forces, once their feet were on Falklands soil. The two men had formed a rapport, meeting every morning to discuss plans over breakfast, and there was none of the inter-service tension between them which had threatened the operation during the planning meetings at Ascension. Both men shared an overriding concern: the lack of air superiority. The task force commanders had frequently reassured them that landings would only take place once domination of the skies had been achieved. Slowly it dawned on Thompson and Clapp that, despite these optimistic forecasts, there would be no air superiority at all. In fact, the reverse was the case: the landings would take place with British air inferiority. To Clapp, there were political reasons for this:

I had got the impression at first that we wouldn't even land unless air superiority was achieved, and I just got the feeling that politically there was no way we could come 7,500 miles, and then go home again. So, having got committed, air superiority or not, we were going in.

In order not to risk the loss of the majority of the men of the landing force, should *Canberra* be sunk by air attack, Clapp and Thompson agreed that 3 Para should be transferred to *Intrepid* and 40 Commando to *Fearless* before the ships moved into San Carlos. Special Forces were also moved, their headquarters transferring from *Hermes* to *Intrepid*. During this operation a Sea King helicopter crashed into the South Atlantic. Twenty-two men were killed, eighteen of whom were SAS men of 'D' Squadron, the group which had taken part in the desperate operation on the Fortuna glacier in South Georgia.

That tragedy apart, the operation to get men ashore went relatively smoothly. Commodore Mike Clapp had spent the time waiting with his force in Ascension training the merchant ships in his unlikely force the rudiments of naval seamanship:

This was one of the great things about the wait in Ascension; we weren't idle and every night all the ships, from *Canberra* right down to the small ones, were going out to sea, manoeuvring, and we worked up, just like naval ships. And so when we came down to the Falklands, instead of having them in convoys as is the traditional fashion, working in very narrow confines of manoeuvring, we could treat them like warships and just give them a station and steam them in and out.

The ships approached San Carlos in darkness. The high hill of Fanning Head, which dominates the inlet, loomed out of the mist and fog towards them. Clapp ordered the ships in his task group to cut their engines. The first boats into San Carlos were to be the landing craft, packed full of men, escorted by HMS *Plymouth* and led by Ewen Southby-Tailyour. The smaller and quieter craft would draw less attention than the vast white hulk of *Canberra*, and the two large ferries, which waited outside the inlet in Falkland Sound.

On board their ships, the men of 3 Commando Brigade made their way towards the landing craft. Barry Norman, trained to jump out of

Landing craft from the assault ship *Fearless* head towards San Carlos packed with men of 3 Commando Brigade. Below: Men wait for the landings in the tank deck of HMS *Fearless*

Anxious waiting: Men of 2 Para on board *Norland* prepare to board landing craft

Above left: Royal Marines drive ashore at San Carlos. The landings were unopposed

Above right: A Royal Marine brings in a captured Argentine from the forward observation post on Fanning Head

Left: Break-out. Royal Marines start the long 'yomp' to Port Stanley

Right: The opposition. Cold, short of food and with inadequate transport, Argentine forces had no wish to come out and fight the advancing British

aeroplanes, found himself jostling his way through the cramped quarters of a North Sea ferry:

To get to this landing craft we had to go all the way down the stair wells and the very narrow corridors of the *Norland*. We thought, God they've got submarines, they've got aircraft and we're fart-arsing about in a car ferry getting on board a marine landing craft in the South Atlantic, and it was cold. We then started the process of getting on board these landing craft and that took quite a considerable amount of time really, when you think we were going into what we thought was an attack. The old butterflies were going in the stomach.

The landing craft came up to the side of the *Norland* and the men scrambled down nets. As the ship rose and sank in the South Atlantic swell the men had to judge when to make the jump into the small boats. Barry Norman saw one man leap at the wrong moment:

And seeing we had bergens (backpacks), of about 100 pounds plus, on our backs at that particular time, it was lucky we only lost one bloke, who fell off and fell between the *Norland* and the landing craft, and he got quite substantial injuries. And that was his war finished, before it even started.

With all the difficulties of transferring from ship to landing craft the landings were delayed. Colour Sergeant Ian Bailey of 3 Para was in HMS *Intrepid*, having cross-decked from *Canberra*. He shared his fellow parachutists' mistrust of sea-borne landings:

They took us down, they showed us three small bath tubs with an engine on the back that we were actually going to go ashore in. Your heads poked over the side, it didn't give you any sense of security at all. And you've got two Marines on the back, the coxswain and his mate, who were actually driving this thing. In very choppy waters – and you put your whole platoon on there. Even when we parachute, you don't put the whole company on an aeroplane, it's all split up.

By the time the men had got through a small opening in the side of the assault ship and made the perilous leap into the landing craft, dawn was breaking over San Carlos. The small fleet, escorted by *Plymouth*, started to move in through the narrow inlet of San Carlos to the landing beaches. As they passed Fanning Head the men could hear the crack of rifle fire and see the streams of tracer from a unit of Special Forces fighting a small Argentine observation post. To Commodore Clapp's relief the Special Forces' intelligence had been correct. Apart from the observation post, there were no other enemy forces in the area.

Soon the first waves of British forces were approaching their landing beaches in San Carlos Water. Barry Norman's craft with members of 2 Para aboard was in the lead:

We saw the land coming out of the gloom, although it was just a haze, because it was quite dark, and all of a sudden, the front of the landing craft actually touched ground. I thought, 'This isn't the beach. Now they've got it wrong. There's no beach. A cock-up right at the start.' And next thing the ramp went down at the front. And we thought, 'No, it's a joke.' And the landing craft commander said 'Out troops'. And I thought, 'I'm not bloody getting out here. The beach is well away yet. We're in the wrong place.' That was the opinion that went through everybody. But then somebody said 'Go', which is our term for jumping out of the aircraft, and we all went. I stepped off the ramp, straight up to my waist in water, which being the South Atlantic, was cold. In fact it was bloody freezing. Before I knew it everything in the crutch had tightened. You felt you had a big lump in the throat, and we were wading ashore.

The first wave of landing craft was followed by the rest of the fleet, sailing slowly into San Carlos Water. It was an extraordinary spectacle. This stretch of water, usually utterly isolated, was now crowded with ships of all shapes and sizes, with helicopters flying from one to the other, and landing craft plying from ship to shore. Dominating the scene was the cruise liner *Canberra*, placed close to the shore in shallow water, to give it maximum protection from air attack.

The fog which had protected the fleet's entry into San Carlos Water began to lift as dawn broke and the sun rose. Major Carlos Esteban, in charge of an Argentine outpost at Port San Carlos, the small settlement overlooking the inlet, had escaped the special forces attack on Fanning Head, only to find himself confronting the invasion force itself:

It was about ten to eight in the morning when one of my advance observers came running down and told me that there was a frigate coming in through the channel. I took the binoculars, ran forward with him, took up his position and observed that a considerable number of ships were entering. There was a large white ship in the middle of the bay of San Carlos, many frigates were protecting it and helicopters were flying around.

Esteban returned to his command post and called up headquarters on the radio. He informed his brigade commander that a mass landing was taking place, and then made preparations to escape:

I was very afraid because the scale of the landing was really very impressive. I remember speaking to the Brigade, trying to tell them everything which was happening, and all the while one of my legs was shaking uncontrollably because I knew I had only forty-one men with which to confront a huge enemy force.

The news of the landing quickly passed up the command chain to the commander of the Malvinas garrison, General Benjamino Menendez, who was in Puerto Argentino (Port Stanley). The General had been informed by the naval Chiefs in Buenos Aires that they considered a landing at San Carlos unlikely. Menendez had, as a result, made few efforts to defend it:

When we received Major Esteban's report we sent it straight away to the mainland. The High Command had already been informed of the fact that I didn't think it possible to carry out any action away from Puerto Argentino.

The job of attacking the British force thus fell to the pilots of the Argentine Air Force and the Argentine Navy, deployed to the south of mainland Argentina in air bases in Patagonia and Tierra del Fuego. Menendez had no intention of ordering a counter-attack from Port Stanley. His troops were told to continue to sit in their dugouts and wait for the British to arrive.

A long period of nervous inactivity was now over for the squadrons of Argentine fighter-bombers stationed in Patagonia and Tierra del Fuego in the far south. At last their waiting was at an end, and they were able to fly and attack the British intruders. Seventy-four strike aircraft, made up of the Argentine Air Force's thirty-nine Skyhawks, eight Mirages and nineteen Daggers (Israeli-built Mirages), as well as the Navy's eight Skyhawks, were available to take part in the attacks. The Argentine forces had conserved their strength for the landings, and had not been drawn out, as the British had hoped, before this crucial moment.

The Argentine aviators had put the time waiting to good use. In the years before the conflict the Argentine military invested considerable sums in British defence technology, in particular in the two Type 42 destroyers, the *Hercules* and the *Santissima Trinidad*. These two ships, equipped with the Sea Dart missile system, held almost all the secrets of the Royal Navy's air defence systems. As a result, Commander Benito Rotolo, in

the 3rd Search and Destroy Squadron of the Argentine Navy, was able to develop and practice a set of tactics to use against the British ships:

These ships had become very important since their acquisition, especially their early warning and detection systems, and we knew how to attack them. We adopted a tactic whereby we could fly over them and fire a volley of bombs. Once we were overhead we felt very secure because that kind of ship didn't have very precise defence weapons.

The Argentine pilots knew that the Sea Dart missile worked well at high altitude. They therefore chose to fly extremely low, safe from the majority of the Royal Navy's defences, and undetected before arrival within striking range of their targets. Only two of the British ships had any effective defence against low-flying jets at close quarters: the Seawolf-equipped destroyers *Brilliant* and *Broadsword*. The others, lacking

sufficient low-level defences, as well as early warning, had to fight it out as best they could.

The news of the British landings reached the mainland air bases early in the morning of May 21. Rotolo and his colleagues were woken up and told the news:

We were told to prepare for the attack on the Islands. We heard that there were British troops disembarking in the San Carlos straits, and we had to intercept the landing ships and warships, causing as much damage as possible in order to prevent the landings.

This was the crux of the Argentine plan: to attack the task force at its most vulnerable, using fighter-bombers, against which the British had least protection. The first wave of naval A-4 Skyhawks took off in two groups of six at 9 am but encountered fog over the sea. Low-level flying was impossible, so the jets turned back, and returned to wait for the weather to clear.

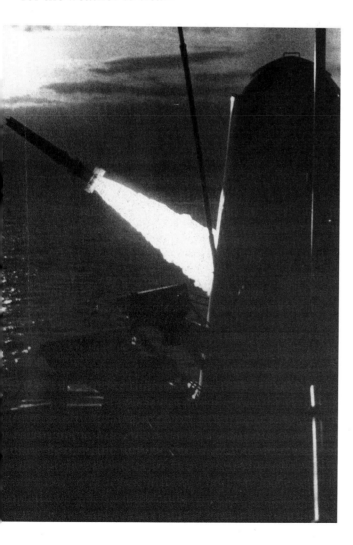

Before the naval squadron had time to take to the air again, the Argentine Air Force launched its attacks, using eight Mirages and six Skyhawks, from the 6th and 5th Fighter Groups. Major Gustavo Piuma, flying on his first active service mission, took off in his Mirage from the Rio Grande base:

As the time for take-off drew nearer the tension mounted. It was mounting because we had never been in a war before; we had been preparing ourselves for one since we were young, since we were cadets, but now we could do something for our country. I think it's natural for men to feel this tension, to feel afraid, for fear is part of our heritage. The only thing we could do was to accept our fear, and try to overcome it. Thanks to the wings we wear on our chests we knew it was only nerves, and when my plane left the ground I felt more at ease, and from that point my fear began to disappear.

The Argentine pilots knew that they were flying at the extremes of their planes' range, over a cold and hostile sea, against a modern navy, in antiquated jets. They were well aware, too, that there was no air-sea rescue service to pick them out of the sea, should they linger too long over the target and be forced to ditch on their return. Captain Alberto Rinke, who flew his Skyhawk in the second wave of attacks on May 21, had no illusions about the risks:

We knew that our chances of being rescued in the sea were nil; even if it had been possible, the rescue would have to have taken place very quickly because of the weather conditions and the temperature of the water. So we knew that whatever kind of fighting, whether air-to-air, or air-to-ground, if we were hit our chances of survival would be very small indeed. That's why we compared ourselves to Roman gladiators who fought in conditions of great danger.

These gladiators of the air were motivated by a deep and abiding sense of patriotism, and a certainty of the justice of their cause. The long period of waiting had given them much time to pause and reflect on their destiny. Major Jorge Senn, a Mirage pilot, volunteered for the battle, despite the fact that his age and seniority allowed him to stay in reserve:

It was a struggle of conscience. I thought I had to do my duty to my country. I was convinced I should fight, but at the same time there was a strong possibility that I would die. There was a continual battle between me and my conscience that nagged me and asked, 'Can you justify doing this for this cause?' It was very difficult for me to leave my family, but later I began to feel patriotic, and that the cause was a noble one.

A British Sea Dart air defence missile. The missile was ineffective against the low-flying Argentine jets

117

As the heavily laden jets, each carrying extra fuel tanks and British-made 1,000-pound bombs, manoeuvred into position on the runways, and then thrust forward to take off on their perilous mission, the pilots felt overwhelming relief that the long wait was over. To Eduardo Senn, it was a religious experience:

I felt a sense of tremendous solitude. It was as if I was taking Holy Communion; and finally I realised that although life is important, I was just passing through, and I accepted that what I was doing was the way it ought to be.

At 10.00 am the first Argentine jets approached the Malvinas. 150 miles before they reached the islands they descended to sea level, in order to avoid detection by the task force's radar. Knowing that the landings were taking place at San Carlos, and aware of the presence of an outer ring of Harrier combat air patrols from the British carriers, the Mirages and Skyhawks approached the enemy flying eastward over West Falkland, hugging the ground to give themselves even greater camouflage. Each pilot observed strict radio silence. Gustavo Piuma's Mirage was the left-hand plane in the group of three. On seeing the first ships in San Carlos Water he broke radio silence and announced that he had seen the enemy:

A missile was fired at me, and that was the first experience I had of being shot at. I manoeuvred the plane to dodge it, and the missile passed me by. But my wingman, who had also been waiting with us for twenty days, was hit by a missile and ejected. In the meantime I finished my attack, and dropped my bomb on a ship. I didn't know whether it hit or not.

The surviving planes returned to base in silence. Piuma's wingman had been shot down by a Seawolf missile fired from HMS *Broadsword*. He did not survive.

The first attack had succeeded in hitting HMS *Argonaut*, a Type 21 frigate, guarding the mouth of San Carlos, with two bombs. Neither exploded, but two seamen were killed. The *Argonaut* was part of the British defences of the approaches to San Carlos. The line, stretching in to Falkland Sound, was made up of the Seawolf destroyers *Brilliant* and *Broadsword*, the Type 21 frigate *Ardent*, the destroyer *Antrim*, together with the older Type 12 frigates *Yarmouth* and *Plymouth*. It was these ships which bore the brunt of the first bombing raids.

Throughout May 21 the Skyhawks and Mirages pressed home their attacks. At 2.30 pm Benito Rotolo took off in a flight of six naval Skyhawks. Approaching the Malvinas he heard the excited and confused chatter of battle over the radio:

Someone shouted 'Harriers!', and someone said 'I'm ejecting', that was the last we heard from them. So I said to my pilots 'Let's go!' . . . We targeted a Type 21 frigate because it was in the middle of Falkland Sound, and that enabled us to make a longer run at it. There were another six ships which started to fire at us. I don't think you really think about anything at a time like that; you're okay as long as you're flying, though you do feel anxious about reaching your target and dropping bombs. Our bombs were aimed accurately at the ship, and the plane behind me, flown by Wing-Commander Lecur, saw the bombs go down. By the time the last plane flew above the ship it was no longer visible: it was all explosions, smoke and water.

Rotolo and his fellow pilots had hit HMS *Ardent*, which had just finished bombarding the airfield at Goose Green. Although they dropped eight bombs on the ship, only two found their target, and of those, only one exploded. But it was the *coup de grace*. The ship had already been singled out for attack by raids before Rotolo. *Ardent* was damaged, steaming to take cover amongst the other warships in the sound, when Rotolo and his men hit her. The damage was so great that the Captain, Alan West, ordered his crew to abandon ship. Twenty-two men were killed.

For the men of the task force, watching as raid after raid came over the 'bomb alley' of Falkland Sound and San Carlos, the sight of the low-flying Skyhawks, Mirages and Daggers was both unreal and frightening. Many watched, in shock, as if the attacks were in slow-motion. There was little that they could do, other than fire at the fast-moving jets with small arms, which had no effect. Surgeon Commander Rick Jolly had just disembarked from *Canberra* when the attacks started:

I was terrified. Because I had the feeling, as all ground troops do, that the pilot of that aircraft can see you and he's coming for you and you are helpless. A little later I realised, of course, that he's just as anxious as you are, and he certainly can't see a little matchstick on the landscape. But that had a very nasty effect, particularly as on the first day of the landing, Friday May 21, we were attacked, or we seemed to be attacked, by a mirage, one of four that were delivering a strafing run against HMS *Antrim*. And I broke and ran from the helicopter and dived into a ditch. Terrified.

When I got back to the aircraft, there was a Royal Marine corporal who'd been firing his machine gun back from the cabin at this diving Mirage, wouldn't speak to me, and I felt very small indeed.

A few minutes later Rick Jolly had the opportunity to atone for his frightened attempt to find shelter from the attack, when he was called to take part in the helicopter rescue of survivors who had jumped into the sea to escape the burning *Ardent*:

A Mirage escapes anti-aircraft fire. The Argentine pilots knew that their chances of survival were very low, but they pressed home their attacks: 'We compared ourselves to Roman gladiators . . .'

When we came to the hover off the port quarter, and found two survivors in the water and a strop, a winch belt, was lowered to the first survivor and he couldn't get into it, I came across on my knees and looked down from the hovering aircraft and saw this young man drowning. And I just knew then that if I didn't do something, he was going to die. And in order to make up for my cowardice earlier, I volunteered to go down, which was pretty silly, because it was a long time since I'd done any winching with the Fleet Air Arm and I wasn't dressed for water at two degrees centigrade. I didn't have a life jacket. And of course, I had my camera in my pocket, which was ruined! But in a sense, I knew I had to do it, and as I went down, I was determined to get this guy out. And I suppose I looked into my soul, then, and was satisfied with what I'd seen. Because it was hard getting out. I had to lift him in a straight bear hug, because he was almost dead, and relaxed as a dead weight when he felt my hand in his back. And I got him up into the helicopter cabin and we jumped on him and he vomited a lot of sea water, and I detected a pulse and thought, 'Oh good, we've got him', when the corporal, my friend, looked at me again with that searching look that Royal Marines have and I knew I was OK.

May 21 came to an end with *Ardent* abandoned and sinking, unexploded bombs inside *Antrim* and *Argonaut*, and the two Seawolf destroyers *Brilliant* and *Broadsword* damaged by cannon fire. Many in the British forces were worried. Captain Coward, in command of *Brilliant*, appealed to Admiral Woodward to bring his aircraft carriers closer to the Falklands so that the Harrier patrols could be more effective. His request was refused. Woodward was prepared to trade his frigates and destroyers for Argentine planes, but would not countenance the loss of a carrier.

Brigadier Thompson, who had been assured at Ascension that the landings would only take place once air superiority had been achieved, watched in angry helplessness as the attacking jets screamed in low over San Carlos:

My overriding concern from day one until about six or seven days after the landing at San Carlos was the air situation, because it seemed to me that at a stroke they could cause enormous damage, and casualties, particularly to ourselves, to the ships and to the brigade, and this could be a turning point in their favour and I was very, very worried. On a number of occasions I represented my worries and so it was known that I was concerned, as was indeed Commodore Clapp.

Below: An Argentine pilot's view of shipping in San Carlos Water, known to the British as 'bomb alley', and to the Argentine pilots as 'death valley'

The crippled and sinking HMS *Ardent*. Right: Damage to the stern of the frigate after the second Argentine air attack on 21 May. Below: HMS *Yarmouth* comes alongside the sinking *Ardent* to take off her crew. A Sea King helicopter approaches her starboard side

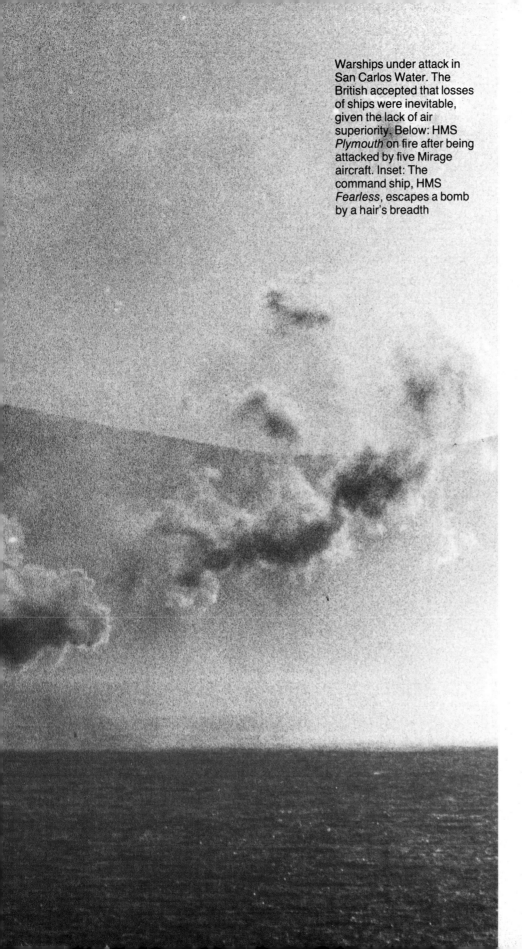

Warships under attack in San Carlos Water. The British accepted that losses of ships were inevitable, given the lack of air superiority. Below: HMS *Plymouth* on fire after being attacked by five Mirage aircraft. Inset: The command ship, HMS *Fearless*, escapes a bomb by a hair's breadth

There was little, if anything, that Woodward, or the High Command in Northwood, could do in response to Thompson's representations. They had hoped that Rapier anti-aircraft batteries would be able to protect the ships in San Carlos. In the event the Rapier missiles proved ineffective. The British were left to sit it out, and hope that the attrition of the Argentine Air Force would render it useless before the loss of ships and stores made the repossession of the Falklands impossible.

The first day of battle ended with the British shocked and worried, but undefeated. The Argentine pilots had been unable to penetrate far into San Carlos, and had attacked the guard ships rather than the most valuable targets, the supply ships. *Canberra* was spared; so too were the ferries, *Norland* and *Europic Star*, and the heavily laden Fleet Auxilliary, *Stromness*. Throughout the day and on into the night men and stores were unloaded. Within twenty-four hours 3,000 men had landed, with their artillery and thousands of tons of their supplies. Under cover of darkness the unloading continued before the cruise liner and ferries withdrew to safety; the high risk of bringing them into San Carlos had been worthwhile.

Argentina paid a heavy price for the limited successes of the day. Ten planes were lost of the thirty-two which attacked. Admiral Woodward used his Harrier force, the outer perimeter of the landing site's defences, to deadly effect. The British plane, using the American Sidewinder missile, dominated the air-to-air combat, as Eduardo Senn discovered during his single attack on the task force:

When we were nearly over Falkland Sound one of my squadron pilots said he could see a Harrier. I told him to be careful, because there were more Harriers in the area, I could see another pack. Then one cut in front of us. I used the after burner, ejected my bombs and steered the plane up vertically, climbing to about 3,500 feet, and from there I saw a Sidewinder, which came out of the side of a Harrier at an angle of almost 90 degrees. I heard an explosion to the rear, and then I decided to eject.

After landing on West Falkland, Senn was rescued by an Argentine helicopter, which had already picked up a British aviator:

As soon as the British pilot saw me we acknowledged each other as fighter pilots; we were wearing the same uniform. Then I offered him a cup of coffee, but he said, 'No thanks', and then, in an outburst of emotion,

HMS *Antelope* explodes. 'I was beginning to convince myself that we weren't going to survive' (Commodore Mike Clapp)

he said, 'I am an only child, I'm twenty-eight years old, I have a girlfriend and this is a shit war.' That was roughly what he said to me. I replied in my broken English that I was thirty-eight years old, I had four children, my father had already died and I had no doubts about why I was fighting, and had no doubts about giving my life for it.

Patriotism and self-sacrifice were not sufficient to win the war. The Argentine pilots needed bombs which worked. Over the next four days they managed to penetrate San Carlos and press home their attacks. In all, eleven ships were hit, sometimes with several bombs, but only three, *Ardent, Antelope* and *Coventry*, were sunk. The others survived because the bombs failed to

explode. Fifteen did not detonate despite hitting their target.

The pilots who dropped the bombs blame their failure on the thin steel and aluminium walls of the British ships. These, they say, failed to retard the bombs sufficiently for their fuses to have time to engage. The British bomb-disposal men working with the task force have a different explanation. Brian Dutton was the Officer-in-Charge of the Fleet Clearance Diving Team. Being British-made bombs, he had a good idea of how they worked, or – in this case – how they did not work:

The Argentinian pilots whom we all admired and who pressed home their attacks very thoroughly, released the bombs too late in flight for the parachute to expel at the rear and for the fuses to be armed at the rear of the bomb. This allowed the bomb to go through the ship's side, and in the particular case I dealt with, in HMS *Argonaut*, it struck the other side of the ship and dropped back in an inert position.

The Argentine pilots knew that the British Sea Dart missiles were lethally accurate at high levels. They chose, therefore, to fly low to avoid them, aware that they could escape detection by the task force's radar, and then strike at the enemy ships without warning and with relative impunity. Finally, to be absolutely sure of hitting the target, they released their bombs at the last moment. The price they paid for this safety and accuracy, however, was the failure of their weaponry. When

Brian Dutton defused a bomb on board *Argonaut* he saw that the fuse, driven by a propeller which spins in the air as the bomb falls to its target, had only unwound four or five times. Given greater time in flight, the fuse would have unwound at least ten times before releasing a striker, which in turn would have sparked the detonator.

Defusing all the unexploded bombs was a difficult, uncomfortable and dangerous job. Men had to work in confined spaces and in freezing conditions, with the constant fear that the slightest false move could trigger an explosion. Brian Dutton's team, in *Argonaut*, defused the bomb amidst piles of the ship's ammunition:

Her back broken, HMS *Antelope* sinks slowly in San Carlos water as the air attacks continue

One of my young men was shifting the ammunition boxes, and he dropped one. And everybody froze, I don't know why we froze, because we wouldn't have been there if the bomb had gone off. You know, it's just an instant reaction. We all looked at each other and then just got on with it. And after that, I don't think anybody really took into account what we were working at. You couldn't afford to think about it.

Unexploded bombs were removed from nine ships by clearance teams. Only one exploded, in HMS *Antelope*, as an army bomb-disposal expert, Staff Sergeant Jim Prescott, attempted to make it safe. Captured on video, the huge explosion was witnessed by millions on television and became an abiding image of the Falklands War. *Antelope*'s back was broken by the force of the blast, and she sank slowly in San Carlos Water the following day, May 24.

Brigadier Julian Thompson was working in his headquarters when he heard *Antelope* explode. At first he thought that the whole ship's company were on board at the time. He was extremely relieved when he learned that the men had, in fact, been evacuated. Nevertheless, the loss of *Antelope* was extremely depressing. He, and the Commodore, Amphibious Warfare, Mike Clapp, had been promised air superiority for the landings. Now they felt they depended on luck, and risked annihilation. At that moment Thompson was at his lowest ebb:

In my more cynical moments, I felt that this brigade, which was all the Royal Marines had to give, was risking being destroyed utterly, and it would never be reconstituted. It was definitely something at the back of my mind that we were going to lose a lot of ships and a lot of men if it all went wrong, because of this business of not having air superiority.

Mike Clapp was on board the headquarters ship *Fearless* when he heard *Antelope* explode:

I was beginning to convince myself that we weren't going to survive. I really couldn't see how we could go on. We'd had incredible luck up until then. The bombs had not been hitting the landing ships; they'd been hitting the frigates and air defence ships, and it just seemed too good to be true that we were still alive.

But luck stayed with the British. By May 25, the air attacks had diminished in intensity in the face of heavy losses. May 25, however, was Argentina's National Day, and was set aside for a major battle, using all the Air Force and Navy's remaining resources. Expecting a major attack, Admiral Woodward deployed *Brilliant* and *Coventry* as a defensive system in the approaches to San Carlos.

Atlantic Conveyor burns after being hit by an Exocet. Her loss was a devastating blow to the British land campaign

Coventry would use her Sea Dart system, and *Brilliant* her Seawolf, thus covering both the high and low-level approaches with a missile trap. Both ships would also be able to provide early warning of attack. The two ships in place, Woodward then moved his carrier force as close to the Falklands as he thought safe, in order to provide extended Harrier cover over San Carlos.

Early in the morning, using a Lear jet adapted for reconnaissance, the Argentine Air Force was able to pinpoint the position of *Brilliant* and *Coventry* in open sea off Pebble Island, forty miles northwest of San Carlos. The information of the position of the two ships was passed from the Air Force's Electronic Operations Centre in Buenos Aires to the 5th Fighter Group at Rio Gallegos. After several abortive attempts to attack, two sections of Skyhawks managed to make a run at the British ships. Neither *Coventry* nor *Brilliant* was able to fire a missile in self-defence. *Coventry*'s defences failed at the crucial moment, and because she was manoeuvring in front of *Broadsword* at the time of the attack, the Seawolf was rendered useless. Three bombs hit the *Coventry*, and all exploded. She sank in less than thirty minutes. *Broadsword* was hit by a single bomb which flew straight through the ship without exploding, taking with it the nose of the ship's Lynx helicopter.

Coventry was the first casualty of Argentina's National Day. The second, *Atlantic Conveyor*, was an even greater blow to the British forces. Argentine naval intelligence had made great efforts to find the battle group's area of operation to the east of the Falklands, in order to launch an Exocet attack on May 25. By keeping a record of the flight paths of Harriers when they arrived on, and departed from, combat air patrols, Argentine intelligence was able to calculate the position of the carriers and the task force.

No reconnaissance flight was possible before this attack. A slow-flying Neptune or Tracker aircraft would have been easy meat for the British Harriers. Instead, two Super Etendards made a long sweep south of the Falklands before heading north towards the task force. Their approach went undetected until 3.36 pm, when they popped up to acquire their targets.

Sub-Lieutenant Andrew Johnstone-Burt, who was in his usual observer position on board HMS *Alacrity*, had a bird's-eye view of the attack. The task force had instituted two code-words for an Exocet attack: 'Handbrake' was a Super Etendard, and 'Ashtray', an Exocet. First the dread word 'Handbrake' was announced:

We then heard the code-word 'Ashtray' passed round the command team, and we knew that there was an Exocet coming towards the task force. A few moments later, we saw *Atlantic Conveyor*, which was on our port bow, hit by a missile in its stern. There was an instant allocation of anti-aircraft weapons to try and see if we could hit the Super Etendard, but it moved away quickly and the Captain rapidly closed on *Atlantic Conveyor* to give assistance.

The aircraft carriers had successfully diverted the two Exocets, by firing chaff rockets; other ships in the task force had followed suit. One Exocet flew harmlessly into the sea, but the other had locked on to the large profile of *Atlantic Conveyor*, which was not equipped with chaff, and could do nothing to avoid attack.

As *Alacrity* drew alongside the stricken *Conveyor*, her hoses ready to dowse the fire, the sea grew rougher. Night was closing in. The huge container ship was foundering; the fire from the Exocet had spread quickly through the aft quarters, and was reaching the higher superstructure of the bridge. Andrew Johnstone-Burt watched as the order to abandon ship led to panic and confusion amongst the civilian crew:

There were several people running around the upper deck in their survival suits, which weren't properly done up, and they'd lowered two ropes and a ladder down the side. They'd released their life rafts, which had come from their canisters and gone down, but they were still connected to the ship, some sixty feet below. We tried to get alongside, and we passed the head rope across to the ship. As we were doing this, we were very close to the ship with our bow to the ship and the life rafts were in between us. There was a sudden explosion and the Captain put the ship astern and we moved away. Unfortunately though we didn't have time to get rid of the head rope. It snapped, fell in the water, and struck one of the survivors who was trying to scramble clear. He was pulled under.

The crew's attempt to get off the burning ship disintegrated into chaos. Some men slid down ropes into the water, others were immobilised on the step ladders hanging over the side, paralysed by fear; some just jumped from the top of the ship. One life raft, positioned at the foot of the ladder, quickly became full. Five or six others, lying astern, remained empty. Andrew Johnstone-Burt threw lines down to the heavily laden raft in an attempt to pull it clear:

But unfortunately, in the confusion there was an individual who was cutting any line that came to the life raft, because he thought that was the line that was connecting the life raft to the canister that was above him on the ship. So this was extremely frustrating from our point of view. We couldn't get close enough, and we just had to watch these people screaming and shouting.

Eventually the crowded life raft was cut free. As the wind rose, however, it was blown towards the *Conveyor's* stern which was rising and falling in the heavy swell. Johnstone-Burt noticed the familiar bearded face of the ship's master, Captain Ian North:

This life raft was now totally overflowing and there were people hanging onto the hand holds around the side. And the life raft disappeared under this pitching stern and re-emerged half empty, and I saw Captain North clinging onto one of these life rafts, and as this life raft re-emerged having been pounded by his own ship, he was not there.

Twelve men died in the Exocet attack. The loss of the ship was a disaster for the British forces now consolidating their position in the Falklands. Although the Harriers she carried had transferred to *Hermes* and *Invincible* six days before, ten helicopters went to the bottom of the South Atlantic with *Conveyor*: six Wessex, one Lynx and three large Chinooks. Tents for 5,000 men were also lost, along with a mobile landing strip for Harriers, and a water distillation plant. When Brigadier Julian Thompson heard the news he was devastated:

We were just putting the final finishing touches to the plans in my headquarters when a man came in and said, 'They've sunk *Atlantic Conveyor*', and all the helicopters bar one had gone to the bottom, so somebody said, 'Well, we'll bloody well have to walk.' Now that was a very immediate blow to one's plans, they were destroyed.

Thompson was forced to rebuild his entire campaign from scratch. He had planned to move 3 Commando Brigade forward by helicopter; now he had to draw up plans in which the men marched to battle across East Falkland:

The whole business of speed, which was crucial, was going to be very difficult to meet. We had to get on as fast as we could once we got started because of the problems of the ships at sea, the problems of keeping men supplied and well and fit in this country. The removal of the ship actually made it difficult to do that, because on board were two very vital bits of kit, apart from the helicopters: one was the materials to build the airstrip at San Carlos, which was going to help us get on, by being able to base aircraft forward, and cutting down the time they had to go back to the carriers to refuel.

Secondly, the tentage that was on board, to which we could have taken people and dried them out, if they were getting very wet and cold, went to the bottom as well. So the whole problem of getting on was made more difficult by the sinking of *Atlantic Conveyor*.

The destruction of *Atlantic Conveyor* illustrated the effectiveness of hitting supply ships, rather than their escorts. But the lesson, if it was learned at all, was learned too late. Argentine men and planes had been lost in a desperate battle against frigates and destroyers. There were now too few left to prevent the task force establishing and supplying a bridgehead.

The British had been fortunate. A combination of mistaken Argentine tactics and good fortune meant that the landings were successful. Had all the bombs exploded, a further eight naval ships would have been lost. The Commander-in-Chief, Admiral Sir John Fieldhouse, was convinced that luck was important to the operation, but not crucial:

You have to remember that we were up against an opposition that had never been to war, and I used to say to myself as I went to bed at night, 'Fortune favours the brave', and it did under these circumstances, and to use another favourite phrase of mine, 'You get what luck you deserve'. Of course we got some luck, but, we deserved that luck. I'd be the last person to say that things didn't go right for us in a variety of directions, but equally they went wrong for us in many directions, but the balance of risk was such that at no stage was I concerned that we were in danger of losing.

Bridgehead at San Carlos. The British were able to consolidate their hold despite the air attacks. Had the Argentine pilots concentrated their attacks on supply ships the outcome of the war might have been very different

20/THE BATTLE FOR GOOSE GREEN

On May 26 2 Para, commanded by Colonel 'H' Jones, set off on foot to attack Argentine positions at Darwin and Goose Green, fifteen miles south of San Carlos. The battle was to be an extraordinary action, in which a small group of motivated soldiers overcame a much larger but less professional force. In the course of the battle many of the battalion's officers, including 'H' Jones himself, were killed.

Before the battle took place there was considerable disagreement about the need for the attack on Goose Green. General Jeremy Moore, the Land Forces Commander, was *hors de combat* in *QE2*, speeding south with 5 Brigade. In his absence, he instructed Brigadier Thompson, in charge of 3 Commando Brigade, to secure a bridgehead on East Falkland, and to prepare to move forward only when the reinforcements had arrived. General Moore expected to take command of the breakout.

Thompson was happy to follow these orders. Without enough helicopters, many of which had been lost in *Atlantic Conveyor*, he was keen to establish as strong a base as he could, before venturing out. The War Cabinet, however, felt differently. The politicians were hungry for success, aware that the longer the force remained in San Carlos, the greater the international pressure for a cease-fire would become. Already Britain was threatening to use its veto in the UN Security Council, should a resolution calling for a cease-fire be adopted. The British public, too, needed results fast if support for the war was to hold up. John Nott allowed no delay:

If I had been Brigadier Thompson, on the ground, I would certainly have wished to establish my bridgehead to the maximum extent before I moved out. So I don't think I would be critical of the position that Brigadier Thompson adopted. Having said that, we were at a critical time internationally, in holding opinion together, and it was therefore imperative that we made a move out of the bridgehead as soon as possible. It may well have been that it led to an attack on Goose Green, twenty-four hours before it would have been prudent to do it. But that is what war is all about. There is never a simple solution to any problem. War is partly confusion, and partly a conflict of requirements.

That conflict led to considerable tension. Brigadier Thompson was unwilling to move forward, and made his feelings plain in a series of difficult telephone conversations with headquarters staff in Northwood. He told the Commander-in-Chief bluntly that his objective was Port Stanley, and that Darwin and Goose Green, to the south, would be an unnecessary sideshow:

I thought so at the time, and I still feel that it was a diversion from the effort, it didn't have to happen. But I can see why there was a requirement for it; I can live with that. At the time I was extremely irritated about it.

Thompson's irritation was not shared by Colonel 'H' Jones, who was itching to move against the enemy. Chris Keeble, 2 Para's Second-in-Command, saw that the difference of view between the two men arose out of a difference of background:

'H' Jones was the leader of a Parachute Regiment and he was working to a Brigade Commander, who was a Royal Marine. And the Royal Marines have a different set of values. And I think both of us regard ourselves internally as an élite. But élite in different ways. The Royal Marines were very concerned about putting us ashore. Establishing a beach-head. Now for the Paras, that was not a point of arrival, that was a point of departure. Here was a place from which we could launch our attack against the enemy. And it was only by attacking the enemy and defeating him, defeating him on the battlefield, that we would resolve this issue. So there was a difference.

When 2 and 3 Para landed at San Carlos and camped for six days on Sussex Mountain, with nothing to do other than watch the air attacks, their frustration grew. Men fell casualty to trench foot, as they sat in their wet and cold dug-outs. Morale started to sink.

Plans for the breakout were proposed and cancelled, as Thompson, faced with the immense logistical difficulties of operating without helicopters, argued for delay. 'H' Jones, growing increasingly impatient, urged attack. David Cooper, 2 Para's Padre, sympathised with the Colonel's desire for action:

He led by example. He literally grabbed men by sheer force of personality and carried them along with him. And that produced a battalion at that time I think I would have set against any other fighting force in the world. Inevitably of course, on Sussex Mountain, he became impatient. Because we were losing men to the weather. We had a limited manpower. We were 8,000 miles from home. Every man really did count. And every man that went down because his feet were no longer such that he could walk on them, was a victory for the enemy.

On May 26, five days after the landing, the arguments ended. The Commander-in-Chief in Northwood issued Thompson with a direct order: get moving. 2 Para's plans to attack Darwin and the settlement at Goose Green were reinstated, and the remaining battalions, 45 and 42 Commando

Argentine dead awaiting burial at Darwin

together with 3 Para, were also ordered to move out of the bridgehead, on a northerly route across East Falkland to Port Stanley. Without helicopters, the men would have to walk. 40 Commando remained to guard San Carlos.

Originally, Brigadier Thompson had argued that the attack on the Argentine garrison at Goose Green and Darwin should be no more than a raid, to give the enemy 'a bloody nose'. 2 Para rejected this. 'H' Jones, despite being aware of the greater size of the Argentine force, and the lack of helicopter transport for his men, was determined to take the battle to the enemy and win it. When the battalion set off on the evening of May 26 on their fifteen-mile night march, they did so with a clear purpose: to capture the enemy positions.

The night march, the first of many long treks for the British forces, was tiring and difficult in the extreme. The men, carrying all their weaponry and ammunition including mortar bombs and grenades, had to walk over wet, boggy and uneven ground. After the night march the battalion rested up in an unoccupied farm, Camilla Creek House, within three or four miles of the start position of the attack. When the exhausted men lay down as best they could, they tuned into the BBC World Service for news. Chris Keeble was horrified by what he heard:

We listened to the broadcast, only to hear that we were being launched against Goose Green. The very thing that we were about to do, had apparently been announced to the world. So we had to quickly readjust our positions, disperse them, and bring our whole planning forward, which cut out a great deal of intelligence acquisition, which we needed in order to do this attack.

News of the impending attack had been leaked from Downing Street. The politicians in the War Cabinet, keen to boost public morale, had made it clear that an offensive would start soon after the landings. The Prime Minister's Press Secretary, Bernard Ingham, had already briefed reporters that '. . . we are not going to fiddle around'; now his press office revealed the destination of the attack, which was duly broadcast by the BBC.

At Camilla Creek House in the Falklands the parachutists noticed that an increase in Argentine helicopter activity followed the bulletin. They were doubly angry: they had deliberately discarded valuable weaponry and travelled light to preserve surprise. Now surprise was lost, and they had insufficient equipment for the battle ahead.

Goose Green and Darwin were indeed being reinforced, but not as a result of the British news reports. On May 25, one day before the broadcast, General Menendez had prepared his own appreciation of the situation, which he sent to Buenos Aires on May 26. He said that the British were likely to take action against Goose Green and that he was taking steps to reinforce the garrison. Menendez ordered troops guarding Mount Kent and Port Stanley to move to the settlement. Due to the shortage of Argentine helicopters, and the complex chain of command, Goose Green was only partially reinforced with soldiers by the time of the British attack. On May 28 the garrison numbered 1,007 men, together with large quantities of artillery and ammunition.

2 Para, by contrast, was made up of only 600 men, with light weapons, three 105mm guns flown in by helicopter and only two mortars. They were, by any standards, an extremely small and ill-equipped force to take on such a well-defended objective. The men were only slightly reassured by the knowledge that they would be supported by HMS *Arrow*'s 4.5 inch gun, and by Harrier air-to-ground attacks.

The plan was to start the battle in the darkness of the night of May 27/28, and to force a corridor through the enemy defensive positions which lay along the narrow isthmus leading to the hamlet of Darwin and the large settlement at Goose Green beyond it. It was hoped that the advance would have reached the civilian settlement by first light. 2 Para's four companies were deployed in the attack. 'A' Company on the left flank moved forward first: its primary objective was the small settlement at Darwin. 'B' Company advanced second, half an hour later, moving forward on the right-hand side of the isthmus. 'D' Company was ordered to follow from the rear, ready to pass through 'B' Company once its first objectives were captured. 'H' Jones commanded the action from his tactical headquarters, 'C' Company.

As with all the best laid plans, the attack, which started at 2.30 am on May 28, went awry. The promised naval gunfire support ceased early because *Arrow*'s gun jammed. The four companies crossed the start line at their allotted times, and initially moved forward well, but soon the fighting became fierce and the advance slowed in the face of heavy enemy fire. The paras had limited stocks of ammunition and were forced to ration what little they possessed. Chris Keeble was watching the battle with 'H' Jones at tactical HQ:

Brigadier Julian Thompson plans the campaign in the operations room in *Fearless*. Thompson came under intense pressure from London to attack Goose Green. He considered such an attack an unnecessary diversion

We were down to relying on courage, bayonets, machine guns and close gutter fighting. That is a hallmark of infantry, at night in confusion and chaos. And that's how it was fought. Trench by trench. Getting closer and closer to a main defensive line around Darwin Hill.

Although many of 2 Para had seen action in Northern Ireland, none had experienced a real battle before. It was a sobering experience for Sergeant Barry Norman:

When you actually see a bloke you've known lying there with a bullet wound in him – all right, I saw the odd Argentine body lying around, but you can't relate to that – and he's bleeding and the medic is treating him, then the thought actually comes home that you know, this isn't an exercise, this is war.

The paras advanced slowly, making their way forward in small groups of four, each group with a machine gun. The teams worked in pairs, using a tactic called fire and manoeuvre. One group advanced, while the other provided covering fire. The forward section then took cover, and the team behind leap-frogged ahead. Yard by yard, the paras made their way through the enemy positions in darkness, applying fire where necessary with ruthless determination. When the men came close to an enemy position, they destroyed it with a phosphorous grenade, or an anti-tank missile. Often, at the last moment, the Argentine soldiers tried to surrender. Usually it was too late. In the frenzy of battle, the British troops had neither time, nor the desire, to pull back from the final, deadly assault.

David Cooper, 2 Para's Padre, accompanied his battalion onto the battlefield. Soon he saw his first dead body. It made him pause and reflect on the motivation of the British soldier:

As I rolled him over to identify him, he had actually had a shot that had just gone through the side of his left eye and taken away the side of his skull. He was a soldier who I knew had got a young family. And I suddenly realised that our strength lay in the fact that we all knew each other, and we would do what was needed because we were friends. Not because the Queen wanted us to do it, or Mrs Thatcher or the CO, but in a large part because we were friends.

By first light it was clear that the advance was bogged down. The battalion was still far from the settlement at Goose Green. 'B' Company on the right was held up at its first objective, the ruins of Boca House. On the left 'A' Company had become badly stuck on its way to Darwin. After crossing some open ground on the approach to a small rise in the ground, known as Darwin Hill, it had become trapped in a gully. Every time the men attempted to climb out of it they were repelled by heavy Argentine fire. 'H' Jones contacted the company commander on the radio and, in a characteristically forthright fashion, ordered the men to get a move on. The reply came back that they were stuck and could go no further. Sergeant Barry Norman was with 'H' at the time:

He wasn't going to accept that, so we got down as close as we could and he said, 'Right, Sergeant Norman, we're going up there.' So, using smoke and what little cover there was, we actually made it to the company's position.

The two men were horrified by what they saw. Organisation appeared to have broken down and morale was low. Casualties and prisoners of war lay scattered haphazardly about the gully. The position was in range of Argentine artillery which was increasingly accurate.

On the Argentine side of the lines few were fully aware of what was going on. Captain Juan Jose Centurion was with his company, in reserve at the settlement of Goose Green. He had seen and heard the intense battle in the distance towards Darwin, the tracer and sporadic flashes of artillery fire lighting up the night sky. At 8 am Centurion was ordered by Colonel Italo Piaggi, the garrison commander, to take his men forward to help block the British attack on Darwin. He set off an hour later:

It was a morning with a lot of mist and drizzle, and visibility was very poor. The situation was extremely confused. Some companies were withdrawing, others remained isolated; there were some detachments which had already arrived back at Goose Green.

Centurion and his men moved forward to reinforce the Argentine positions holding the British off Darwin Hill. They set up their machine gun positions in slit trenches, commanding the approaches to the hill, and immediately joined the battle:

As the British tried to advance we opened fire. We fought a fairly intense battle, with some advantage because we managed to check the British detachment straight away and hold them back.

'A' Company, trapped in the gully, were now coming under fire from Centurion's machine gun trenches, as they sought to break out from the gully. 'H' Jones took charge. After a heated discussion with the company commander, he told Barry Norman how he wished to proceed:

The funeral of British
soldiers killed in the battle
for Goose Green, 29 May
1982

Colonel Jones said: 'Right, the only way we're going to do it is over the top.' So we lined up in extended line, and we went over the top with mortar smoke coming down onto the position to provide a screen. But that particular day, even for Falkland standards, the wind was exceptionally strong.

The wind blew the smoke-screen protection away from the men, and left them vulnerable to direct fire from the Argentine defensive positions. Three men were caught in the open as the smoke cleared. They were shot dead immediately.

Colonel Jones, leading the advance, turned round and shouted to Sergeant Norman that he intended to outflank the Argentine positions which were holding up the British attack:

He said, 'Follow me', which I did. We then turned right and the Argentinians were firing at us from the high ground to the left. We ran across the top feature, as fast as we could, and then down, into dead ground from the Argentinian position. And I thought he was going to stop, but he didn't. He just continued running.

Sergeant Norman followed Colonel Jones. As he ran behind him he heard a British voice shouting a warning that they were threatened by a second Argentine trench to their left. Norman immediately dived for cover, firing at this second enemy position, which was occupied by Captain Centurion's men. Barry Norman was relieved to see that 'H' Jones had made it to dead ground ahead of him, where he was safe. Instead of stopping and taking cover, however, the Colonel just kept on going:

To my utter amazement I looked again and he was just checking his sub-machine gun, to make sure he had a full magazine on, and he went charging up the hill, to the trench which I was firing at . . .

The higher 'H' Jones ran up the slope towards the trench, the more he was exposed to the Argentine position to his rear. The enemy immediately opened fire. Norman attempted to warn him:

I shouted to him, 'Watch your fucking back!' And he totally ignored me. Whether or not he heard me, I don't know. I think he ignored me, personally. And the higher he went up, the nearer he was to this fall of shot. All of a sudden his body and the fall of shot coincided and he was hit in the back. The momentum of the shot actually forced him forward and he fell just within inches of the Argentinian trench he was actually going for.

Leading a platoon attack, the Colonel of the battalion had been killed. It was typical of 'H' Jones and typical of the Parachute Regiment. To the

Argentine defenders it was extraordinary that a colonel should be leading such an attack. Captain Centurion, who witnessed Jones' death, was impressed and perplexed by the display of heroism:

He (Colonel Jones) found my detachment by chance; I arrived not ten minutes before him, and took up the advantageous position, really by a stroke of luck. I think of Colonel Jones as someone who proved himself to be an excellent commander. Although he possessed innumerable resources: 66mm rocket launchers, his unit had Milan anti-tank weapons, mortars, and some artillery support, he personally took part in a machine gun battle fighting with hand grenades.

Such conduct was unheard of in the Argentine Army, and for that matter, in all of the world's fighting forces. Battalion commanders were simply not expected to charge enemy machine gun nests. The conventional wisdom was that,

Col. 'H' Jones

134

although they moved forward with their troops on the battlefield, they did so prudently, and in no circumstances did they lead their men over the top. But the rejection of conventional wisdom was second nature to Colonel Jones, and lay at the heart of the Parachute Regiment's philosophy. Chris Keeble was waiting back at 2 Para tactical HQ:

It was at that point that I heard some words that I shall never forget, which were 'Sunray is down', which was the signal that something had happened to 'H', and that the prearranged plan of my assuming command would have to go into operation, and my heart beat fast as I heard those words, and tried to take in what it really meant. That this is really happening, I'm now in command of this. I've got to somehow sort out this attack, which was clearly stalled, and hadn't made the progress we wanted in broad daylight on a terrain that was completely bare. There was no cover. There were no hedgerows, no trees, nothing. It was like a billiard

table and blowing right across it was this polar wind, fifty or sixty knots, that just burnt off any heat that we had. And we were getting casualties. And 'H' was dead, our leader.

'H' Jones' attack, for which he was awarded a posthumous Victoria Cross, had broken through the stalemate. By 11 am 'A' Company had captured the high ground of Darwin Hill, and 'B' and 'D' Companies, working together, had taken Boca House. The settlement of Goose Green was now threatened by the British.

The position facing Chris Keeble as the day progressed was not good, however. After a night and a day's fighting, the paras were running short of ammunition. The enemy had not surrendered, despite a successful attack by three Harriers in the afternoon on a group of 37mm anti-aircraft guns. The guns had been used to fire directly at the British ground forces, with deadly effect. One in six of Keeble's men was either killed or injured. He was aware, too, that 112 civilians were locked up in Goose Green's Community Hall, and that he was limited in the fire he could bring down on the settlement. There was very little that he could now do to win the battle.

Taking shelter in a gully, surrounded by the garbage of war – discarded rifles, bandages and spent ammunition cases – Keeble pondered his dilemma in solitude:

I thrust my hands into my pockets, because they were so cold, and my fingers caught a piece of plastic that I had in my pocket, a laminated prayer, from a French soldier. I had a kind of bargain with God, you know, I'll carry this prayer, if you look after me. I knew this prayer well. And I suddenly thought, I need to say this, and in that darkness I knelt down, in this gorse, and I said this prayer, which was essentially abandoning myself to God and seeking his will and whatever the outcome was, I'd live with that. And a most amazing kind of transformation occurred. From feeling cold and fearful, and uncertain and frightened, I suddenly felt joyful, hopeful, warm and very clear about what we should do. And I turned round and went back to the boys. I said, 'I'll tell you what we're going to do. I'm going to seek a surrender, tomorrow morning.' And they were astounded, inevitably, and I said, 'Trust me,' in the way in which I felt I needed to trust my God, in this case.

Keeble gathered together some prisoners of war and ordered them to go back to their own defences, to speak to their leaders and tell them that the commanding officer of the British battalion would come to meet them the following morning. That night there was an undeclared cease-fire as the two sides tended to their dead and wounded.

Opposite above left: An Argentine soldier, one of the many who surrendered at Goose Green, prepares a meal in the settlement's sheep-shearing shed

Below: Argentine dead at Goose Green

Above right: The pathetic belongings of an Argentine conscript killed in the fighting at Goose Green

Keeble was anxious not to do anything which might provoke the Argentine forces.

The next day, May 29, Major Chris Keeble, his Artillery Officer, and the BBC radio correspondent, Robert Fox, met the commander of the Argentine garrison, Colonel Italo Piaggi, in a hut by Goose Green airfield. They talked for some time, discussing the options. The two British officers were filthy after forty hours of fighting; their faces blackened and smeared with combat paint, their uniforms covered in the mud and grime of the battlefield. In stark contrast the Argentine officers were immaculate in freshly pressed uniforms.

Keeble made it plain that if Darwin was not captured by 2 Para, another battalion, and if necessary another brigade, would follow behind to ensure a surrender. This simple argument convinced Piaggi and his men:

They conceded and said, 'Fine, OK. But can we surrender with honour?' And so we agreed that they'd have a parade and they'd form up and sing their songs and lay their weapons down and surrender the garrison. And that's what happened.

The paras were amazed at the size of the force which surrendered. One thousand and fifty Argentine troops marched out of the settlement to lay down their arms. Before he saw them, Barry Norman had been disappointed by the news that the enemy was about to surrender:

The grass roots people in the battalion didn't want the Argentinians to surrender. We wanted to go in and take Goose Green because of the people that had died the previous day. When we actually saw the numbers of people coming out of the settlement, we were glad, and everybody was glad that they actually surrendered. They were just coming out in droves.

The decision to surrender was welcome, but humiliating for the Argentine forces. Although the number of troops was indeed large, it was made up of many men who were unable to fight: Air Force technicians, and support personnel. The reinforcements who had just arrived had no time to participate in the battle. They and their valuable helicopters went straight into captivity. Captain Juan Jose Centurion felt great bitterness when he heard the order to surrender:

I think that for any professional soldier surrender never enters into his plans. He always has a sort of motto, in all fighting divisions: victory or death, so it was very hard. But you must bear in mind the human factor: we had been under a lot of strain. Everyone had lost at least five kilos in weight. And our equipment was poor; we only had one heavy mortar. Our radio batteries had gone flat, and so command was very difficult.

But the British had not had an easy victory. Seventeen men, thirteen of them officers and NCOs, had been killed in the battle. Any doubts which Chris Keeble may have had about the value of the operation, with its heavy cost in human life, melted away when he saw the liberation of the Falkland Islanders from their imprisonment in the Community Hall:

We went into the church hall and released the civilians, who came out into the sunlight, blinking and crying and the children running around. After all, they'd been imprisoned for about a month. And we had cups of tea and we hugged each other. And oh, I felt, all my anxieties on the way down about was this an authentic operation? Was this really right? You know, the paradox between being a Christian and being a soldier, and all those kind of anxieties, were blown away in that landscape when I, with 2 Para and the others, restored freedom to a bunch of people who had lost it. I felt good.

The bodies of the dead parachutists were flown back to San Carlos for the burial service at Ajax Bay. Chris Keeble, David Cooper the Padre, and a small group of parachutists accompanied their fallen comrades. David Cooper read out the names of the dead:

It didn't surprise me to see a number of soldiers, very hard men in some cases, with tears streaming down their faces. And it did seem that I'd stumbled almost inadvertently on a means whereby soldiers could almost, within a controlled environment, come to terms with their experiences. Nobody thought it odd that somebody was crying in the service, or at least that tears were coursing down their face.

The British, while demonstrating their overwhelming military superiority in battle, had learned many lessons. It was clear that fighting in daylight, against heavy fire over open ground, was too dangerous. Henceforth, all attacks would take place at night.

Whether a military necessity or not, the battle for Goose Green was a tremendous boost to British spirits. The War Cabinet was relieved to realise that the quality of the Argentine fighting man was not as high as some had feared, and that his morale was obviously poor. The politicians were certain that the decision to order the attack had been the right one. The military agreed: moral ascendancy over the enemy, which would make so much difference in later battles, had been decisively won.

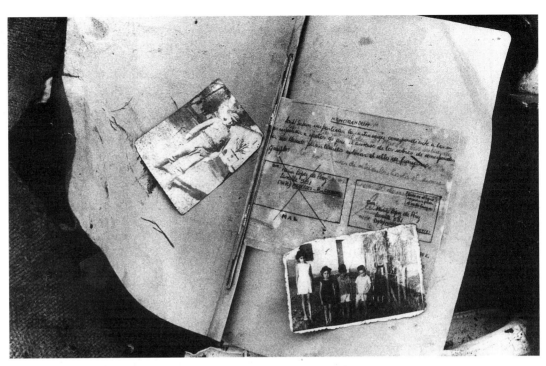

21/DISASTER AT FITZROY

Sir Galahad burns after the Argentine attack on 8 June. Inset: A Sea King hovering at the stern of the blazing ship winches a survivor to safety

THE first land battle in the Falklands took place in the absence of the Commander of the Land Forces, Major-General Jeremy Moore. He had decided to accompany 5 Brigade on the journey south aboard the liner *QE2*, rather than make a more rapid transit by air, and drop by parachute on to British-held territory in the Falklands. It was a decision which he came to regret deeply. Stuck on board the ship, away from the action, he was unable to intervene in the arguments over the move to Darwin and Goose Green, and could not mediate between Brigadier Thompson and the politicians in London.

General Moore's decision to travel with 5 Brigade was understandable. He had ordered Thompson to establish a bridgehead; he had no reason to expect the Brigadier to move forward as rapidly as he did. He was needed at task force headquarters to help plan the campaign with the Commander-in-Chief, Admiral Fieldhouse. The General also believed he would have the advantage of the peace and quiet on board *QE2* to plan the campaign.

The result was that he arrived in the Falklands on May 30 *in medias res* only two weeks before the Argentine collapse. 2 Para had fought successfully for Darwin and Goose Green; three other battalions assigned to 3 Commando Brigade, 45 and 40 Commando, and 3 Para, had advanced rapidly on foot to their objectives: Teal Inlet and Douglas Settlement. The men had 'yomped' in Marine parlance, 'tabbed' in Para talk, all the way, carrying their kit with them in a classic demonstration of their supreme strength and fitness. At the same time 42 Commando flew to Mount Kent and secured the peak, after it had been captured by the SAS.

Mount Kent, only twelve miles from the Islands' capital, was an obvious point for the Argentine military to defend with all their strength. Whoever held this mountain had a vantage point which towered above all the hills encircling Port Stanley. One of the British commanders described it as being 'at the top of the staircase' which led down to Stanley. General Menendez had initially posted a force on the mountain. With typical ill-luck, however, he had sent all the defenders to reinforce Goose Green, where they were immediately captured, together with their helicopters. Mount Kent, undefended, fell into British hands without a single casualty.

The beleaguered General Menendez watched the enemy advance on his defensive position in Puerto Argentino. There was little he could do.

Canberra (left) and *Queen Elizabeth 2* (right) at Cumberland Bay, South Georgia, during the transfer of 5 Infantry Brigade

When General Galtieri issued him with orders for an immediate counter-attack he refused, and threatened to resign unless the order was withdrawn. Menendez sent a gloomy report to the Junta in Buenos Aires:

I said that in order to launch a counter-attack we needed means that were not at our disposal, and that in my opinion the troops were in no condition to march, because the logistics and the heavy artillery could not be moved. After the reinforcement of Goose Green we had no helicopters; we had no air defence to cover the march, no suitable vehicles for the Malvinas terrain, and no possibility of travelling by boat.

The problem facing the two armies was the same: a lack of helicopters to move men and supplies. The British overcame this by the fitness of their troops, and by the judicious use of the few helicopters available. The Argentine troops, deprived of sufficient food by the blockade; cold and miserable in their wet shelters; demoralised first by lack of action, and later by artillery bombardment, had neither the ability nor the inclination to march towards the enemy.

On May 27 *QE2* steamed into Grytviken Bay in South Georgia with 5 Brigade on board. The men then transferred to *Canberra* and *Norland* for the journey to the Falkland Islands. The War Cabinet had no intention of exposing Britain's prestige liner to the risks of Argentine air attack.

On 5 Brigade's arrival in San Carlos a new command structure was imposed on the land forces. General Moore was now in charge, reporting to Admiral Fieldhouse, the Commander-in-Chief in London. Under Moore were two brigadiers, Julian Thompson, already half-way to Stanley with 3 Commando Brigade, and the newly arrived Tony Wilson, in command of 5 Brigade. The land force headquarters was set up on HMS *Fearless*, taking over directly from the amphibious headquarters, which had commanded the landings. It was generally agreed that the constant chopping and changing of the structure of 5 Brigade, and the late imposition of a new command structure, was a mistake. In future wars, the Ministry of Defence decided, there would be a clear command structure, with a two-star general

The Commanders. Left: Brigadier Julian Thompson confers with Major-General Jeremy Moore during the advance on Stanley. Right: Brigadier Tony Wilson ponders his advance over a mug of tea

in command at the scene of the battle from the beginning.

2 Para, recovering from the arduous battle for Goose Green, was ordered back to 5 Brigade, under the command of Brigadier Tony Wilson. Wilson, a softly spoken aristocrat, was already under something of a cloud when he arrived in the Falklands. After the less than successful brigade exercises at Sennybridge in Wales, concerns were expressed at a senior level about the suitability of his appointment. A second Brigadier travelled with Moore's staff on *QE2* to replace Wilson should it become necessary. This must have done little to boost the commander of 5 Brigade's confidence, and relations on the journey south between the staffs were strained.

5 Brigade's precise role in the Falklands was unclear. At first the Brigade, now made up of Gurkhas, together with the Welsh and Scots Guards, was expected to act as a garrison force. While *QE2* travelled south General Moore refined his tactics. The strength of the Argentine garrison in Port Stanley, and the General's belief that it was

commanded by a fearsome General (he had been wrongly informed that another Menendez, of a more blood-thirsty disposition, was in command), led him to decide that a two-brigade attack was essential. 3 Commando Brigade was to approach Stanley from the north; 5 Brigade was to advance from the south, via the settlements at Fitzroy and Bluff Cove.

The men of 2 Para did not welcome the news that they were rejoining 5 Brigade under Tony Wilson's command. As Chris Keeble recalls, they were suspicious of his proposed strategy:

There was some friction between his rather Camberley (staff college) approach of manoeuvring his brigade across country and our rather more outrageous *coup de main* style of operation. He presented his plan and we presented ours. And he then said our plan was preposterous and he would set off now to put his plan into operation and we'd be hearing from him. And he left.

Chris Keeble and his men were fired up by their first battle, and wished to get on. Many of them doubted the need for 5 Brigade at all, and believed that they should advance straight for

Stanley, without – in Chris Keeble's view – the rather cumbersome approach developed by General Moore and his staff.

There was tremendous energy in 600 paratroopers who wanted to do it now, rather than go through the more cautious, ponderous, logistic build up. Nibble at this. Nibble at that. The safe approach that was being espoused by the General. We wanted to move fast. We wanted to move now. I think there would have been tremendous energy to do it. Whether it would have been successful, who knows? But we'd done something pretty outrageous at Goose Green. There was the spirit and the willingness and the experience to do it again. I think we could have done it.

With the benefit of hindsight, Lord Lewin now wonders whether the sending of 5 Brigade was at all necessary:

I think perhaps it was a pity that 5 Brigade was committed at all. And that the troops who started the action weren't allowed to continue it to the end.

The logistical problems of unloading the paraphernalia of an entire brigade, and moving it across the inhospitable Falklands, were immense. Wilson ordered the Welsh Guards Battalion to advance on foot to Goose Green, following the route over Sussex Mountain which 2 Para had taken only five days before.

The march was a disaster. The men, burdened by their heavy equipment, found the going extremely difficult after only a few miles. Their problems were compounded by the breakdown of the sno-cats, brought to the Falklands specially to move the brigade's equipment. According to Brigadier Wilson it quickly became apparent that the march was impossible:

What became patently obvious was that the route was impractical to take large quantities of rations, or far more important ammunition and heavy equipment over: and that we simply could not do. And there is a point at which just sending a soldier over, really makes no sense at all, because the soldier, unless he's got all the back-up he needs at the far end, is going to be worse than useless and just another mouth to feed.

The failure of the march over Sussex Mountain soon led to allegations that the Welsh Guards were not march-fit. Certainly, the men of the Paras and the Marines, who had marched long distances, were ready to pour scorn on the failed effort of their colleagues in 5 Brigade. The imputation of unfitness is rejected outright by Brigadier Wilson:

You'll always get this kind of cap-badge rivalry and people who reckon that they can do things that other people can't do. All I can say is that in the army everyone takes the same battle test standards and has to pass them. Pure simple physical fitness. OK, some people may be more highly tuned than others, but they were certainly not unfit in any way at all. No. That's nonsense.

Although the Welsh Guards were fit, it is unlikely that they were at the same peak of battle-readiness as the Paras and Marines. They had, after all, just come off a ship after a long journey. Before that they had been stationed in London on ceremonial duties.

Whatever the causes, 5 Brigade was unable to advance on foot to its first objective. Other ways had to be found to move the men forward, at a time of acute helicopter shortage. At this time, Brigadier Wilson accepted a bold plan put forward by Chris Keeble, for a rapid advance of the brigade beyond Darwin and Goose Green. The extra problem of moving the men forward compounded Wilson's difficulties, and led to the need to use *Sir Galahad* and *Sir Tristram*, which were bombed at Fitzroy, to reinforce the forward positions.

Keeble's plan was simple but brilliant. He suggested to Wilson that they should telephone the settlements at Bluff Cove and Fitzroy, thirty-five miles from San Carlos, to establish the exact whereabouts of the enemy. If there was only a small garrison there, the plan was to follow the call with a *coup de main* attack using the sole Chinook helicopter available to the British forces. On June 2 Wilson, having thought it over for a day, accepted the idea. By good fortune a single telephone line still existed which ran from Fitzroy to a settlement called Swan Inlet House, about half-way along the southern coast towards Stanley. 2 Para put a small party together which flew to Swan Inlet House, seized it and telephoned Fitzroy. The news came back from the surprised locals that there was no permanent Argentine garrison and that the single bridge connecting it with Bluff Cove and Stanley remained intact, though demolition charges had been laid.

Wilson seized a Chinook, filled it with as many Paras as possible and ordered them forward. Fitzroy and Bluff Cove were captured. The news of the rapid advance was not welcomed with the expected rapture at land force headquarters. General Moore and his staff were well aware of the problems of moving men forward to reinforce the advance party. Some felt that the operation

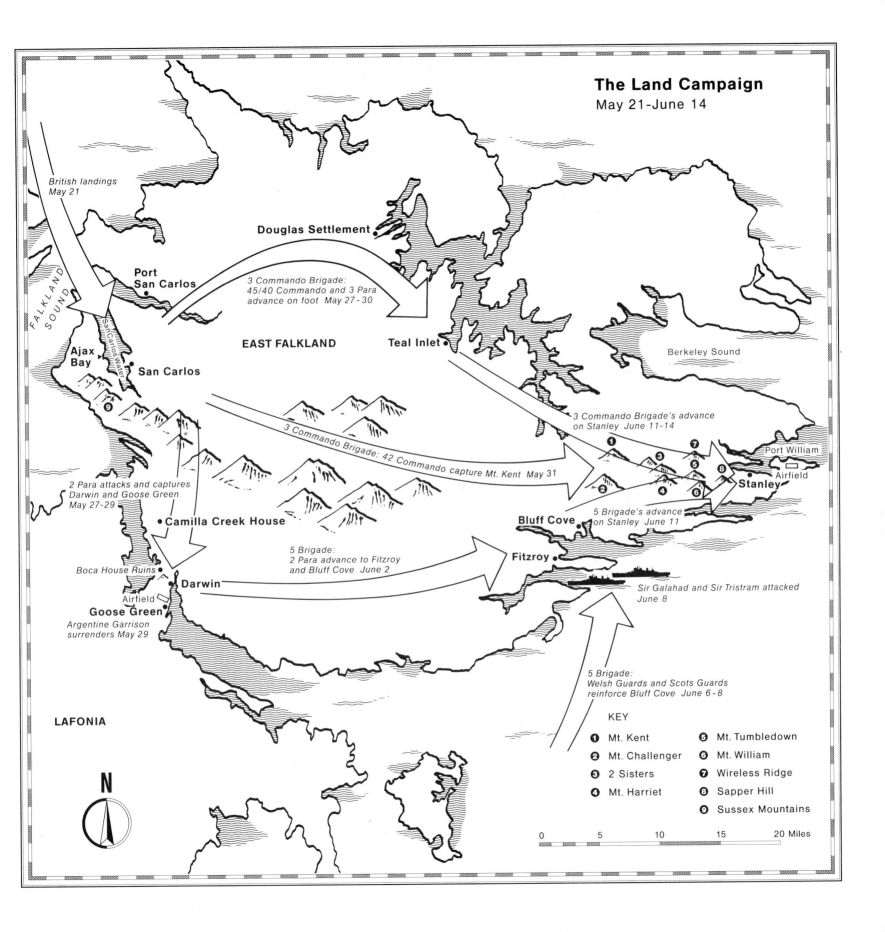

The Land Campaign
May 21-June 14

British landings May 21

FALKLAND SOUND

Douglas Settlement

Port San Carlos

3 Commando Brigade: 45/40 Commando and 3 Para advance on foot May 27-30

San Carlos Water

EAST FALKLAND

Teal Inlet

Berkeley Sound

Ajax Bay

San Carlos

3 Commando Brigade's advance on Stanley June 11-14

3 Commando Brigade: 42 Commando capture Mt. Kent May 31

Port William

Stanley

Airfield

2 Para attacks and captures Darwin and Goose Green May 27-29

Camilla Creek House

5 Brigade's advance on Stanley June 11

Bluff Cove

Boca House Ruins

Airfield

Darwin

5 Brigade: 2 Para advance to Fitzroy and Bluff Cove June 2

Fitzroy

Sir Galahad and Sir Tristram attacked June 8

Goose Green

Argentine Garrison surrenders May 29

5 Brigade: Welsh Guards and Scots Guards reinforce Bluff Cove June 6-8

LAFONIA

N

KEY
❶ Mt. Kent   ❺ Mt. Tumbledown
❷ Mt. Challenger   ❻ Mt. William
❸ 2 Sisters   ❼ Wireless Ridge
❹ Mt. Harriet   ❽ Sapper Hill
          ❾ Sussex Mountains

0   5   10   15   20 Miles

had been reckless, and that Wilson had sanctioned it with insufficient reconnaissance of the surrounding area. Much valuable helicopter time, needed to supply the advance party already in a key position on Mount Kent, would now have to be transferred to the southern flank.

5 Brigade was now desperately exposed. The small advance party of 2 Para at Fitzroy and Bluff Cove had to be reinforced quickly. As helicopters were unavailable, the only way to take men forward was to use task force ships. When the Commander-in-Chief in London was informed of the need to reinforce he told General Moore that he did not wish major ships to be risked. British intelligence had discovered that the Argentine forces at Port Stanley had a land-based Exocet launcher which threatened the approaches to Fitzroy and Bluff Cove.

The ships most suitable to carry the Welsh and Scots Guards to Fitzroy, *Intrepid* and *Fearless*, would have to remain well out of Exocet range and could not be used on the final stages of the journey. Landing craft had to be used instead to ferry the men on the last leg of the journey from the assault ships to Port Pleasant, a shallow creek just by Fitzroy. As the landing craft could only carry a small number of troops, several journeys had to be made under the cover of darkness.

Ewen Southby-Tailyour, with his detailed knowledge of the coastline, volunteered to take the first group of Guardsmen from *Intrepid* to Port Pleasant in landing craft. The night of June 5 turned out to be the worst of his life. After the 1st Battalion, Scots Guards, had boarded *Intrepid* and the ship set off on its journey, Major Southby-Tailyour was summoned to the bridge. The Captain told him that the landing craft would leave the assault ship to the west of Lively Island, some seven hours sailing to Port Pleasant. Southby-Tailyour was appalled. He considered the long unprotected journey far too dangerous. A row ensued, in which the Captain argued that to lose *Intrepid* would be tantamount to losing the war. Southby-Tailyour replied that losing the landing craft and a battalion of the Scots Guards would be as bad. The argument became extremely heated:

I was frightened personally, I was frightened for the Scots Guards. My final words to the Captain were, 'I think the whole fucking thing stinks and what's more, sir, I want you to remember this, if we don't make it.' He told me to leave his bridge, quite understandably.

The Captain did not give way. The four landing craft left the assault ship west of Lively Island and headed for the coast. Lively Island was still occupied by Argentine forces. By good fortune, the enemy failed to detect the vulnerable group of landing craft as it passed by. A seventy-knot wind blew up, and it started to rain. The small craft could only make headway at four or five knots.

Five hours later, exhausted and soaked to the skin, the Scots Guards waded ashore at Port Pleasant. Major John Kizely was in command of a company. His job was to prevent the men from dying of exposure:

It was very cold, very wet and I was told by the commanding officer that if there were any casualties, by exposure or anything else, it wasn't possible to get anybody taken out by helicopter. It was far too stormy for that. So, we dug in during the whole of the night and one couldn't let anybody just stop and lie down in a sodden condition, because they'd have had exposure very quickly indeed. So one kept going until one had proper shelters built and some cover.

Southby-Tailyour was convinced that a repeat of that night's landing craft passage, to bring the remaining men of 5 Brigade to Bluff Cove, would be too dangerous. As the advance group based at Bluff Cove did not have any communications with San Carlos, or with their own tactical headquarters at Goose Green, or with the ships of the task force, he returned by helicopter to land forces HQ the next morning to make his point. On arrival, he was reassured to find out that the assault ship *Fearless* would bring the remaining Welsh Guards much closer to the shore, while remaining out of the range of missile attack. The plan was that Southby-Tailyour would return to Bluff Cove, and go out that night and meet the ship with the landing craft he had used to ferry the Scots Guards ashore.

When Southby-Tailyour returned to Bluff Cove in the evening he was horrified to find that his landing craft had been requisitioned for use elsewhere. He was, as a result, unable to go and pick up the Welsh Guards from *Fearless*. Only half the men, using two of *Fearless*'s own landing craft, were able to make it ashore on the night of June 6. The other half had to return to San Carlos and seek alternative means of transport. By this stage Northwood was becoming increasingly concerned about the use of the assault ships. Admiral Fieldhouse advised that they should not be risked at all in future. Commodore Clapp, in charge of the amphibious operations, decided that the landing

A Sea King, pressed into service to move supplies during the land campaign. After the loss of *Atlantic Conveyor* there was a desperate shortage of helicopters to take men and ammunition forward

ship *Sir Galahad* should be used instead. The Welsh Guards disembarked from *Fearless*. Together with 5 Brigade's Field Ambulance, two Rapier batteries and other support units they started to board *Galahad*.

On June 7 *Sir Tristram*, *Galahad*'s sister-ship, sailed into Port Pleasant, the inlet at Fitzroy which leads to Bluff Cove, and started to unload her stores of supplies and ammunition. The unloading of the ship proceeded in broad daylight, under the watchful eyes of an Argentine observation post looking down from Mount Harriet. It was considered by 5 Brigade's staff to be an acceptable risk, as there were no men aboard. The task was not completed by nightfall. That evening Southby-Tailyour dined with the Captain of *Sir Tristram*. The Captain asked the Royal Marine what the chances were of an air attack the following morning. Southby-Tailyour told him that it was a strong possibility.

While Southby-Tailyour was dining with the Captain of *Sir Tristram*, *Sir Galahad* was being loaded with the Welsh Guards, their equipment, and the other supply units at San Carlos. Loading took some time, and the ship's departure was delayed.

Late in the night on June 7, the Captain of *Galahad* asked if he might wait an extra day, in order to be able to approach Fitzroy and have sufficient time to unload in Port Pleasant under the cover of darkness. Commodore Clapp refused his request. Aware of the pressure of time, Clapp ordered him to proceed to Fitzroy at the first opportunity.

5 Brigade's communications with San Carlos were extremely poor. Because a signals link had failed, it was impossible to pass a message from the advance party at Bluff Cove back to tactical headquarters, let alone divisional headquarters, and vice-versa. As a result, nobody at Fitzroy or Bluff Cove was aware of the despatch of *Sir Galahad*. Brigadier Tony Wilson, in San Carlos on the morning of June 8, was never told of the reinforcement by his staff.

When the men at Fitzroy and Bluff Cove woke up that morning they were astonished to see the landing ship sitting at anchor in the narrow inlet, close to *Sir Tristram*. It was an obvious target. Even those who had no great military knowledge could see the danger. The Padre, David Cooper, was standing with 2 Para's medical officer when he saw the ships:

A squadron of Argentine A-4 Skyhawks similar to that which attacked *Sir Galahad* and *Sir Tristram* at Fitzroy

Day broke and we looked out and were staggered to see two ships in the bay. And Steve Hughes the doctor said, 'Well, you know, I wonder how long it'll be before they're bombed?' We'd seen the effectiveness of the Argentines and we knew that Fitzroy was in sight of the high ground round Stanley.

Up on the high ground, in the Argentine observation post on Mount Harriet, Major Carlos Arroyo had been aware for some time of the British presence:

We had visual access to the whole area, including Bluff Cove and Fitzroy. On the morning of June 7 my observers told me that there was shipping movement in the area. I verified what they told me and passed the news on to the High Command. Owing to the weather it was impossible to carry out any air raid that day.

On June 8, when *Sir Galahad* arrived, the weather had cleared. Visibility and flying conditions were very good. On board the landing-ship the men lounged about. Some watched videos in the NAAFI canteen, others rested with their equipment. Many had a nagging fear of air attack. Down in the cavernous and darkened tank deck, Sergeant Peter Naya, a medical orderly with the field ambulance, sat and waited for the order to disembark:

You were always aware of a risk of air attack. This threat was always with you, all the time. Because we had jumped from one ship to another to another, and you could see the damage done by cannon fire, rockets and what have you to these ships. And indeed the *Galahad* itself, at that time, had sustained some damage, bomb damage.

The officers in command of the troops on board *Sir Galahad*, two majors in the Welsh Guards, were extremely reluctant to disembark at Fitzroy despite the obvious danger. Their destination was Bluff Cove, a sixteen-mile march away. They had no wish to repeat the fiasco of the march over Sussex Mountain nor did they wish to endanger themselves by travelling on landing-craft with their ammunition. Major Southby-Tailyour warned them that the men should get off the ship as quickly as possible. They refused to move.

Unfortunately the argument came down to relative ranks, and the fact that I was a Major, and they were Majors, meant that it was not going to be acceptable as an order. Well, my rage knew no bounds, frankly.

There was nothing he could do to persuade the men to leave the ship. When some troops were eventually ordered to disembark, one of the ship's doors jammed, and the operation was halted.

In the far south of Argentina, Commodore Ruben Zinn's squadron of eight Skyhawks took off and headed for the Malvinas. The Skyhawks' mission was one part of a two-pronged attack, involving the bulk of the Argentine Air Force's remaining serviceable planes. Zinn's section was to attack British shipping reported by the observation post on Mount Harriet. Another section of Mirages and Daggers was ordered to bomb ships in Falkland Sound, and act as a diversion to draw off Harrier patrols from the attack on the ships at Fitzroy. Three of Zinn's squadron were forced to turn back because of problems with their in-flight refuelling. The others pressed on:

We flew over the East Malvinas Island, from north to south looking for the ships. When we were about to give up the search, an officer, the youngest, spotted one of the ships' masts, tucked away in the irregular coastline ... it was visible because we were flying at very low altitude. So he said 'to the right!'. The whole squadron turned to the right, and we entered the bay at very low altitude, and when we got there we found the two ships. We immediately dived and attacked them.

Zinn and his men hit both *Sir Tristram* and *Sir Galahad*. There were massive explosions, and the ships began to burn furiously. Peter Naya was looking through the open tank deck, just as the Argentine planes passed overhead:

Almost simultaneously, about three or four people shouted, 'Hit the deck!' Even I shouted, 'Hit the deck!' And bang that was it. All hell broke loose. We'd been hit. The one fear you had all the time, the one dread actually materialised. It happened. All kinds of emotions come up on you then. Personal anger at being in that position and not being able to do something about it. You know, being stuck in this tank deck. And it's hard to describe when these kinds of weapons explode. They've got enormous power; fantastic power. You know, these modern weapons are designed to kill. That's what they're there for. The fireball it created, the heat it generated. The shrapnel, the debris that flies. The secondary detonations of ammunition. Quite enormous, awesome, that's when the devastation starts.

The scream of the low-flying jets followed by the crump of detonation alerted those on shore to the attack. A BBC video crew, filming with 5 Brigade, happened to be on the spot at the time. The crew recorded the devastating effect of the attack. Their film was shown a few days later: it was one of the very few occasions where the full horror of war, with dead and wounded, was actually witnessed by the British public.

Immediately Ewen Southby-Tailyour heard the attack, he ran down to the beach, and saw both ships burning. His worst fears had come to pass. Men were beginning to come ashore, some terribly burned, others suffering the effects of the blast, with limbs smashed up, some with their legs and arms torn off. Southby-Tailyour stripped off to the waist and carried stretchers for two hours:

I was so angry that I had to, in a way, get rid of my anger by doing something physical. Not only was it physically demanding, it was, too, the most emotionally sapping thing I have ever done in my life. Yes, it was awful. And I felt slightly guilty, because I feel that I could have insisted with even more vigour that those guys got off.

On board *Galahad* and *Tristram* men were desperately trying to escape from the flames. The first explosion had lifted Peter Naya, in *Galahad*, and thrown him across the tank deck. The interior of the ship was plunged into blackness by a thick pungent smoke. As Naya picked himself up and sought to make his escape, he could hear the screams of the injured and dying caught in the rear of the ship, together with the noise of secondary explosions from the burning stores of ammunition and fuel on board:

My face was rubbing the deck because there was a gap of perhaps two, three or four inches of fresh air. With all the smoke and heat rising, there's a little gap of fresh air down there, and you can barely see a foot ahead. I'd memorised the internal sections of that tank deck; I knew that to the port side, half-way up the ship, there was an exit, that led up to the deck. So I made a bee-line for that. Dragging people. Climbing over dead people. People hanging on to you, trying to get out, whilst all this burning was going on. It was terrible really. The instinct for self-preservation and survival is very strong.

When Naya reached the deck he was confronted by the sight of men with appalling injuries. As a medical orderly, he set to work doing what he could to apply immediate first aid:

You came across people with hands, fingers blown off. Arms blown off. Bellies hanging out, you know. It's so quick. It's so sudden. You think, God, you know, you'd never seen anything like it. And the burns, tremendous burns, black, you know. British soldiers standing there and looking ashen, black, charred. With no skin left whatsoever. The skin burnt off where it was exposed.

Within minutes Naya's limited store of medical dressings was used up. More bandages and drips were brought to him by the surviving Welsh Guards, and he established a first aid post at the bow of the ship. For two hours he treated the injured as best he could, improvising where necessary, using makeshift splints from wooden pallets to bind broken and mangled limbs. Sea King helicopters ferried the injured to the shore:

We were passing casualties up to them. We had very badly injured people. We even tried to create makeshift slings, improvised hoists and things to get them off. We were physically manhandling people up to the helicopter, dumping them on board. And they were ferrying to and fro to the land. Dumping them off. Coming back for more.

Peter Naya was one of the last men off the burning ship. For his courage and help to the injured and dying he was awarded the Distinguished Conduct Medal.

On shore David Cooper, 5 Para's Padre, tried to arrange medical facilities for the survivors arriving from the burning landing ships:

At that time brigade headquarters from 5 Brigade were in Fitzroy as well. And I'd found them to be something of a really non-decision making concern at that time. I established a helicopter landing site by the settlement, with the help of a lieutenant from 9 Squadron, Royal Engineers, and with the defence platoon from 9 Squadron we ferried casualties from the helicopters into the village hall, where such medics as there were gave them the treatment. I then established another helicopter pad at the other side of the village where those who'd been treated were flown out and back to Ajax Bay. The walking casualties I put along a hedge. And I remember being absolutely stunned when I was walking down a track and a figure came round the corner, soaking wet, with a blanket round him. And he was Chinese.

Several of the casualties from *Galahad* and *Tristram* were civilian Chinese, recruited in Hong Kong to work for the Ministry of Defence.

150 Welsh Guards were flown to the field hospital at Ajax Bay in San Carlos Water, where they were tended by Rick Jolly and his men:

I had to take this heart-rending decision to get rid of those with less than ten per cent burns. And walking around in the gloom of Ajax Bay and apologising to these young men, who were standing there blowing on their fingers, which had skin hanging off them like wet tissue paper. Trying to explain why we were doing what we were doing, I found them wonderfully brave in their attitude to me, when in their sing-song voices they would say, 'Don't worry about me, Sir, you look after my mate. Have you seen him, Evans?' And my heart went out to them. They made it possible for me to clear the decks and allow us to look after the seventy-five or so very badly injured. The worst, of course, being Simon Weston. And to ensure the following day that we were able to get them out to the hospital ship *Uganda*.

Brigadier Tony Wilson, in command of 5 Brigade, had no idea that *Sir Galahad* was at Fitzroy, let alone that she and her sister-ship *Sir Tristram* had been bombed. Flying back from a conference on board *Fearless* at San Carlos, he saw the flames from the burning hulks of the two ships flickering in the darkness. On arrival at Bluff Cove he learned the bad news: that fifty men had died in the attack, the majority of them Welsh Guards.

It was a blow to the campaign, which at first seemed extremely serious. General Moore personally informed the Commander-in-Chief in Northwood, telling him that he considered that the battle to retake Port Stanley might possibly be delayed by four days. He urged that the casualty figures be underestimated, in order to encourage the belief amongst the Argentine military that the main thrust of the attack would still come from the south. Somehow, this request became confused, and the Ministry of Defence in briefings deliberately sought to exaggerate the number of dead and wounded, in the hope that this would lull the enemy into a false state of security. The news of a disaster with high casualties did nothing for public morale, and the correct figure of dead was issued to end speculation on June 11.

The events at Fitzroy were the product of many causes, some of them going back to the very start of the campaign. 5 Brigade was cobbled together at the last minute: it suffered, as a result, from poor organisation; it was less fit and battle-ready than 3 Commando Brigade; its communications equipment was not good; the men had difficulties marching over the terrain; and the loss of *Atlantic Conveyor* meant that there were too few helicopters to move them. In the bloody chaos and confusion of war these factors led with a terrible inevitability to disaster.

David Cooper stood and watched the burning ships with the Captain of *Sir Galahad*:

And we stood there and talked and he'd got tears streaming down his face, and I had too. And I remember him saying, 'I told them to get off, and they wouldn't get off.' And he kept going back to that refrain ... It was our Government who sent the forces to the Falklands. But within all that, there are different levels of command and there must be responsibility. Our experience of the Welsh Guards was that they were a very fine battalion of infantry. But I don't know how well they'd been briefed. They clearly didn't appreciate the threat that Argentine air power presented. And wherever you look, I think, ultimately there is still a responsibility on the commander on the spot. Just as there is responsibility for more senior commanders, not to put forces into a position where this kind of disaster can happen.

Although there was no public apportioning of the blame for the disaster, many in the armed forces believed that 5 Brigade's organisation was poor, and that it was an act of negligence to leave the men on board ship so long in the face of an obvious danger. That view is shared by Lord Lewin:

General Wolfe, who was a great amphibious operations man, said that the admiral must lose no time in running into the enemy's port and getting his troops on shore. And they ran into the port. But they didn't get the troops on shore. And they were caught.

The casualties at Fitzroy were high by the standards of the Falklands conflict, accounting for nearly a quarter of the total number of British deaths. By the terrible standards of modern war, with all its destructive potential, they were very small. The incident became, in the public mind, such a disaster, partly because of the deliberate playing up of casualties by the Ministry of Defence, and partly also because of the terrible and striking nature of the images which were seen by millions on television.

Fortunately for General Moore, the land campaign was hardly affected, and his strategy of a two-pronged attack from the north and the south could continue. Two companies of 40 Commando were quickly flown forward to replace the Welsh Guards disabled in the attack, and planning for the final push continued. It was delayed by only two days.

Sir Galahad continues to burn as British forces prepare for the final push to Stanley. The disaster at Fitzroy did not greatly hamper the British campaign

22/THE FINAL PUSH

42 Commando secure Mount Kent

HIGH on Mount Harriet Major Carlos Arroyo watched the attack on *Sir Galahad* and *Sir Tristram*. He and his men were keen to take advantage of the British set-back, and launch an attack immediately:

It seemed to us to be the optimum moment to leave our positions and go to the attack when we saw the vulnerability of the English ships. Initially I was a little afraid, but when I saw the battle was going in our favour due to the action of the aircraft, I was longing to go and attack the English.

General Benjamino Menendez quickly learned of the successful bombing of the enemy ships at Fitzroy. To the disappointment of his men on Mount Harriet, however, he decided against a counterattack. The British position was too far from his artillery at Puerto Argentino, there was no air cover for his troops, and the British had, by this time, defended the high ground around the settlement at Bluff Cove.

In Buenos Aires, the Argentine Military Council discussed various grandiose plans for a counter-attack against the British. The Junta was encouraged by the reports of heavy British losses at Fitzroy, which were hugely exaggerated in the Argentine press. That, together with the firm belief that the British carrier *Invincible* had been hit by Skyhawks in a raid on May 30, contributed to a pervasive sense of unreality. It was manifested in its most extreme form by General Galtieri, who ordered the garrison at Puerto Argentino to be prepared to fight to the last man, and under no circumstances to surrender.

In fact, the morale of his troops occupying the Malvinas had taken a nosedive. The commanding officers did little for the welfare of their men. The conscripts, left in their freezing dug-outs to fend for themselves, were forced to steal food from their own depot, or to break into unoccupied houses and loot them. Many lived on the meat from sheep which they caught and killed.

There were 12,000 Argentine soldiers, 11,000 of them fighting troops, the rest support staff, defending Port Stanley. They were deployed around the capital, ready to repel attacks from every point of the compass. General Menendez, expecting the main British thrust from the west, was also concerned that the enemy might land forces on beaches south of Stanley in a surprise amphibious assault. He made his dispositions accordingly. On the outer perimeter, part of the 7th Infantry Regiment made up a defensive line, holding Mount Longdon and Wireless Ridge. To the south, the 5th Marine Battalion occupied Mount William and Mount Tumbledown. In the west companies from the 4th Regiment held the peaks of Two Sisters and Mount Harriet. The 3rd and 6th Regiment were ordered to defend the southerly approaches to Stanley, where the British landings were expected. At the same time Menendez instructed his engineers to scatter mines wherever they could. Minefields were placed at every conceivable place where a British assault might be expected.

Stanley, or Puerto Argentino, was completely surrounded by defences in a 'hedgehog' formation. Although the Argentine forces lacked heavy artillery pieces and ground attack aircraft, the rocky peaks of the encircling mountains were ideal defensive positions. They offered a clear view of the approaching enemy, wide and unimpeded fields of fire, and very good cover.

General Moore and his two Brigadiers faced a daunting problem. The enemy was well dug in, in dominant positions around Stanley. Once these were taken, it was presumed that the Argentine forces would withdraw into Port Stanley. The possibility then arose of street fighting in the town. Many of the inhabitants were still living there, and would be at risk from artillery and small arms fire in the fighting.

The General's greatest headache was the problem of logistical supplies. Although reinforcements of Sea King and Wessex helicopters had arrived a week before on board *Canberra* and *Atlantic Causeway*, there were still insufficient numbers to carry as much ammunition for the guns as was considered necessary. The loss of three Chinooks from *Atlantic Conveyor* had been a grievous blow. Chinooks could carry more and operate longer than the other helicopters. In desperation, Admiral Woodward released six anti-submarine Sea Kings for use inshore as transport. Even this was barely sufficient. Men were ordered to carry gun ammunition for their rifles and machine guns up to the forward positions. When casualty-evacuation helicopters came forward to remove wounded men, they brought with them boxes of ammunition and exchanged them for the injured. Gun ammunition had priority over absolutely every other load, even rations. Frequently men had to go without resupply of food for two or three days.

In planning for the final battle Moore's staff calculated how much ammunition would be needed by the British artillery. The gunners

Royal Marines board a
Wessex helicopter at San
Carlos, before the move
forward to Stanley

requested 1,000 rounds forward with each gun to start the battle. Even with all the available helicopters it was worked out that it would take ten days to move that quantity forward. The campaign could not be delayed that long. Moore halved the number of rounds per gun to 500, and the immense work of moving the ammunition forward began.

The first attacks were planned to take place on the night of June 11 against the outer perimeters of the Argentine defences: the key peaks of Mount Longdon, Two Sisters and Mount Harriet. General Moore reorganised the brigade structure. After the debâcle at Fitzroy, and the evident lack of a decisive and clear command structure within 5 Brigade, he was, apparently, little pleased with Brigadier Wilson's performance. Once again 5 Brigade was torn apart and its battalion structure changed, to the benefit of Brigadier Thompson's 3 Commando Brigade. 2 Para, which had been switched to 5 Brigade, was now ordered back to 3 Brigade. The surviving companies of the 1st Battalion Welsh Guards were also assigned to Brigadier Thompson's unit.

It was a further blow to Brigadier Wilson, whose campaign had not been going well. To make matters worse he came down with a severe head-cold. In the stress and strain of battle he became convinced that cap-badge politics, and not strategic logic, were dictating the General's decisions. He suspected that Moore, a Royal Marine, was favouring his own men at the expense of 5 Brigade. In particular, Wilson was incensed by the allocation of helicopter time. It seemed to him that 3 Commando Brigade was receiving much more than its fair share:

I think we started to suffer to some extent from what appeared to be a cap-badge rivalry, when it seemed that most of the resources were being allocated to the other brigade. And therefore my people started to feel that they were not only deprived, but had been, shall we say, cast into the role of the Cinderella of the Falklands.

Without much sleep, in the tension of war, tempers became frayed, and feelings hurt. Ten years later it seems that General Moore's decision to reinforce the Commando Brigade at 5 Brigade's expense was entirely justified. The move along the southern flank was planned as a deception, and did not constitute the main thrust, which was to come from the north, where Brigadier Thompson's force was advancing. It was quite logical, therefore, to ensure that 3 Commando Brigade was supplied before 5 Brigade.

Late on the night of June 11 the attacks on Argentine positions began. Much patrolling had taken place in advance of the attacks, to probe the enemy defences and establish their strength, and the position of machine guns and minefields. Special forces, too, had been operating behind the lines for some time. The patrols had a dual purpose: to gain intelligence, and to wear the enemy down by surprise attacks, and by the constant noise of battle through the night.

When the first British shots were fired in the final assault, on the night of June 11, intelligence about the Argentine forces gave an almost complete picture of their strength and defensive positions. It was clear to the British commanders and their men that the enemy forces had immense superiority in numbers and that their weaponry was as good as, and in some cases – such as night-sights – superior to their own. Crucially, however, their morale was extremely poor.

3 Para were given the most difficult task of the final assault: the capture of Mount Longdon. Before the attack the battalion advanced to the start line through forward Argentine positions, from which enemy troops had hastily withdrawn. The disarray of the encampments, with their litter of dead sheep, discarded ammunition and sleeping

bags, and the stench of human excrement, was a clear sign of the weak spirit of the Argentine troops. But when the attack began, 3 Para soon got into difficulties. They were attacking up the spine of Longdon, which resembles the uneven back of a dinosaur. The many large rocks provided cover, but channelled the men into a narrow line of attack. They were vulnerable to fire from all sides. Corporal Ian Bailey's section was in the lead:

Over to our left we heard an explosion, and this actually was one of our men stepping on a mine, unfortunately. This woke them up, and that's when literally all hell broke loose. Everybody, I think, that was on the mountain could see us. And they started firing at us. A lot of small arms, grenades, anti-tank weapons, whatever they had, they were throwing at us. Some were going high, some were actually making contact with us as well.

The Argentine positions were extremely well dug in. In the dark the advancing parachutists failed to destroy them completely. The occupants of the dug-outs, by-passed by the British, crawled out and opened fire from behind. The paras were hemmed in, caught in a narrow couloir, and under fire from all sides. The Argentine defenders above tossed down grenades at their attackers, which bounced down the rocks before they exploded. Although the soggy earth tended to absorb some of the force of the explosion, the brittle rocks were shattered into a lethal cloud of splintered fragments. Many men were injured.

3 Para's advance up the mountain was, unsurprisingly, extremely slow. The formidable combination of grenades, heavy machine guns and anti-tank weapons in well-fortified positions was almost insurmountable. The battle dragged on from 9 pm until 7 am the following morning. During the battle the paras were split up, and were unable to perform their usual tactics. Ian Bailey, separated from his section, 5 Platoon, joined up with 4 Platoon. As he did so, the platoon's commanding officer was wounded, and Sergeant Ian Mackay took over:

Ian and I then had a talk about this one particular position that was causing us a problem, across open ground. And myself, him and three or four of the boys, we were going to move across into a better position, with covering fire, from the rest of the platoon. We got up, moved across, firing, getting down, firing. And we were still going across the open ground. I actually took a round then in the hip and went down. It's like going into the ring with Mike Tyson. He just hits you and you don't know it and you go down. I

Sergeant Ian Mackay, who won a posthumous VC during 3 Para's bloody battle for Mount Longdon could still hear firing going on, and Ian was still going on, and took out another position. You could hear him firing, taking out positions, asking for support from other people. But at this stage, of the three lads to my left, one had been killed, another had been injured and another was in cover and couldn't get round the feature to give Ian covering fire. But Ian went on alone and took out further positions.

Storming a machine gun post on his own Ian Mackay was killed. He was awarded the Victoria Cross for his heroism. Ian Bailey was hit by a further two bullets as he tried to reach cover. He was taken back down the mountain while the fighting continued. He received the Military Medal for his part in the action.

The casualties in the battle for Mount Longdon were extremely high, the highest of any land-based unit in the battle for the Falklands: twenty-three dead and at least thirty-five wounded. When the paras reached the top of the mountain and looked down in the morning light, they realised their achievement. The Argentine forces had spent two months fortifying the peak; they had been extremely well dug in, and were provided with first-class weaponry. They lost the battle because they did not have sufficient aggression, nor the will to defend the barren rocks until the last.

The battles and skirmishes during the final assault fell into a clear pattern. They started with a fierce initial defence, in which the defenders demonstrated their ability to take on the British army and cause it immense difficulties; then, having shown their strength, the Argentine morale crumbled, as though the men did not believe the fight for the Malvinas really merited the full scale battle and loss of life a real defence required.

While 3 Para was struggling for Mount Longdon, 45 Commando quickly captured the twin peaks of Two Sisters. The Argentine defenders here had little stomach for a fight. The skirmish took place in two stages: first a single company, 'X' Company, advanced and captured the approaches, then the two remaining companies, 'Y' and 'Z', came up to take the peaks. They were spotted and pinned down by enemy fire. Lieutenant Clive Dytor, 'Z' company commander, decided on bold action. Shouting the company cry, 'Zulu, Zulu, Zulu', he got up and started running forward. When he looked round he saw his whole company following. They too were shouting 'Zulu, Zulu...' The company swept forward and took its ridge. 'Y' Company followed and captured the other peak. The battle was over almost before it began.

Further south, 42 Commando attacked Mount Harriet, approaching the Argentine defences from the rear, in a classic surprise attack. Colonel Nick Vaux was in command, fighting for the right-hand objective of Julian Thompson's brigade attack. On two successive nights before the battle he had sent patrols through the mine-fields to find a way through the back of the enemy defences. On each occasion a marine had his foot blown off by a mine, but the patrols pressed on regardless and established the best position from which to mount the attack. Corporal Steve Newland had taken part in both patrols on Mount Harriet and had seen the full extent of the Argentine defences. He was aghast to hear that he was being marched up it again:

We'd got out with our lives the first time, and now they were telling us we were going to have go back and take it out again. Which was like death twice over if you like. That was the hardest bit to take in. Because we were trying to convince everybody that this was a bad place to go. Obviously they weren't having any of that. We were going anyway.

Newland and his fellow marines knew that their company was one of two taking part in an assault against an enemy force of three hundred men, one third greater than their own strength. When the order came to advance they approached the enemy's rear in complete silence:

Then we got within about 100 metres of them, and suddenly they must have seen us, and the place just lit up like a *Star Wars* film. There was red and green tracer going everywhere. So we hit the deck. I can remember a guy screaming – he had a really distinct voice – 'Fix bayonets'. So he was in amongst it somewhere. And it was all like slow motion, but not slow motion.

Newland's section made quite good progress advancing up the hill until they were held up by a sniper. Every time one of the men tried to break cover the sniper shot at them, and then moved, making sure it was impossible to pin-point the firing position. Newland decided to advance on his own, to find and destroy the enemy.

I sneaked up to the top of the ridge line. And peered round a large rock, trying to stay as near to the ground as possible. As I looked round this corner, in front of me was a table-top shelf made out of granite. And behind it was a troop of enemy. They were lined out with two guns, one on one side, and one sort of tucked into the right. And in between were all these soldiers. And basically when one of our guys moved, one of these blokes would just take one shot. And then duck down behind a rock. As soon as another moved, another guy would have a turn. So it looked to our lads, on the other side of it, like there was only one sniper. In fact, there was a troop sat there. And what they were trying to do was to sucker them into breaking cover. Come out into the open. And then take them to pieces with these two machine guns.

Newland had hoped that he would be supported in his move forward, but when he looked round he saw there was nobody behind him. He decided to attack the troop on his own:

I went round the back of this large rock that I'd just looked round. Changed my magazine, took out the two grenades I had left. Basically pulled the pins on 'em. Stepped round the corner, sent the white phosphorous grenade into the middle, for the people on the gun in the middle, and the high explosive grenade to the gun on the end, and then stepped back round the corner. Counted a time delay. Waited for both bangs. Then I just stepped round the corner and anything that moved got three rounds.

Steve Newland then retreated to a safe position, and ordered his section to put two anti-tank rounds into the Argentine position for good measure. The two rounds exploded above him, and he started to descend the hill to his former position:

I'd shot one of these guys but I'd only hit him in the shoulder. As I walked round this rocky outcrop he was laid on his side and just squeezed off an automatic burst. He spread a line of bullets across from left to right and two of them hit me, one in each leg. He died after that, because I had a bit of a 'sad' on at the time. In fact, he died quite rapidly after that.

This mixture of brutal aggression and an almost foolhardy courage was typical of the British forces. Few prisoners were taken; no quarter was given. Once experienced, the Argentine defenders had little taste for more, and were understandably quick to surrender. Newland, badly wounded in both legs, had to make his way down from Mount Harriet to find a first aid post:

I threw my weapon down, stood up to see if my legs would still work, decided that the muscles wouldn't work properly but I could swing my legs from the hip and sort of walk a bit like Frankenstein. I did that and then I put my arms to the side like Jesus on the Cross. So that there was no doubt in anybody's mind if they saw me, that I was unarmed.

He staggered down the hill, and was rescued by his comrades.

View of Mount Tumbledown (left) and Mount William (right), seen from Mount Harriet

Major Carlos Arroyo was at the other side of Mount Harriet when the assault began, in the Argentine forward defences. Because the attack was on the rear, he did not take part in the fighting until the following morning. Then, hemmed in by artillery and mortar fire, there was little he could do but give up:

It hurt me a lot to have to take the decision to surrender, but the situation then gave no alternative, and all I could have achieved was further casualties in my personnel, who were already in a very bad state. But I was very sad to surrender.

Without helicopters, the bulk of which had by now been destroyed by the British, General Menendez and his local commander, Brigadier Joffre, were unable to move reinforcements forward to help defend against the first wave of British attacks. Brigadier Joffre was startled by the uncanny ability of the enemy to pinpoint his position:

We think the British had an enormous amount of information about our plans. We don't know if they obtained it for themselves, or with the timely help of the United States. They knew too much about the location of our troops and helicopters. We were no longer able to move our troops as we had planned.

Although the United States had moved a spy satellite to cover the Falklands, after repeated requests, it supplied little intelligence which the British had not been able to discover for themselves using special forces. The Argentine High Command was convinced, however, that the British were being supplied with all their intelligence by the Americans. It led to considerable bitterness and recrimination after the war.

The morning of June 12 dawned with the British in command of all their objectives, and dominating the final approaches to Stanley. 3 Commando Brigade was now established on a ridge of hills running north to south across East Falkland only six miles from the capital. The Argentine forces had put up a stiff resistance, and had taken comparatively heavy casualties: fifty men had been killed. The British had not come off lightly, with twenty-five men dead, the vast majority, twenty-three, killed on Mount Longdon.

Argentina did have one success that night. An Exocet, dismantled from a frigate, and reassembled on the back of a lorry, was fired at HMS *Glamorgan*. The ship had been firing at Argentine positions in support of the British attacks, and was returning to the task force when the attack took place. As dawn was fast approaching, *Glamorgan*'s Captain decided to risk a short cut across the 'no go' area around Port Stanley, in order to be out of range of morning air attacks as fast as possible. Commander Julio Perez and his crew were waiting with their Heath-Robinson Exocet launcher:

After waiting for many nights, when the ship entered our firing range we were very excited; and I remember clearly that we were very moved, just hearing the roar of the missile and watching the gases expelled.

The launch team ran to a small promontory to see the course of the missile flying towards its target:

Though we knew the flight's duration, it seemed like hours, its flight seemed never-ending. When it impacted we felt a mixture of joy and sorrow. We were happy because we had hit a ship which we were firing at, and at the same time we felt sorrow for all the lives that were at stake.

Damage to the helicopter hangar of HMS *Glamorgan* caused by the last Exocet attack of the war, 12 June 1982. The Exocet was launched from the rear of a truck in Port Stanley

Thirteen men were killed, including Lieutenant David Tinker whose controversial diary of the war was published soon after the conflict. The ship itself was not too badly damaged, and was able to sail back to the safety of the task force.

General Moore hoped to continue the final phase of the attack, this time using both 3 Brigade and 5 Brigade, on the night of June 12. Brigadier Wilson, however, asked for a postponement of twenty-four hours. His men had not had sufficient time in which to plan their attacks, nor to look over the ground they were due to attack. Moore agreed to the delay, and the final attacks on the mountains overlooking Stanley itself, Wireless Ridge, Tumbledown and Mount William, started on Sunday June 13. The General was hopeful that the Argentine garrison might give up before the final assault:

As we stepped forward each time, we got closer and closer, we were looking down his throat and practically had his teeth prised apart by this time, and I had hoped that he might surrender at that point; he was clearly losing and being beaten, but it didn't happen and we pushed on.

2 Para in the north were ordered to capture Wireless Ridge, which they did without much difficulty, fighting against tired and demoralised troops. In the south the Scots Guards attacked Mount Tumbledown which was occupied by Argentine marines of the 5th Regiment, professional soldiers of a very high standard.

After a short diversionary attack by the Welsh Guards, fortified with 42 Commando, the Scots Guards started their advance on Tumbledown. The mountain was typical of those on the way to Stanley: another rock and stone-strewn ridge, which offered the defenders every advantage, and the attackers none. The forward company of the Scots Guards managed to reach their first position, just before the approaches to the summit, without a shot being fired. Two companies then continued to move forward in darkness, lit up occasionally by the explosions and flares from the diversionary raid to the south. Major John Kizely was leading a company forward:

From about 300 yards in front of us, about twenty or thirty rifles and machine guns opened up, all at one time. It was quite cleverly done. And then of course, we went into our battle procedure for dealing with that sort of thing. The platoon commanders started getting their platoons moving forward, trying to win the fire fight against the enemy and then move on. But they had considerable fire power and whenever you tried to

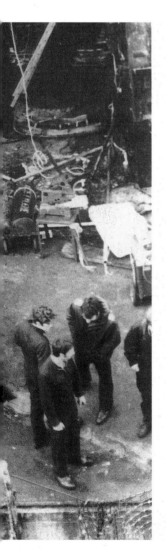

move you weren't able to. You were pinned down. We were starting to take casualties. And for quite a long time, it bogged down, the attack. And we were lying there with our own artillery fire starting to come down, but very much on the receiving end. We thought we were going to be cutting through them like a knife through butter. But as it was, there we were on the receiving end and that just wasn't in the script.

There was a considerable delay while the Guards summoned up more artillery fire, and arranged for it to land in the right place and at the right time. By early morning a slow advance had started once more. The Argentine defenders, fighting valiantly, were close to running out of ammunition. They called for reinforcements and resupply, but none came. Instead Menendez ordered them to withdraw. The Scots Guards, with John Kizely in the lead, continued to press forward:

That part of Tumbledown is a series of false crests, and you never quite know when you're at the summit of it. But I remember topping a crest which I thought would be just another false crest, and it wasn't, it was the summit. And I looked down and there, not very far away, was Port Stanley. The lights were on in the streets, the houses. You could see the headlights driving up and down the streets. And it was quite surreal, really, because there was civilisation. People were going about their normal business and here on the top of a hill, there was a bunch of people trying to kill each other. And I was gob-smacked by it. And I stood stock-still, just for a moment. But it was a very stupid thing to do, because immediately there was artillery and a burst of machine gun fire and of the seven people who were up there on the top of the hill with me, three were immediately shot and wounded.

But Tumbledown had been captured, and the British now dominated the approaches to Stanley. In the early morning of Monday June 14 the Gurkhas advanced, in their first action, on Mount William, next to Tumbledown. To their chagrin, they encountered no opposition. Meanwhile the Welsh Guards were standing behind, ready to move forward to Sapper Hill, the ridge closest to Stanley. Just as Brigadier Wilson was giving the orders to the Welsh Guards to press ahead he received an urgent message from General Moore ordering him to hold the attack. Wilson, deeply suspicious, probably believed that Moore wanted to bring 3 Commando Brigade forward across his front on Tumbledown and Mount William, to take Sapper Hill in place of the Welsh Guards. This could then allow Brigadier Thompson's brigade to lead the final push into Stanley. In the heat of the moment, with the excitement of the possibility of final victory as he pushed to Stanley, Wilson told the Guards to proceed to their objective. They went forward and took Sapper Hill. This now put 3 Brigade in the pole position for the final attack on Stanley, planned by General Moore for the evening of June 14. It now looked as though Brigadier Wilson's men, and not Thompson's 3 Brigade, could be the first to raise the Union Flag over Stanley.

But it was not to be. Shattered by the rapid British advance, and aware of the decline in his forces' morale, General Menendez decided to have a serious talk with General Galtieri. It was ten o'clock in the morning of June 14:

I decided that I had to talk to General Galtieri, so I left Brigadier Joffre minding the post and went to the radio station. I finally got through to General Galtieri and explained the situation as I saw it. I suggested, and I was later criticised for this, that perhaps we should accept the UN Resolution 502. I was told that this was impossible. At the end of our conversation I told him that, as he was in Buenos Aires, I would take on full responsibility.

The decision to surrender was not one which he could avoid. Men were now leaving their positions and running for the shelter of Stanley; even the élite 5th Infantry Battalion had broken up, and was fleeing for safety. Just after his telephone call with Galtieri, Menendez was told by a fellow member of his civil administration, Captain Barry Melbourne-Hussey, that the British had contacted him to offer terms for a surrender. Melbourne-Hussey, a fluent English speaker, had been listening in to British appeals for a surrender for some time, on a radio link established by an SAS Colonel, Mike Rose, using the civilian medical radio net. Menendez decided to accept the offer:

I called a General on the continent who was my superior in the operations centre, I told them that I had already spoken to General Galtieri, and based on that conversation I was going to accept the offer of a cease-fire. He told me that he agreed with me, and that the decision was the right one.

Menendez ordered Captain Melbourne-Hussey to pass a message to the British in which he agreed to discuss terms, and asked for a preliminary meeting at 3 pm.

At the same time that General Menendez decided to surrender, the British forces, poised for the final strike from their captured hilltops overlooking Stanley, saw the Argentine enemy in flight: pulling back off the hillsides and heading for the town. The news was relayed to the two Brigadiers and General Moore, who were holding their own meeting to discuss the situation. Moore flew back to his tactical headquarters, unaware that Menendez was considering a surrender:

Although people had been standing around on Mount William, there was no sign of any sort of surrender or anything at that time, so I did actually walk around, kicking the turf and cursing and saying 'Why cannot this bloody man see that he's got to surrender? He's absolutely surrounded, we've got him absolutely beat, he's got to surrender', and then somebody came with a message, that there were people running off and there were white flags appearing in Stanley.

The white flags were metaphorical; there were none, but the decision to surrender was genuine. Moore ordered all firing and air attacks to cease forthwith. He then urgently told Julian Thompson to get his men going, fast. Thompson complied. Just as his forces reached the outskirts of Port Stanley, by the racecourse, Thompson was ordered to stop. The idea was to allow some separation between the British and the Argentine armies while the delicate negotiations took place. 2 Para, who were in the lead of the march for Stanley, were very suspicious of Thompson when he relayed the command to them. They suspected that General Moore and Brigadier Thompson, both Marines, might wish their own men to have the honour of being first into recaptured Stanley.

Chris Keeble, the Second-in-Command of 2 Para, ordered his men to halt at the race track. The journalist, Max Hastings, was with him at the time.

And Max Hastings gave me one of his kind of steely-eyed looks, and I could see what he was thinking. That he was not in the military and he was wearing one of those old airborne jackets which he took off in a very deliberate way, to kind of say, well I'm not a soldier, and he turned on his heel and walked on down the road into Stanley, which enabled him to liberate it.

Hastings was the first member of the British forces to enter Stanley. It was a terrific scoop for the veteran war correspondent, who filed his story for the *Evening Standard*. It was also carried by almost all the Fleet Street papers.

General Moore arranged for a Spanish-speaking officer, Captain Robert Bell, together with Colonel Mike Rose, to attend the first meetings with General Menendez in the afternoon. Colonel Rose, who had experience of negotiating for the release of hostages during the Iranian

Argentine Prisoners of War are led down from Mount Harriet after 42 Commando's assault

Below right: Men of the 2nd Battalion Scots Guards celebrate the capture of Mount Tumbledown

Far right: An Argentine conscript lies dead after the final British assault on the mountains overlooking Port Stanley

British troops of 3 Commando Brigade march into Port Stanley after the Argentine surrender

Opposite above left: Major-General Jeremy Moore, Commander of the British Forces on the Falkland Islands, holds up the instrument of surrender

Opposite above right: Defeated and demoralised Argentine troops wait for the opportunity to lay down their arms

Opposite below: The Union Flag flies once more over Government House, Port Stanley

Embassy siege, had already started the surrender discussions on a positive note. Throughout the preliminaries he insisted that the cease-fire was being sought because the Argentinians had already demonstrated their bravery; any more deaths at that stage would be pointless. General Menendez accepted this point wholeheartedly. Although he wished to surrender, he would only do so if the Argentine forces could retain their sense of honour:

I spoke to Colonel Rose and told him that there was a very important issue for us soldiers; we wanted to take our flags back to the continent. Thus started our conversations. Colonel Rose made some inquiries, using a radio which fascinated me because of its very small size and amazing power, and we reached an agreement and decided to meet again at 1900 hrs with General Moore in order to sign the document.

General Moore and Commodore Mike Clapp, in the absence of Admiral Woodward, flew into Stanley in the middle of a snowstorm to accept the Argentine surrender. They went to the Secretariat building where the ceremony was to take place. Moore ordered all cameras away; he was determined that Menendez would feel no sense of public humiliation. The General was ushered into an upstairs room in the large building and waited for the arrival of the Argentine General. Moore was flabbergasted when his opponent eventually came in:

Out stepped these gentlemen in what I would call service dress, impeccably turned out, creases in their trousers, shiny shoes, and it was as though they were the victors and we were the victims.

The British commander was doubly surprised. During the long journey south in QE2 he had carried a photo of the man he thought to be General Menendez, in order better to appreciate the character of his opponent. Montgomery had done the same in the Second World War, keeping a portrait of Rommel in his caravan. When the real General Benjamino Menendez appeared, Moore realised that he had been studying the wrong picture. Instead of the blood-thirsty warrior he had been led to expect, he was confronted by a small and mild-mannered man, more like a bank manager than a war leader.

General Moore was quick to tell Menendez that the British were impressed with the honourable and brave way that the Argentine forces had fought the conflict, and that he would do nothing to humiliate them. Reassured, Menendez took out his pen to sign the document, but before he did so he read it through for one last time. He stopped and asked for the word 'unconditional' to be removed. Moore had no qualms about this, despite London's desire for an unconditional surrender, and crossed the troublesome word out. Menendez then signed the document. The war was over.

It had been close run. Some of the British batteries were down to only six rounds of ammunition per gun. At sea, Admiral Woodward and his task force were taking a hammering from the heavy South Atlantic winter seas. The carriers would not have been able to last much longer. The British were thankful that street fighting in Port Stanley had been avoided.

After tea General Moore took a walk through the streets of Stanley. Buildings were burning, others were crammed with Argentine soldiers who had fled the mountains, and had found shelter where they could. The place was a terrible mess. Moore made his way to the West Store, Port Stanley's single large shop, where he was able to meet some of the Islanders.

I thought, 'What does a General say on an occasion like this? I haven't a clue.' So I walked in and, I don't know, I suppose it just came off the top of my head, I said, 'Hello, I'm Jeremy Moore, sorry it took us three and a half weeks to get here.' And they all fell about, as though it was the funniest thing they had ever heard.

The *Canberra* returns home. After ninety-four days at sea the cruise liner is greeted by a helicopter display, hundreds of boats and thousands of the families of the men of 3 Commando Brigade

EPILOGUE

AFTER the battle of Waterloo, the Duke of Wellington surveyed the scene of carnage: 'Nothing except a battle lost can be half so melancholy as a battle won,' he observed. The victorious British troops were overcome by a similar sentiment as they entered Stanley. The sight of the thousands of cold and bedraggled Argentine soldiers, filthy in their cold and wet dug-outs, was dispiriting in the extreme. Chris Keeble, who led his men into Stanley immediately the surrender ceremonies had been finished, contemplated the men who had been his enemy only hours before:

Defeated, disillusioned, just like cattle, numb, distraught, bemused. And they just filed up, delivered their weapons, and hung around waiting to be sent home.

Their officers, by contrast, appeared smart and well fed. It was this contrast which made the British see why the victory at the end had been relatively easy: the crucial leadership function had broken down; the officers had deserted their men.

The news of the surrender of the Argentine forces was received with more obvious joy, 8,000 miles away in London. In the afternoon of June 14 the Prime Minister interrupted a debate in the House of Commons. She told MPs that the Argentine forces '. . . are reported to be flying white flags over Stanley'. Her announcement was greeted with loud cheers from both sides of the House, and energetic waving of order papers. Michael Foot, the Leader of the Opposition, immediately rose to congratulate Mrs Thatcher.

The Prime Minister received almost universal praise for her handling of the conflict. Not one of the many senior officers and civil servants who worked under her voiced any serious criticism of the way in which she led the country during the conflict. Lord Lewin declared that there was no other politician with whom he would have preferred to have worked. Sir Anthony Parsons, who did not see eye to eye with her on other matters, thought she was superb. In war Mrs Thatcher had found her *métier*. The need for grasp of detail, relentless hard work, personal courage, the unyielding pursuit of an objective, and the refusal to compromise were all hallmarks of her political style, and were all ideally suited to the moment.

The Falklands War benefited the Prime Minister and the Conservative Party. Although there is some debate about the precise effects of the conflict on the outcome of the General Election in 1983, there is little doubt that her reputation was enhanced, and her popularity increased by the successful outcome of the war. Sending the task force was a calculated risk. Mrs Thatcher was advised many times of the difficulty of the job which it faced, and the dangers of committing British forces to battle so far away without sufficient air defences. Some may question the morality of gambling with Britain's prestige and standing in the world, for the sake of political survival. If she had failed, she and her Government would have been finished; the country would have been humiliated in the eyes of the world. Mrs Thatcher risked all and won.

Great Britain's stature in the world, and particularly in the United States, was enhanced as a result. Sir Nicholas Henderson, Britain's Ambassador in Washington, reported an immediate and tangible increase in the respect with which his country was held in America. In the years that followed men like Caspar Weinberger and Al Haig went as far as to attribute the first glimmerings of reform in the Soviet Union to the West's demonstration, in the Falklands, that it was prepared to stand and fight aggression.

If such views are far-fetched, Mrs Thatcher herself was convinced for a time that the 'Falklands Factor' had brought about a sea-change in British attitudes and reversed decades of national decline. Only weeks after the battle for Port Stanley she told a rally at Cheltenham that a threatened rail strike was not on. 'Now, once again,' she said, 'Britain is not prepared to be pushed around. We have ceased to be a nation in retreat.' In the years that followed, however, the Falklands ceased to be a *leitmotif* of her speeches or her party's campaigns. For the public, the tensions of the war became a distant memory, with little if any domestic or international significance.

For Mrs Thatcher, however, it remained one of the episodes in her leadership of which she was most proud. Showing the film producer, David Puttnam, and the composer of popular musicals, Andrew Lloyd-Webber, round Chequers at Christmas 1982 she pointed proudly at a chair and announced, 'This is the chair I sat in when I decided to sink the *Belgrano*.' But no patriotic equivalent of *Chariots of Fire* was produced to glorify the Falklands.

Not all those who served the British cause in the Falklands War prospered. John Nott announced his decision to retire from politics soon afterwards. Although he denied any link between the decision and his time as Defence Secretary, it was clear that his proposed Defence Review was dead in the water. The Royal Navy had triumphed: Australia gracefully withdrew from the purchase of the carrier *Invincible*, and the Royal Marines' assault ships, *Fearless* and *Intrepid*, were reprieved.

Brigadier Tony Wilson, the Commander of 5 Brigade, resigned his commission and left the army when he returned to Britain. He, too, made plain that the decision had been taken long before the campaign, and had nothing to do with the difficulties of leading a brigade which had been systematically pulled apart and haphazardly reconstituted in the weeks before the battle.

Most of the senior British officials and military who participated in the campaign did prosper from its successful outcome. In the New Year's Honours list in 1983 decorations, Knighthoods and Peerages were showered by a grateful nation on the task force commanders, the diplomats and civil servants who had won the war. At the same time as the Honours were announced, Mrs Thatcher herself was waiting in some trepidation for the report of the Committee of Privy Councillors which had been established shortly after the war was over. Its purpose had been 'to review the way in which responsibilities of Government in relation to the Falkland Islands and their dependencies were discharged in the period leading up to the Argentine invasion . . .'. The Committee, chaired by Lord Franks, was given the difficult task, as one commentator put it, of 'reviewing a putative diplomatic failure in the light of a decisive military success'.

When the Report was published, on January 18 1983, its contents – apart only from the final paragraph – were hailed as a masterpiece of clarity and objectivity. Lord Franks and his committee demonstrated, in a rare and illuminating insight into the workings of the most secret parts of Whitehall, that the Falklands War was the result of confusion and chaos, of years of neglect and botched policy making. The final paragraph, however, was also a masterpiece; but a masterpiece of bureaucratic obfuscation:

We conclude that we would not be justified in attaching any criticism or blame to the present Government for the Argentine Junta's decision to commit its act of unprovoked aggression in the invasion of the Falkland Islands in 1982.

Lord Callaghan described the conclusions as 'throwing a bucket of whitewash over the rest of the report'. He pointed out that nobody was

seeking to blame the British Government for General Galtieri's decision to invade. Mrs Thatcher and her colleagues, as the report showed, deserved blame for their failure to take the necessary steps to *deter* the invasion.

The country was in no mood, after a decisive military victory, to point the finger of blame. As *The Times* commented, 'The Committee had to be set up, if only to provide some objective commentary on a national drama which had brought the country to a pitch of emotional intensity unwitnessed for twenty-five years.' Lord Franks and his colleagues read the mood of the country correctly when they presented the report. It was not the appropriate time to lambast the Prime Minister. Mrs Thatcher was let off the hook.

In Argentina the news of the crushing defeat was greeted with rioting in the streets. The Junta, which had led the country to a massive humiliation, was soon forced out of office. When the country's prisoners of war were repatriated on board British ships, the true story of the incompetence of the leadership and the poor treatment of the conscripts became public knowledge. A Commission was established to try the leaders of the Junta; only Brigadier Basilio Lami Dozo and the Air Force emerged with any credit. Admiral Anaya, the man whose dream had led to Argentina's repossession of the Malvinas, and his dupe, General Galtieri, both received short prison sentences.

The Junta was replaced by a democratically elected Government, led by Raoul Alfonsin. The question of the Malvinas soon ceased to be a burning political issue, as people sought to forget the nation's humiliation. Nevertheless, a decade after the conflict, the Argentine people remain as convinced as ever of the justice of their cause. If the war had achieved anything, it had brought Argentina democracy, and focused attention on a dispute which many feared would die through British prevarication and international apathy.

The British use of armed force to remove the Argentine forces did nothing to solve the long-term problem. Like other relics of imperialism, there appears to be no solution to the question. Argentina's claim remains as strong as ever, while Britain has declared herself no longer prepared to discuss a transfer of sovereignty. Instead, as the Islanders have always wished, the Government has adopted a policy of 'Fortress Falklards'. In 1982 work started on a hugely expensive and ultramodern base at Mount Pleasant. It was completed two years later, and is now reputed to cost £200m a year to run.

Few of the men who fought in the war, or the families who lost loved ones, feel their effort and sacrifice was in vain. Jorge Luis Borges described the conflict as 'two bald men fighting over a comb', but those involved on both sides believed important points of principle were at stake: for Argentina, the profound national belief that the Malvinas were part of the nation's rightful heritage; for Britain, the strong desire to show that aggression should not be seen to triumph.

The cost for those who were injured or lost their menfolk was, and remains, very high. 655 Argentine servicemen died in the war; the British lost 252 men. Hundreds more were injured, in body and mind. In Argentina there has been almost no support for 'los chicos de la guerra', the conscripts who returned in shame from a war which their country had lost. Many remain unemployed to this day, hanging around on street corners in Buenos Aires, relying on crime and drugs to keep them going. In Britain there is much greater provision for the men and families who still suffer the after-effects of the war. The South Atlantic Fund, a charity established after the war, received millions of pounds from the public, and has made generous donations to the bereaved and their families, and to those suffering from battle injuries, whether physical or mental. There is, too, now a much greater understanding of, and sympathy for, the effects of battle on the mind, or 'post-trauma stress disorder', from which many of the Falklands veterans have suffered.

The most lasting impression of the war which remains for the veterans is one of comradeship. Those of religious persuasion, like David Cooper and Chris Keeble, were faced with a paradox which has haunted them ever since: that war in its destruction and violence brings out the best in men. They saw and experienced a closeness, a mutual dependence and a common aim which transcended their own lives, and the lives of those with whom they fought. To David Cooper, this is the tragedy, that 'men give so much for war, and give so little for peace'. The only comparison he could make with the comradeship of war was with another more creative human experience: 'The whole emotional and physiological event of giving birth and the relationship which exists is the only thing that I can think of which comes in any way near to the kind of closeness that exists among soldiers.'

Mrs Thatcher acclaims the British victory outside Number 10 Downing Street

Chronology of the Falklands War

1592 English sea-captain John Davies discovers Falkland Islands

1770 Spain expels first British settlers

1771 British settlers return after Spain apologises; they stay only a few years

1820 *November 6* Argentina raises flag in the Malvinas/Falklands

1829 First Argentine Governor, Louis Vernet, takes office in the Malvinas/Falklands. USS *Lexington* later destroys Argentine installations, declares Islands without Government

1832 Buenos Aires appoints new Military Commander. He is killed two months later in a mutiny

1833 *January 3* Britain occupies Falkland Islands

1840 Islands formally established as a Crown Colony

1963 Resurgence in Argentina's interest in the Islands

1965 Royal Marine garrison established on the Islands

December 16 UN passes Resolution 2065 calling on Britain and Argentina to resolve their differences

1966 *January 14* Great Britain agrees to negotiations. Sixteen years of bilateral talks follow

1968 *February 27* Four members of Falklands Executive Council leak details of secret Anglo/Argentine 'Memorandum of Understanding' to MPs. The Memorandum agrees to a transfer of sovereignty. Falkland Islands Emergency Committee formed to lobby against transfer

November Lord Chalfont visits the Falklands to explain Government policy. His reception is 'less than enthusiastic'

December 11 Cabinet decides Falkland Islanders' wishes must be paramount in any settlement

1969 Talks between Argentina and Britain over Islands resume

1971 Agreement reached with Argentina on communications; Argentina takes over transport links with the Falklands

1976 *February* Argentine destroyer fires on RSS *Shackleton*

March 23 Military coup led by Jorge Videla overthrows Peronist Government

December 20 HMS *Endurance* discovers Argentine base on Southern Thule

1977 *November 21* British Government orders naval deployment of one submarine and two frigates to vicinity of Falkland Islands during negotiations in December

1979 *September 20* Lord Carrington recommends leaseback to Prime Minister and Cabinet Defence Committee

1980 *April 15* Talks held at UN between Britain and Argentina, with Islander representation

November 22–29 Nicholas Ridley visits Falkland Islands. Islanders make plain their dislike of leaseback

December 2 Leaseback rejected by House of Commons

1981 *June 30* British Government confirms decision to withdraw HMS *Endurance* as part of major defence review

December 8 General Leopoldo Galtieri takes office as President of Argentina, replacing Lt. General Roberto Viola in a coup. Admiral Jorge Anaya is Commander-in-Chief of the Navy; Brigadier Basilio Lami Dozo is Commander of the Air Force. Planning begins for the recapture of the Malvinas

December 16 Constantino Davidoff departs on first mission to South Georgia

1982

January

9 British Embassy lodges formal protest with Argentine Foreign Ministry over Davidoff visit to South Georgia

12 Joint armed forces committee in Buenos Aires begins military planning for the invasion of the Malvinas

24 First of a series of articles by Iglesias Rouco in *La Prensa* newspaper which reveal military action to recover Malvinas being considered by Junta

February

9 Prime Minister Margaret Thatcher confirms decision to withdraw HMS *Endurance*

27/28 Richard Luce and Enrique Ros meet at United Nations, New York, for 'talks about talks'

March

1 Argentina issues unilateral communique rejecting outcome of UN talks

3 Prime Minister Margaret Thatcher urges 'contingency plans' in case of increased Argentine hostility

5 Lord Carrington rejects idea of sending a nuclear-powered submarine to the South Atlantic

19 Constantino Davidoff's party of scrap-metal workers lands at Leith in South Georgia. Britain issues formal protest

20 Admiral Jorge Anaya orders Vice-Admiral Juan Jose Lombardo to bring forward his plans for the invasion of the Malvinas

22 HMS *Endurance* is ordered to proceed to South Georgia to remove scrap workers. Orders later rescinded

25 South Georgia incident escalates as Argentine ship *Bahia Paraiso* arrives at Leith and reinforces scrap workers

26 Argentine Junta decides on military action. In London Ministry of Defence advises against preparation of a task force and tells Lord Carrington that HMS *Endurance* will be withdrawn after crisis is over. MoD also advises Prime Minister that if Argentina occupies Islands 'there could be no certainty' that a large task force could retake them

28 Argentine invasion fleet sets sail for the Malvinas

29 Prime Minister and Lord Carrington agree to the sending of a nuclear-powered submarine to the South Atlantic

31 British intelligence learns that an Argentine invasion force is on its way. The Prime Minister accepts naval advice to prepare a task force

April

1 President Reagan fails to persuade President Galtieri to cancel military action

2 Argentine force invades the Falkland Islands. Governor Rex Hunt surrenders

3 Mrs Thatcher announces to House of Commons the despatch of a large task force. UN Security Council approves Resolution 502

5 British task force leaves port. General Al Haig, US Secretary of State, announces mediation effort. Lord Carrington announces resignation

8 Al Haig arrives in London on the first leg of his shuttle

10 Al Haig travels to Buenos Aires and begins talks with Argentine Junta

12 Britain declares 200-mile maritime exclusion zone in force around the Falklands. Al Haig arrives in London for last round of talks with Mrs Thatcher before travelling on to Buenos Aires

16 Al Haig makes a final visit to the Argentine Junta. Talks end without a settlement three days later

17 Admiral Sir John Fieldhouse, Commander-in-Chief of the British task force, holds council-of-war at Ascension to plan the repossession of the Falklands

20 War Cabinet orders recapture of South Georgia

25 South Georgia is recaptured

28 Britain announces Total Exclusion Zone around Falklands

30 British Carrier Battle Group penetrates Total Exclusion Zone. United States declares support for Britain

May

1 Military action begins. British aircraft and ships bombard Port Stanley airfield. Argentine jets attack British ships. Argentine navy begins pincer attack on British task force. Nuclear-powered submarine, HMS *Conqueror* trails Argentine cruiser *General Belgrano*

Acknowledgements

2 Argentine navy cancels pincer attack on British task force. President Belaunde of Peru announces renewed peace intiative. British Foreign Secretary Francis Pym holds talks with Al Haig in Washington. Cruiser *General Belgrano* is sunk by HMS *Conqueror* outside the Total Exclusion Zone

4 HMS *Sheffield* is hit by Exocet missile

12 *QE2* sails from England with 3,500 men of 5 Brigade

20 UN Secretary General announces collapse of UN peace effort

21 British landings take place in San Carlos in the Falkland Islands. Argentine air attacks begin

25 *Atlantic Conveyor* is hit by Exocet and sinks

27 2 Para advances on Argentine garrison at Goose Green

29 Argentine garrison at Goose Green surrenders

30 3 Commando Brigade advances to within 25 miles of Port Stanley

June

1 5 Brigade reinforcement arrives at San Carlos

3 2 Para advance and capture Fitzroy and Bluff Cove

8 Royal Fleet Auxiliaries *Sir Galahad* and *Sir Tristram* bombed at Fitzroy

11/12 British forces capture Mount Longdon, Two Sisters, Mount Harriet

13/14 British forces advance and capture Mount Tumbledown and Wireless Ridge

14 Argentine forces surrender to Major-General Jeremy Moore

25 Governor Rex Hunt returns to Port Stanley as Civil Commissioner

July

6 Prime Minister announces appointment of Lord Franks to head Committee of Privy Councillors reviewing Government policies before the conflict

1983 *January 18* Franks Committee report released

Sources

The accounts of the Falklands War quoted in this book are taken from television interviews for the series, *The Falklands War*, a Fine Art Production for Channel Four. The interviews were transcribed by Barbara Dean.

The extracts from debates in the House of Commons are taken from *The Falklands Campaign, A Digest of Debates in the House of Commons, 2 April to 15 June 1982* (London, HMSO 1982).

Mrs Thatcher's comments about the conflict are taken from *Independent Television News* broadcasts: her rebuttal of the idea of failure, *News at Ten* April 3 1982; her remarks about the rail strike, *News at Ten* July 7 1982. Her pointing out the seat where she made the decision to sink the *Belgrano*, mentioned in the Epilogue, is drawn from *One of Us*, by Hugo Young (Macmillan, London 1989). The comments on the Report of the Franks Committee quoted in the epilogue are taken from a paper by Dr Alex Danchev, *The Franks Report: A Chronicle of Unripe Time* (University of Keele 1990).

Details of the number of bombs which failed to explode in task force ships were provided by Lt Cdr Brian Dutton DSO QGM RN (Ret.).

The main source used for the events leading up to the invasion was the *Falkland Islands Review*, Report of a Committee of Privy Councillors (Franks Committee Report) (HMSO, Cmnd. 8787, London 1983).

The author also acknowledges *Signals of War*, Lawrence Freedman and Virginia Gamba Stonehouse (Faber & Faber, London 1990); *Task Force: The Falklands War 1982*, Martin Middlebrook (Revised Edition, Penguin Books, London 1987); and *The Fight for the 'Malvinas'*, also Martin Middlebrook (Viking, London 1989).

The author has used many other sources, in particular:

Above All Courage, First-Hand Accounts from the Falklands Front Line (Sidgwick and Jackson, London 1985) whose author, Max Arthur, recorded the experiences of some of the participants in the television series, and led us to Peter Naya, David Cooper, and Steve Newland

The Battle for the Falklands Max Hastings & Simon Jenkins (Michael Joseph, London 1983)

Caveat Alexander M. Haig Jr. (Weidenfeld and Nicolson, London 1984)

The Disappeared, Voices from a Secret War John Simpson and Jana Bennett (Robson Books, London 1985)

Events of the Weekend 1st and 2nd May 1982 Third Report of the House of Commons Foreign Affairs Committee, Session 1984–5 (HMSO, London 1985)

The Falklands, The Secret Plot Oscar Cardoso *et al.* (Preston Editions, East Molesey 1983)

The Falklands Campaign: The Lessons Secretary of State for Defence (HMSO, London 1982)

The Falkland Islands as an International Problem Peter Beck (Routledge, New York 1988)

Fighting for Peace, Seven Critical Years at the Pentagon Caspar Weinberger (Michael Joseph, London 1990)

The Franks Report: A Chronicle of Unripe Time Paper by Dr Alex Danchev delivered at Conference on the Falklands Conflict, University of Keele, September 1990

Gotcha: The Media, the Government and the Falklands Crisis Robert Harris (Faber & Faber, London 1983)

The Land that Lost its Heroes: The Falklands, the Post-war and Alfonsin Jimmy Burns (Bloomsbury Publishing, London 1987)

One Man's Falklands Tam Dalyell MP (Cecil Woolf, London 1982)

The Little Platoon, Diplomacy and the Falklands Dispute Michael Charlton (Basil Blackwell, Oxford 1989)

No Picnic: 3 Commando Brigade in the South Atlantic: 1982 Julian Thompson (Leo Cooper, London 1985)

One of Us Hugo Young (Macmillan, London 1989)

Operation Paraquat Roger Perkins (Picton Publishing, Chippenham 1986)

The Right to Know: The Inside Story of the Belgrano Affair Clive Ponting (Sphere Books, London 1985)

The Royal Navy and the Falklands War David Brown (Leo Cooper, London 1987)

The Secret Story of the Malvinas War Admiral Jorge Anaya (unpublished)

The Sinking of the Belgrano Arthur Gavshon and Desmond Rice (Secker & Warburg, London 1984)

Weapons of the Falklands Conflict Bryan Perrett (Blandford Press, Poole 1982)

Photo Acknowledgements

Colour Section

Associated Press: 74 (bottom); Denys Blakeway: 75 (top); Camera Press: 78, 80 (bottom); Imperial War Museum: 73, 74 (top), 75 (bottom), 76/77 (centre and right), 78/79 (centre and right); Rupert Nichols: 76

Black and white photos

Associated Press: 54/55 (bottom), 57 (bottom), 66/61, 96; Denys Blakeway: 20, 93, 104/5 (top and bottom left); Camera Press: 2/3, 12/13, 14/15 (centre and right), 16/17 (centre), 25, 34, 36, 42, 46 (left), 48, 51 (right), 54 (top), 70/71, 86/87, 109, 146, 161 (bottom), 162, 164; Diario y Noticias: 6, 18/19; Peter Holdgate MoD: 110, 112, 114/115 (top left and right, bottom left), 120, 132/133, 150, 152, 155, 158/9 (left), 160; Imperial War Museum: 1, 30/31, 46 (right), 50/51 (centre), 55 (top), 63, 65, 66/67, 68, 69, 82, 84 (bottom), 100, 104/105 (bottom right), 113, 116/117, 118, 119, 120, 121, 122/3, 125, 126/7, 129, 130, 134/5, 137, 138/9, 140, 141, 145, 149, 153, 156, 159 (top and bottom), 161 (top left and right); Navy News: 103; Popperfoto: 14 (left), 27, 45, 57 (top), 58/59, 84 (top), 106, 114/115 (bottom right); Press Association: 64, 94/95, 124

Index